MOSES

*Typical Mediator
of the Old Covenant*

*BERNARD
WOUDENBERG*

REFORMED
FREE PUBLISHING
ASSOCIATION
Jenison, Michigan

All Bible quotations are taken from the King James [Authorized] Version

Reformed Free Publishing Association
1894 Georgetown Center Drive
Jenison MI 49428
616-457-5970
www.rfpa.org
mail@rfpa.org

Cover design by Erika Keil
Interior design by Katherine Lloyd / theDESKonline.com

ISBN: 978-1-944555-78-8
ISBN: 978-1-944555-79-5 (ebook)
Library of Congress Control Number: 2021945582

CONTENTS

A NOTE FROM THE PUBLISHER

Rev. Bernard Woudenberg was a minister in the Protestant Reformed Churches of America (PRCA) and served in several pastorates during his forty-year ministry: Creston PRC (Grand Rapids, Michigan); Edgerton PRC (Edgerton, Minnesota); Lynden PRC (Lynden, Washington); and Kalamazoo PRC (Kalamazoo, Michigan) where he retired.

In God's providence Rev. Woudenberg was not able to see the publication of this book; on November 17, 2020, he passed away at the age of eighty-nine, twelve days after the death of his wife, Frances, Rev. Woudenberg's companion of sixty-seven years.

Rev. Woudenberg loved the study of dogmatics, so much so that he sat through Rev. Herman Hoeksema's dogmatics course three times—as an undergraduate at Calvin College in Grand Rapids, Michigan; while he attended the Protestant Reformed seminary; and during his first pastorate at Creston PRC.

But one of Rev. Woudenberg's greatest loves was Old Testament history. When Rev. George Ophoff, professor of Old Testament history in the Protestant Reformed seminary, suffered a stroke in 1958, Rev. Woudenberg took over his Old Testament history class, Rev. Woudenberg only having graduated from the seminary two years earlier.

It was also in 1958 that Rev. Woudenberg became the first contributor to the rubric "Cloud of Witnesses" in the *Standard Bearer* magazine. Over the next thirteen years, Rev. Woudenberg would write more than 200 articles under this rubric, many of which covered the life of Moses and became the subject matter of this book.

With *Moses*, we desire to introduce readers to a Protestant Reformed writer with whom they may not be familiar, and to make accessible a book on the timeless subject of the true Mediator. Moses was a typical mediator of the old covenant and Rev. Woudenberg offers a fascinating account of his life. Rev. Woudenberg begins with the Lord's preservation of an infant Moses from drowning in the River Nile and covers the history through to Moses' final ascent to the top of Pisgah as a one hundred twenty-year-old man. And although Rev. Woudenberg at times uses poetic license to convey thoughts and actions of characters in this history, we are convinced that this book will benefit all readers.

When we as the New Testament church hear the words of God's law as the children of Israel heard them at Mount Sinai, we too become the humbled people who are unable to stand in the presence of their God:

> It was a humbled people that came to Moses that night and said, "Speak thou with us, and we will hear: but let not God speak with us, lest we die" (Ex. 20:19). Suddenly they had come to realize that they were in need of a mediator. By themselves they could never stand in the presence of this just and mighty God. They needed one to take their place and bring their cause into the presence of God. As never before, they began to see Moses as their savior, the one who could bring their cause to God, a figure and a type of the promised Redeemer, Jesus Christ.[1]

---

1 From chapter 22, "God Speaks at Sinai," page 136.

Chapter 1

SATAN DECLARES WAR AGAINST THE CHURCH

13. And he said unto Abram, Know of a surety that thy seed shall be a stranger in a land that is not theirs, and shall serve them; and they shall afflict them four hundred years;
14. And also that nation, whom they shall serve, will I judge: and afterward shall they come out with great substance. (Genesis 15:13–14)

8. Now there arose up a new king over Egypt, which knew not Joseph.
9. And he said unto his people, Behold, the people of the children of Israel are more and mightier than we:
10. Come on, let us deal wisely with them; lest they multiply, and it come to pass, that, when there falleth out any war, they join also unto our enemies, and fight against us, and so get them up out of the land.
11. Therefore they did set over them taskmasters to afflict them with their burdens. (Exodus 1:8–11)

The book of Exodus opens amid the roaring flames that heated the brick kilns of Egypt. Blood, mixed with tears and sweat, tinted the new mortar under the cruel lashes of the taskmasters. Slowly the walls of Pithom and Raamses rose from the desert floor, troves for the treasures of Egypt (Ex. 1:11). They were made by the groans and anguished cries of a people sorely oppressed. This was the work of slaves, and the slaves were the children of Israel, the members of God's chosen nation. We look on in amazement, and we ask, "Why?" Why such grievous affliction? Why was it even necessary for Israel to be in Egypt?

1

To this latter question, Joseph already had given an answer. He had told his brothers, "And God sent me before you to preserve you a posterity in the earth, and to save your lives by a great deliverance" (Gen. 45:7). There was at that time a famine, ordained by God, covering the face of the earth. God had sent Joseph beforehand to make preparations by putting in storage of the bounties of Egypt. Thus many thousands of people were being saved from death; and thus also the children of Israel were brought to abide under the care of their brother amid the plenty of Egypt. But yet, this answer by itself does not satisfy us. Surely God could have made some other provisions for Israel whereby she might have stayed in Canaan. The food could have been sent to them by camel; or, at least, they could have returned to Canaan as soon as the famine was over. It was evidently the will of the Lord that Israel should remain in Egypt for an extended stay. This much was implied when God spoke to Jacob on the way, "Fear not to go down into Egypt; for I will there make of thee a great nation" (46:3).

A deeper reason for Israel's extended sojourn in Egypt we may find by examining the preceding history of Jacob's children. For many years already they had been associating with and intermingling with the Canaanitish peoples of the land. The result was that they were falling deeper and deeper into sin. Witness the massacre of Shechem, and the sins of Judah with Tamar, to say nothing of the countless iniquities that Joseph as a boy had faithfully reported to his father. The distinctiveness of the family of Israel as a people dedicated unto God was swiftly disappearing. Given a generation or two more among the wicked inhabitants of Canaan, it would have been completely gone. It was necessary for the survival of Israel as a distinctive nation that she should be removed to a portion of the earth where she could dwell alone, until such a time as the Canaanitish people had filled their cup of iniquity and could be destroyed. For this the land of Goshen in Egypt was suited, and God provided that they might dwell there. In a sense it was a chastisement for their sins and a banishment from the promised land; but at the same time it was a deliverance from the countless temptations that they were not yet strong enough to bear.

But there was also another reason why Israel was sent into Egypt. Perhaps it was the most important reason of all. Already many years before, God had made it known unto Abraham. "Know of a surety," he said to Abraham, "that thy seed shall be a stranger in a land that is not theirs, and shall serve them; and they shall afflict them four hundred years; and also that nation, whom they shall serve, will I judge: and afterward shall they come out with great substance" (Gen. 15:13–14). God was planning to deliver his people out of bondage. He would reveal himself as Jehovah, the God who is ever faithful to his promises, by judging the oppressors of his people, by delivering his people with many miraculous wonders out of the power of their enemies, by feeding them with bread from heaven in the wilderness, by giving to them the revelation of his commandments, and generally by making them partakers of many glorious, typical blessings. God was planning to reveal his gospel more clearly than ever before through many marvelous demonstrations of his grace and power. For this the scene was being set when God sent his people into Egypt.

For a time, even after the death of Joseph, the life of the children of Israel was peaceful and quiet. Joseph's work and influence had been very great. The Egyptians continued to show their appreciation for what he had done in their attitude toward his family. True, the Egyptians did not seek to associate with the Israelites, for they were shepherds, and the Egyptians considered that a disgrace. But the children of Israel were left unmolested to dwell amid the fertility of Goshen. Their sheep were well fed, and they had opportunity to learn about farming and many other trades from the highly civilized Egyptians. They prospered, and the Lord multiplied their number so that they became very great.

This very ease of life, however, eventually became for them a temptation in itself. The children of Israel became attached to the land of Egypt. Life was pleasant, and they enjoyed Egypt's rare and delicious foods, its fish, its cucumbers and melons, its garlic and leeks. Seldom did they think anymore of the promised land of Canaan as something to be desired. They had little longing to return. Joseph's coffin was still with them, but its testimony they neglected. In effect, they disdained the covenant promises of God because of their love for the fleshpots of Egypt.

But God looked down from heaven and saw the complacency of his people. He also knew what should be the cure. He set on the throne of Egypt a new king "which knew not Joseph" (Ex. 1:8). It was not that this king did not know about Joseph, who he was and what he had done. Joseph's renown was too great to be forgotten even after several hundred years. But this king did not care. He felt no real appreciation for Joseph and no obligation to his heirs. He looked upon the Israelites as aliens, intruders in his land. He hated them and determined that they should be enslaved. He had been given over unto a reprobate mind by God.

The new Pharaoh called together his people and counseled them thus: "Behold, the people of the children of Israel are more and mightier than we; come on, let us deal wisely with them; lest they multiply, and it come to pass, that, when there falleth out any war, they join also unto our enemies, and fight against us, and so get them up out of the land" (Ex. 1:9–10). With these words we gain an insight into the character of Pharaoh. He was a man of extreme jealousy. This gave rise to endless confusion and contradiction within him. On the one hand, he was extremely envious of the prosperity of the Israelites. They had evidently become much stronger than the Egyptians themselves were. This Pharaoh could not bear. It touched his national pride. But, on the other hand, Pharaoh also realized how much the prosperity of Israel contributed to the well-being of Egypt. The Israelites were strong and willing workers. Should they choose to leave the land it would be an irreplaceable loss. Basically, however, Pharaoh was motivated by a hatred for Israel's God. It was well known in Egypt that Israel's strength was due to the greatness of their God. The driving ambition of Pharaoh's heart was to prove that he could dominate over Israel and her God. In his wicked ambition, Pharaoh became a fool.

The folly of Pharaoh soon became evident in his plan of action. He set taskmasters over the Israelites to afflict them, forcing them to work for the Egyptians. Had Pharaoh been a wise and discerning man, he would never have followed this course. He would have seen that, as long as the Israelites were left in peace, they were losing all desire to leave the land. They were a quiet and submissive people who readily obeyed the proper authorities. Moreover, while working willingly, they were contributing much more to the Egyptian economy than they ever would under force. But God's goal was the opposite of Pharaoh's, and, as always, he used the folly of the wicked to bring it to pass. Under the oppression of the Egyptians, the children of Israel began to look once again at the promise received through their fathers that they would be delivered from this land. Their earthly prosperity being threatened, they looked more and more to the deeper covenant joy that they had in the presence of their God. God used Pharaoh to bring his chosen people unto a gradual transformation of life. In this way they were blessed and grew stronger than ever before.

The more Pharaoh saw his goal receding, the more he became determined in his folly. The Israelites had been assigned the task of building Pithom and Raamses, treasure cities for Egypt. In this work the Egyptians pressed them harder and harder. The lives of the children of Israel became bitter under the rigor of their bondage. They labored from morning till evening under the burdens of brick and mortar and in the most menial tasks of the field. But it only served to thwart the plans of Pharaoh and to realize the will of God, for Israel grew and multiplied as never before.

Finally, Pharaoh became desperate. The glory of Egypt was dimming before the growing strength of Israel. Drastic measures had to be taken. He issued an order that seemed certain to cut short the growing strength of Israel. He summoned the two women, Shiphrah and Puah, who were in charge of the Hebrew midwives, and ordered them to slay all of the male children at birth. The plot was meant to be a secret one. All of the midwives of Israel were to be commanded to watch carefully when attending a birth to note immediately whether the child was male or female. If it were a female child, she might be allowed to live; but if it were a male child, he was to be stifled before the parents even knew whether he lived. In this way the strength of the Hebrews would be curtailed, while the women would remain to perform the work. Supposedly these measures would be stopped as soon as the strength of Israel was sufficiently reduced.

What Pharaoh failed to consider was the faith of the Hebrew midwives. They believed in God and would not willingly take part in the destruction of his people. Moreover, the Hebrew women were strong and healthy, usually requiring very little assistance in delivery. When summoned to a home, the midwives merely lingered on the way until after the child was born. Once the parents knew that the child lived, it was no longer required that the child be slain.

It was not long before Pharaoh learned that his command was not having effect. In a fit of anger, he summoned Shiphrah and Puah and accused them, "Why have ye done this thing, and have saved the men children alive?" The women answered, "Because the Hebrew women are not as the Egyptian women; for they are lively, and are delivered ere the midwives come in unto them" (Ex. 1:18–19).

The wickedness of Pharaoh would not be stemmed. Casting all pretense of secrecy aside, he issued this inhuman command to the Israelites: "Every son that is born ye shall cast into the river, and every daughter ye shall save alive" (Ex. 1:22). It was Satan declaring open war against the church.

Israel's life in Egypt had become very bitter. She labored in bondage, with persecution and pain. Not only did her people suffer, but the lives of their children and of their nation were being threatened. But behind it was the will of their God: "For whom the Lord loveth he chasteneth, and scourgeth every son whom he receiveth" (Heb. 12:6). He was turning the hearts of Israel back to him again. Once again the children of Israel looked upon the coffin of Joseph and with joy remembered its testimony of faith: "God will surely visit you, and ye shall carry up my bones from hence" (Gen. 50:25).

Chapter 2

PRESERVATION OF MOSES

1. And there went a man of the house of Levi, and took to wife a daughter of Levi.
2. And the woman conceived, and bare a son: and when she saw him that he was a goodly child, she hid him three months.
3. And when she could not longer hide him, she took for him an ark of bulrushes, and daubed it with slime and with pitch, and put the child therein; and she laid it in the flags by the river's brink. (Exodus 2:1–3)

Toil and tears had become the lot of the Israelites in Egypt. For many years it had been different. They had reaped the bounties of the land, and under the blessings of their God had prospered. But now a new Pharaoh had arisen who was determined to break the power of Israel's God. First there was the extra toil in brick and mortar and menial labor of the fields. More and more the taskmasters of Egypt bore down upon them, intent on breaking their strength; but Jehovah held them up, and the nation grew the more. Next there was the command that all of the male children should be stifled at birth, but against it the faith of the midwives prevailed. Finally, the command went out to all the land that the baby sons of the Hebrews should be cast into the river. Pharaoh and the God of Israel were engaged in open combat.

"And there went a man of the house of Levi, and took to wife a daughter of Levi" (Ex. 2:1). It is a homely tale. In another setting it might appear peaceful and serene; but the place was darkened Egypt, and the time was that of Pharaoh's implacable hatred. What did such a marriage have to offer? Only days of exhausting labor, nights of trembling, and bitter tears. Still, for simple Amram and Jochebed there was hope and promise. It was not that they thought the luxuries of Egypt could somehow compensate for the sorrows, as was true with only too many of their nation. It was not that they believed that there would be found some goodness in Pharaoh that would cancel out his wickedness. Amram and Jochebed had the hope and promise of faith. They believed in God and in the promises that he had given unto their father Abraham, to be a God unto him and unto his seed after him through all generations. They waited for the deliverance that was sure to come.

The birth of a first child to Amram and Jochebed was an occasion of great joy. Although the oppression of Pharaoh was already severe, it had not yet reached into the intimate circle of the home. In their homes the Israelites still had opportunity to find joy and peace. The child was a girl, and they named her Miriam, "the beloved one." But time went on and the wickedness of Pharaoh began to cut closer and closer. It became evident that he was intent on destroying the nation and had designs to cut off all of the male seed. Jochebed conceived again and bore a son, but now the joy of birth was gone. There was no assurance that the child's life could be spared, and they named him Aaron, meaning "uncertainty." Yet, perhaps through the faithfulness of the midwives, the child was kept alive. Spurred on by his lack of success, Pharaoh in his ragings was approaching the point of madness. Finally, he issued the command that thereafter all of the male children who were born of the Hebrews should be thrown into the River Nile. This command was not limited to the midwives or parents; it went out unconditionally through all the land. It was the duty of everyone to see that it was enforced. When Jochebed conceived again, there was little room for joy, only the silent prayers that the child in birth might be a girl. But the will of God was not so. In due time, a son was born. The situation was very dire, for the agents of Pharaoh were throughout the land. If this son would be found with them alive, the consequences would be severe. But these faithful parents would not bow in fear before the tyranny of wicked Pharaoh. They saw, we are told, that their son was a goodly child. Now it may be, as many say, that this son was beautiful to look upon. But what Amram and Jochebed saw was much more than that. It was what Stephen pointed out many years later: the child was pleasing to the Lord. These believing parents recognized that their son was a covenant child of God. They could not give him over to death. No matter what the consequences might be, their faith demanded of them that they do all in their power to keep him alive.

We might be inclined to ask why God ordained that Moses should be born just then. A few years earlier, Moses' birth would have preceded this most cruel and wicked command of Pharaoh. Moreover, it appears that a few years later the law fell into disuse and became a dead law upon the books. Moses was born during the time when it was being painfully enforced. Actually, of course, it is foolish for us to question the wisdom of God. His way is always best and must be received as such by faith. It makes no essential difference whether we can understand it or not. Nonetheless, in this case the wisdom of God is evident. Pharaoh had determined to destroy the church of God, and God would expose his folly. Out of the very period of Pharaoh's most fanatical effort, God would raise the man through whom Pharaoh's might would be utterly destroyed. In fact, in the midst of his most vile efforts, Pharaoh himself would be used to prepare that one through whom these efforts would be brought to naught. God would make it clearly evident that none can withstand his will. As God, he is very great.

For a time, it appeared to Amram and Jochebed as if they would be able to keep their child safely in their own home. Careful measures were taken to prevent anyone from even knowing that the child had been born. He was kept as quiet as possible behind closed doors, and the older children were warned not to tell anyone of his presence. For about three months these efforts were successful. However, the task was becoming ever more difficult. The child's voice was becoming stronger, his growing body more active. It became apparent to the parents that they would not be able to keep the child hidden much longer from those who passed by in the streets. Something different had to be done. If it were not, the child would soon be discovered and killed.

Burdened by her responsibility, faithful Jochebed went down to the riverbank one day and gathered a large bundle of bulrushes. These she took home, and she set to work. With painstaking care she wove the weeds into a closely knit basket. Thereupon she coated the inside of the basket with a smooth coat of pitch and slime until she was sure that it would be completely waterproof. Into this basket or ark Jochebed placed her son. Her plan was this: They would find a desolate stretch of riverbank by which people very seldom passed. Each morning, early, before anyone else was astir, they would take the little ark with the child and allow it to float on the water within one of the thick clumps of reeds that grew all along the Nile's banks. Being made from bulrushes itself, the ark would be very difficult to see. Should the child cry, it would be much less likely to be heard there in the desolate riverbank than at home close to the busy streets. Finally, each day Miriam would be sent apparently to play by the river but actually to keep a close eye on the little basket as much as possible, keeping it from being harmed. Each night the child could be returned again to the home after dark. Perhaps the location of the basket was changed from day to day to ward off all suspicion.

This action of Jochebed, we are told in Hebrews 11, arose out of faith. It was not as though the child would now be free from all threats of danger. One could imagine countless things that might easily happen. What if the current should catch the basket and carry it away; or a storm should break and fill the basket until it sank; or if, perhaps, the crocodiles of the river should discover the precious contents? These dangers were very real, but to Jochebed they were far to be preferred to the dangers represented in the Egyptians that passed every day by her door. She felt as David did after he numbered the people, that it was better to "fall into the hand of the Lord"

(1 Chron. 21:13). Realizing that she could protect her child no longer, she placed him in the care of the Lord.

How long this plan was successfully followed, we do not know. However, one day as Miriam was sitting on the river's brink, she looked up to see a company of women approaching. Her heart skipped a beat with fear, for these women were evidently Egyptians. Moreover, from the royal dress of the one it was apparent that she was from the court of Pharaoh, evidently the king's daughter. She was coming to the river to bathe. Quickly Miriam withdrew herself so as not to draw attention to the place where the ark was afloat in the reeds. If the child would fall into the hands of these hated Egyptians, surely it would be the end. But alas, the quick eyes of Pharaoh's daughter were not to be deceived, not even by the clever camouflage of the bulrushes. She sent one of her maidens to fetch the basket and looked within.

Trembling with fear Miriam watched, expecting any moment to see her young brother thrown heartlessly into the river. She wondered within herself what she should do. The child was crying, and Miriam was quick to note that on the face of the Egyptian women there were not sneers but smiles, not anger but sympathy. She heard the words of Pharaoh's daughter, "This is one of the Hebrews' children" (Ex. 2:6), and there was kindness in her voice. Miriam caught the implication: the child was to be kept alive. Quick of wit, Miriam approached the woman and said, "Shall I go and call to thee a nurse of the Hebrew women, that she may nurse the child for thee?" (v. 7). Suddenly the possibility appeared that the child could be restored to their home, safe from all threat of death.

Pharaoh's daughter looked at the young girl standing eagerly before her and immediately the whole situation became clear. The girl was evidently the child's sister, engaged in a plot to preserve the babe from death. Did not the girl's eagerness manifest a personal interest in the child's care? Did not her very features resemble those of the child? The girl wanted to return her brother to their mother. But, then, it made no difference. The child was fair to look upon, and she had determined to take it into the palace for her own. As yet the child was too young. It needed a nurse. Who would care better for him than his natural mother? She told the young girl, "Go," and soon the girl returned with her mother. Pharaoh's daughter gave to Jochebed her instructions, "Take this child away, and nurse it for me, and I will give thee thy wages" (Ex. 2:9).

There was little cause for concern that evening in the palace of Pharaoh. True, one Hebrew child had been spared from death, and that with the approval of Pharaoh, for he could hardly deny the plea of a favored daughter. But what did it really matter? That child was but one among many, and plans were already in the making to have the child educated in Pharaoh's own schools. The situation was well under control. What Pharaoh did not realize was that behind that one seemingly insignificant exception was the will of Israel's God. Moses, the child drawn from the river, would rise up to put to naught all of the boasting of that evil kingdom. The very efforts of Pharaoh were hastening Egypt's destruction. As the psalmist wrote many years later, "Why do the heathen rage, and the people imagine a vain thing? The kings of the earth set themselves, and the rulers take counsel together, against the LORD, and against his anointed, saying, He that sitteth in the heavens shall laugh: the Lord shall have them in derision" (Ps. 2:1–2, 4).

Chapter 3

MOSES CHOOSING TO SUFFER WITH GOD'S PEOPLE

24. By faith Moses, when he was come to years, refused to be called the son of Pharaoh's daughter;
25. Choosing rather to suffer affliction with the people of God, than to enjoy the pleasures of sin for a season;
26. Esteeming the reproach of Christ greater riches than the treasures in Egypt: for he had respect unto the recompence of the reward. (Hebrews 11:24–26)

22. And Moses was learned in all of the wisdom of the Egyptians, and was mighty in words and in deeds.
23. And when he was full forty years old, it came into his heart to visit his brethren the children of Israel. (Acts 7:22–23)

And it came to pass in those days, when Moses was grown, that he went out unto his brethren, and looked on their burdens. (Exodus 2:11)

It was an anxious, wondering, fearful Jochebed who hurriedly followed her daughter Miriam toward the group of Egyptian women standing by the bank of the Nile. In the middle of the group was Pharaoh's daughter, and at her feet was the ark of bulrushes that Jochebed knew so well. Even as Miriam had excitedly related, these women had discovered her son. But once she had approached the women, Jochebed's face lost its look of fear, her eyes began to sparkle with joy, and her heart breathed a prayer of thanksgiving, for Pharaoh's daughter spoke, "Take this child away, and nurse it for me, and I will give thee thy wages" (Ex. 2:9). Jochebed's son was not going to die; in fact, he was to be returned to her own home. The providence of God had provided for it, and the authority of Pharaoh's throne had commanded it.

Once again peace returned to the humble home of Amram and Jochebed. No longer did they need to fear the footsteps that passed by their doorway. The child had been given an Egyptian name, Moses, and was known as a son of Pharaoh's daughter. An edict of the throne protected him. Even the threat of poverty and hunger had disappeared. At regular intervals funds were received from the palace sufficient for all of the child's needs and enough for the family besides. Only one cause for concern remained: Moses could not remain always with his parents. Pharaoh's daughter wanted him for her own. She would allow Moses to remain with his parents only through the tender years of early childhood when he needed special care. After that he would be taken away to be placed in the courts of Pharaoh's heathen palace. There he would be in the midst of the world, far removed from all of the children of God. Very early Amram and Jochebed began to prepare the child for that day. There was no time to spare. From the moment the child Moses began to show signs of comprehension, they taught him the truth of the covenant and began to warn him concerning the dangers that he in a peculiar way would have to withstand. Never was Moses allowed to think that his life would be easy or that his instruction in the truth could be allowed to wait.

We do not know how frequently during these early years Jochebed was required to bring the child to the palace so that Pharaoh's daughter could cuddle him and play with him like a toy. Neither do we know how often a royal embassage approached their humble home to see if the child was being properly kept. Those were times of fear, for it was never known whether or not the time had come when Moses was to be taken away. At such times, while the parents stood quietly by in the silence of fear, they realized how powerless they were. The life of their child was in the hand of the Lord. For them there was only one comfort. From his earliest years Moses had shown an unusual interest in all that his parents sought to teach him. Eagerly he listened as they told him over and over again of all that had been passed on from the fathers before them. He memorized and retained all that was known about their God and his gracious covenant promises. He never neglected the opportunity to learn, seeming to understand that for him it was of special importance. It was evident to the parents that the Spirit of the Lord was upon him. In this they found comfort and gave God thanks. Their prayers never ceased to ascend unto heaven in Moses' behalf.

Finally, the much-feared time came. Pharaoh's daughter decided that Moses should be taken to make his home in the palace. With heavy hearts the family made the last preparations for his departure. There were the last words of instruction and warning; there was the last kneeling together in prayer; and then there were the last fare-wells. With tear-blurred eyes the parents watched their child being led away. He looked so small, so much in need of his parents' care, so incapable of standing in the midst of an evil world. As the small figure faded into the distance, they knew that his heart yearned for them even as theirs did for him; but henceforth all they would be able to do for him would be to pray. Only the grace of God could enable him to endure.

It was a strangely different world in which the child Moses now found himself making his home. In place of the unadorned Hebrew hut, there was the regal splendor of the palace. In the place of the simple religious instruction of his parents, there were elaborate discourses by the most learned men of the ancient world. In place of the intimate family circle, there was the great household of Pharaoh with countless servants ready at any time to do his every bidding. Gone were the watchful eyes of his parents, ready to reprimand him for what was wrong as well as to encourage him in the right. Gone was the intimacy of a home united in love and spiritual devotion. Gone was mutual awareness of a God who has made the world and to whom all of the allegiances of life belong. The new surroundings were entirely different. There were governors and tutors who, even though he was young, were concerned with nothing more than winning his favor. There were spectacular rituals and ceremonies that, although engaged in with much pretentiousness, were in reality mostly shams. Amid all of the pomp and splendor of the court, there was a basic shallowness of life in which everyone lived for himself.

Of greatest importance for Moses in his young life was the opportunity that came to him for learning. As a member of the royal family, it was expected that he would eventually become a leader and a judge among the people. The whole of his life was centered in preparation for this. For such preparation there was no better place than ancient Egypt. It was by far the most advanced of all of the ancient kingdoms. It abounded in the knowledge of mathematics, astronomy, and chemistry. Many of the things known by them we in our day might consider to be more recent discoveries. They were learned in music and poetry, having libraries with thousands of volumes. The best of the instruction that this country could afford was given to Moses. Blessed with extraordinary ability by God, he advanced very rapidly in his learning. Stephen, many years later, expressed it like this: "And Moses was learned in all of the wisdom of the Egyptians, and was mighty in words and in deeds" (Acts 7:22).

The struggles that went on in the heart of Moses during these years we can only imagine. Were there days and weeks on end when he was torn between the immense learning of his teachers and the simple faith he had learned from his parents? Were there times when he was sorely tempted to throw himself into all of the sensual pleasures that were waiting for him in that heathen court? Were there moments when his pride whelmed up within him urging him to grasp the opportunities afforded, to make for himself a name in the midst of the world? Were there nights when he tossed upon his bed with heavy heart because he had allowed himself to follow much farther in the ways of the world than in his heart he knew was right? Yet through it all Moses' faith prevailed. It had to, for he was a child of God. As he grew in years he began to realize more and more that all of the learning of the Egyptians did not have the fundamental depth and soundness of the simple faith that he had learned from the lips of his parents. The Egyptians had much knowledge and many pleasures, but in their hearts they had no peace. Living in the midst of the world, Moses was not of the world. He could not think of himself as the son of Pharaoh's daughter. All of the treasures of Egypt held no real attachment for him; its pleasures he could not enjoy. Within his own heart he always remained the son of simple Amram and Jochebed, a Hebrew and a child of God.

Slowly the years went by, and Moses came to maturity. Still Moses took no permanent position in the government, nor did he engage himself in a marriage. Was this not contrary to the efforts and urgings of his foster mother and many others of the royal court? Surely for a man of Moses' ability the opportunities were many. As he grew, Moses withdrew more from public life. His heart was with the Hebrews laboring in the field. These were his people, and he could not forget them. His prayer and longing was for their deliverance. Already to Abraham it had been told that after four hundred years deliverance would come. Moses could not bind himself to the Egyptians. He had to make plans so that he could go with his people.

Gradually Moses took to walking out in the fields, and especially to those places where the Hebrews were working. His sympathies were there, and he could not keep himself away. There he saw it in all of its gruesome detail—the labor and toil, the sweat and the blood, the bodies weary and fainting, red with the stripes of whips. Time and again he flinched as he gazed on the blows of the taskmasters; he groaned within himself along with the cries of the workers; he fled with unbelievable anguish to the peace and quiet of the palace. Still he went again and again to stare with glassy eyes. With a pained and weary heart he watched, and what made it so hard was that these were his brethren, the children of his God.

Slowly the mind of Moses began to evaluate the facts. God had foretold this all, and the time for deliverance was approaching. The nation of Israel was great and mighty in spite of her cruel oppression. All she needed was a leader, and then who could prevent her from returning to Canaan? With the blessing of Almighty God upon her, no one could keep her from going.

Again Moses' mind turned to consider his own life. There was first his miraculous preservation from death but a few months after he was born, which spoke so evidently of the gracious providence of God. Then there were the early years of concentrated instruction by his parents in all of the truth of God's covenant. Finally, there were the years of specialized preparation in the palace to qualify him as a leader of people and a judge among men. What did it all mean? Could anything be more evident than that God was preparing him to deliver his people from bondage? The very thought excited the ambition of Moses as nothing before had ever done.

Still, there were two things that marred Moses' plans for the future. The first was for him the most painful. The children of Israel refused to recognize him as their brother. Perhaps they knew that he was a son of Amram and Jochebed, but that no longer made any difference. When he came into the fields with his royal Egyptian dress, they eyed him with suspicion. While *they* labored in bondage, *he* was refined in labor and dress. While the taskmasters beat them into submission, they treated Moses with utmost respect. All of Moses' sympathetic looks and words would not relieve their suspicions. As long as this were true, they would never receive him as their leader.

And then there was the one other difficulty that remained: God had not called him to be Israel's leader. All of his plans were built upon his own suppositions. Until the Lord spoke, he could only wait.

So the years passed by as Moses planned and waited—waited for a calling from God.

Chapter 4

MOSES REJECTED BY HIS BRETHREN

23. And when he was full forty years old, it came into his heart to visit his brethren the children of Israel.
24. And seeing one of them suffer wrong, he defended him, and avenged him that was oppressed, and smote the Egyptian:
25. For he supposed his brethren would have understood how that God by his hand would deliver them: but they understood not. (Acts 7:23–25)

11. And it came to pass in those days, when Moses was grown, that he went out unto his brethren, and looked on their burdens: and he spied an Egyptian smiting an Hebrew, one of his brethren.
12. And he looked this way and that way, and when he saw that there was no man, he slew the Egyptian, and hid him in the sand.
13. And when he went out the second day, behold, two men of the Hebrews strove together: and he said to him that did the wrong, Wherefore smitest thou thy fellow?
14. And he said, Who made thee a prince and a judge over us? (Exodus 2:11–14)

Moses had come into his fortieth year of life, and he formed a lonesome figure in his wandering through the land of Egypt. In position and appearance he was an Egyptian, and one of the highest rank. He was known as the son of Pharaoh's daughter. But as he advanced in years he had withdrawn himself more and more from the life of the court. He had refused to take a position in the government for which he had prepared. He had neglected to take to himself a wife from the daughters of the land in spite of his foster mother's urgings. Seldom was he to be found in the social functions of the palace, and there was no effort on his part to make friends with any men of his own rank. Most of his time seemed to be spent in wandering through the fields and close by the construction projects where the Hebrew slaves were working. Also there he cut a solitary figure. The Egyptian taskmasters showed him a fawning respect. They recognized his influential position in the court, but he evidenced little appreciation for them. Occasionally he spoke a kind and sympathetic word to one or another of the slaves. Their responses were curt, if not openly hostile. The Hebrews knew that he was of their own blood, but he had lived too long among the Egyptians to be trusted. His Egyptian clothes and customs made too much of a rift for them to ignore. He did not toil in slavery as they did, and how could mere words remove that difference? Let Moses speak as he would; to them he was an Egyptian and not to be trusted.

Little did anyone realize the turmoil that lived in Moses' breast. From the Egyptians he received countless offers of kindness. They sought to give him friendship, power, and glory among the mightiest of the land. In the court of Pharaoh, personal opportunities never ceased to come his way. But Moses had no appreciation for these offers of the Egyptians. He did not want to live as the son of Pharaoh's daughter. He was a Hebrew. His love was with the people of his birth. They were the chosen people of God. For them in their bondage he grieved. For their deliverance he longed and prayed. He remembered the promise of God to Abraham that after four hundred years they would be returned to Canaan, and upon that promise he rested his hope. Time and again he had counted the years and found that the promised day was drawing nigh. There remained only one thing for him to do: he had to find his place in the Hebrew nation so that the deliverance might not pass him by. Was it not quite evident? Israel needed a leader to guide and direct the forces of the nation. Was there anyone more suited for that than himself? He had the training. He had the ability. He alone of Israel was prepared for work such as that.

It was Moses' firm conviction that he was to lead the people of God. Only one thing stood in the way: the Israelites would not have him as their leader. They would not even acknowledge his membership in the nation. They looked upon him with distrust and suspicion. And then there was one more thing that troubled him. God had not confirmed this calling. Thus Moses waited for a change of attitude among the Hebrews and for a word of confirmation from God.

Slowly the feeling of eagerness and anticipation built up in the breast of Moses. As he watched the suffering and oppression experienced by his brethren, he became more and more convinced that something had to be done very soon. When one day he watched an Egyptian beating an Israelite unmercifully and without due cause, he could contain himself no longer. He would prove to this fellow Israelite that he was not an Egyptian at heart; he was ready and willing to take the part of the people of God. Moses was determined, but he was careful not to neglect due caution. Vigilantly he looked about him. No Egyptian must see or know what he was about to do. The way was clear, for no one else was in sight. Quickly Moses stepped forth and, laying hands on the Egyptian, slew him. With continued caution he carried the body away and buried it in the sand where it would not soon be discovered. Only then did he notice that the Hebrew had already departed.

With a light heart Moses returned that evening to the palace. He felt flushed with joy in his accomplishment. Was not the man whom he had rescued even now spreading the word through the land of Goshen? Was not the news being received with amazement and joy by all who heard it? Now all Israel would know with certainty that he had forsaken the riches of life among the Egyptians to unite himself with them in their suffering. Surely their attitude toward him would be different on the morrow. Would they not eagerly receive him as one of them, and maybe even suggest that he be their leader? With only a slight tinge of fear and misgiving, Moses passed the hours of that night.

In the morning he left the palace with a greater enthusiasm than he had known for many a year. Perhaps he would never return. If the Israelites received him with the gratitude that he expected, he could go to dwell with them. It would maybe be only a matter of days before the people would be sufficiently organized to rise up in rebellion against the Egyptians. With the blessing of God upon them they would throw off the yoke of Egypt and return with power into Canaan.

As Moses approached the place where the Israelites were working, he looked about him for signs of the new and appreciative attitude. It was then that he saw a new opportunity for him to establish himself more firmly with his people. He saw two Hebrews striving together. The day before, he had availed himself of the opportunity to show himself to be a strong and able defender of the people of God. Now he would show himself as a wise and discerning judge. He would watch to see which of the two was in the wrong and then take steps to reconcile them to each other. By this they would know for sure that he was capable of being their leader.

Finally, Moses approached the two brethren that were struggling together. With a tone of voice as gentle and understanding as he could make it, he addressed himself to them. "Sirs," he said, "ye are brethren, why do ye wrong one to another? Wherefore smitest thou thy fellow?" (Ex. 2:13).

But the response was far different from what Moses had expected. The man who was evidently in the wrong turned upon him. There was no shame, no guilt, no repentance upon his face. There was only a bitter sneer, and from him came the retort, "Who made thee a ruler and a judge over us? intendest thou to kill me, as thou killedst the Egyptian?" (Ex. 2:14), and with a rude shove he pushed Moses away.

In amazement and dismay Moses looked about him at the others, but wherever he looked it was the same. There was no kindness, no gratitude, no sympathy or understanding. On the faces of all were to be seen only sneers, distrust, hatred—the same as before, only now even more bitter. Moses turned and fled.

There are disappointments in the lives of men that at the time often seem impossible to endure. We think of Elijah when he was driven all alone into the wilderness until he cried unto God that he might die. We think of Peter that night after he had denied his Lord when he went out to weep wretchedly bitter tears. Such was the despair that tore at the heart of Moses as he was retreating from the sneers of his brethren. The whole of his life had served to the building of the dream that now lay crumbled about him. It had been the one thing only that he had really desired, because he believed in God and loved the people of God. But he had underestimated the ingratitude and hardness that still dominated the hearts of Israel. They did not want a deliverer. In spite of all their hardships, they were still bound with lust to the fleshpots of Egypt. That was their reason for rejecting the love of Moses.

Still, as Moses retreated, there was one thought that he could not drive away. In his ears continually rang the question, "Who made thee a ruler and a judge over us?" For that question he could not find an answer. He had no appointment either of man or of God. What he had done, he had done on his own, and he had no right. He was an intruder and an impostor. Uncalled of God and unwanted of the people, he had received only what he deserved.

Moses now faced the question of where to go. If his brethren held no love or respect for him, they would soon report his misdeed of the previous day to their overlords. Soon even Pharaoh would know and he would be called to give an account. Perhaps even now the summons was awaiting him. He could go to the palace and defend himself. His word would undoubtedly stand against the accusation of a mere Hebrew slave. In that way his position in the palace and in Pharaoh's family would be secured. But that would require of him a false oath before the king. It might stand before man, but for it he would be held guilty by God. Even more, it would mean that he would be forever separated from the people of God. The Israelites would recognize him as guilty even if Pharaoh did not. All possibility of his being restored to the covenant people of God would be forever gone. When their deliverance would come, it would pass him by.

The only other alternative would be for him to flee the land. This would be sure to incur the wrath of Pharaoh, for it would be as much as an admittance of guilt. It would constitute a public acknowledgment that he had taken the part of a Hebrew slave over against the ruling power of the Egyptians. Never again would he be able to return in peace to the palace. The riches and glory of the royal palace would be forever lost. He would be a hunted man, unwanted in all of the land of Egypt.

We read concerning Moses in Hebrews 11:27, "By faith he forsook Egypt, not fearing the wrath of the king: for he endured, as seeing him who is invisible." Moses stood before a choice between Pharaoh and God. Only by remaining in Egypt and defending himself with a false oath could Moses maintain the position of favor before Pharaoh that he had known all of his life. In fleeing, he would incur Pharaoh's wrath, and he would be disowned as the son of Pharaoh's daughter. Henceforth his life would be worth nothing more than that of any Hebrew slave. But with Moses there was an awareness of more than just the attitude of Pharaoh toward him. He was conscious of the presence of the invisible God. As powerful a ruler as Pharaoh might be, the favor of God was to Moses much more important, and God would never condone an oath falsely sworn. Moses was a man of faith, and the presence of the invisible God could not be forgotten.

It was a solitary figure that made its way toward the wilderness of Midian. He had thought to be going this way at the head of a great nation, but he was now going all alone. He had thought to be going in power, but now he was fleeing for his life. He had thought to be going in joy, but now his heart was rent in sorrow. There was yet very much that Moses had to learn.

Chapter 5

HUMBLING OF MOSES IN MIDIAN

> Now Moses kept the flock of Jethro his father in law, the
> priest of Midian. (Exodus 3:1)

With anguish and confusion weighing upon his soul, Moses made his way toward the wilderness of Midian. He wandered almost aimlessly. His thoughts were not on the place to which he was going but upon all that he was leaving behind. Behind him were all of the privileges of his childhood. No longer would he know the luxuries of Pharaoh's court, the schooling that he had enjoyed and mastered, the servants anxious to do his every bidding, the countless opportunities of influence and advancement. Behind him were all the dreams of his youth. More and more through his young life, his mind had been dominated by plans of what he would do for the children of Israel. He had thought to unite himself with them. He had thought to lead them in a glorious demonstration of power. He had thought to be their savior. But now these dreams were all shattered and were being left behind. Behind him—and this hurt most of all—were being left the people of God. The Israelites were his brethren and the fellow objects of God's promises. His heart had cried for them in their suffering, and his prayer had been for their deliverance. But now he was leaving the land, and they were being left behind in bondage.

Quite conscious was Moses all of the time that he had made an irrevocable choice. He was not sorry that it had been made, but moment by moment he began to realize the more the greatness of the consequences. By fleeing the land, he was acknowledging before everyone that he was guilty in the murder of the Egyptian taskmaster.

It meant that a member of Pharaoh's own household had taken the part of the Israelites over against the Egyptians. It was a personal disgrace to Pharaoh, and it surely infuriated him. Pharaoh would have been willing, even anxious, to have Moses remain and deny the charges so as to spare the reputation of the royal court. But that would have required a false denial on Moses' part, and, because he feared God, Moses knew that the present course was best.

Weary from pondering all this, Moses came to rest at the side of a well in Midian. Little did he realize how carefully the invisible hand of God's providence was guiding him. While in Egypt, Moses had been close to the people of God. Perhaps he had been allowed from time to time to return to the spiritual fellowship of his parents' home. Now he was leaving this sphere of covenant fellowship to go, as it were, into banishment alone. But God would not leave one of his chosen vessels completely isolated from the communion of saints. In Midian there dwelt the descendants of Abraham through Keturah, a small remnant of which still remained faithful to the faith of their father. Chief among them was Reuel, a friend of God as his name implied. He served in the capacity of priest to the faithful. It was toward the home of this man Reuel that Moses was being led by the hand of God's providence.

As Moses sat by the well, the daughters of Reuel approached to perform the daily task of watering their father's flock. There follows a meeting that reminds us of the experiences of Eliezer and Jacob in Haran. There were also those in Midian who were antagonistic to Reuel and his household. It was their custom, when Reuel's daughters came to water the flock, to drive them away, forcing them to wait until everyone else was finished. So did they also on this day when Moses sat watching. However, within Moses there was a heart of kindness such as is peculiar to the people of God, whether Eliezer, or Jacob, or Moses. He could not endure merely to look on amid such apparent rudeness and injustice. Although weary, he still presented an imposing figure as he approached the men. There was the dignity of one raised in the royal court. There was the confidence of one who understood full well what he was doing. There was the determination of one incensed with a feeling for justice. With a few sharp and threatening words he sent the men scurrying away. Nor did his regal bearing prevent him from stooping to the menial task of filling the troughs with water. With dispatch the daughters of Reuel were soon on their way. Enthused, as only young girls can be, they related to their father how they had been saved by an Egyptian from the customary rudeness of the shepherds. Not wanting in hospitality and gratitude, Reuel quickly sent the girls again to invite the man to come to their home and stay.

Surely it was not long before Reuel and Moses discovered the common ground that lay between them. They feared and worshiped the same God. Soon Moses discarded his courtly robes for the clothing of the field to engage in the duties of the household. Time went on and Moses was united in marriage with Zipporah, one of Reuel's daughters. God had provided him with a place where he could dwell. In the household was the fear of God, and Moses could remain there without fear.

Still, although Moses was supplied with the needed communion of saints, there was a facet of his spiritual life that neither Reuel nor Zipporah could share. They were descendants of Abraham through Keturah and could not appreciate the central place that Israel and his children held in the covenant of God. They felt no special sympathy for the Israelites who labored in the bondage of Egypt. They had no strong desire for the day when the children of Jacob would be delivered from the hand of Pharaoh. They did not see the need for Israel being returned to Canaan. But these were the things that dominated the mind of Moses. Moses tried to explain his concern to them, but they did not understand, and they even resented the prominent place that Israel held in his heart and mind. Moses soon learned that this burden of his heart had to be borne alone. More and more he began to withdraw himself with the flock into the solitude of the wilderness, there to commune with his God all alone.

The early years of Moses' sojourn in Midian were hard and bitter years. Outwardly he seemed to have adapted himself to the quiet life of a herdsman, but inwardly his heart was often in turmoil. The royal robes of the court could be laid aside, but a man's nature cannot be shed like a garment. The dreams and ambitions of his youth had been many years in developing; they lingered with him still. As he guided Reuel's sheep, he thought repeatedly of the greater flock that he had longed to lead along those same roads. With pent-up feelings approaching resentment, he questioned why it could not have been so. Had not he had the ability, the preparation, the qualifications to lead the people of God? And according to prophecy, was not the time drawing nigh when Abraham's seed should be delivered? Earnestly Moses sought for the answers. With a sorrow so great that it hurt, he thought on his rejection by the Israelites. Why had they refused to receive him as one of their brethren? Why had they defended the Egyptian over against him? Perhaps he had been a bit hasty. Maybe he should have been more careful. But was that sufficient reason for them to treat him as they did? Time and again Moses felt as though he should hasten back to Egypt to see if he could not establish himself again. But he could not. Pharaoh would seek for his life, and his brethren would not receive him. Those years were to Moses years of banishment. He felt rejected on every side. A son was born to him and he named the child Gershom, "for he said, I have been a stranger in a strange land" (Ex. 2:22).

Slowly the years passed by, and with them Moses' outlook made a change. His confidence began to waver and slowly to slip away. Amid the solitude of the wilderness, the ability he had thought himself to possess did not seem quite so convincing. He had been mighty in word and in deed while attending the schools of Egypt, but was that sufficient to lead the people of God? A voice from the past that had long remained in the mind of Moses as an uncomfortable whisper began to grow into a loud, accusing roar, "Who made thee a ruler and a judge over us?" Those had been the last words spoken to him in Egypt, and for them he had never found an answer. Try as he might, he could not escape their implication. How long did he try to forget them? How often did he try to resist their meaning? We of course do not know, but if we may deduce from our own experiences, the admission must have been hard in coming. But Moses was a child of God, and the time of confession had to come. He had been an impostor. He had gone beyond his right. There was no more room for bitterness. There was no more room for resentment against others. If he was in banishment, it was a banishment that was just.

That was undoubtedly the time of Moses' greatest anguish. His days were dark from the sorrow of sin; his nights were sleepless in the light of God's holiness. He had learned to know himself as never before. He was a sinner. He had sinned, not so much against the Egyptian, nor against the Israelite, but against God. How presumptuous it had been for him to endeavor to establish himself as a leader in Israel; how foolish to think that he could save the people of God. It would have been just had God allowed him to die by Pharaoh's sword. Salvation would come to Israel, but not by his hand; it would be solely by the hand of the Lord. Moses came in repentance to God, and there he found peace. Was it not in that day when his second son was born? He named the son Eliezer, "for the God of my father, said he, was mine help, and delivered me from the sword of Pharaoh" (Ex. 18:4).

Forty years passed by in Midian, and Moses was a changed man. Gone was the refinement, the eloquence, the dignity of the court. In its place appeared a common man, almost crude after the manner of a shepherd. His clothes were poor, dirty, and torn from much wandering in the wilderness. His words were simple and few. Self-confidence had given way to timidity. The years had left their mark. The ambition and enthusiasm of youth had subsided into quietness and patience. He now was a man content to be a mere shepherd. To all appearances the advantages of Moses' youth had been wasted. What good was all of his schooling and royal upbringing, out here in the barren wastes? Where in it all was the wisdom of God?

Also inwardly there had come a change. Still there was the same faith and hope that had been with him from his youth. The instruction of his parents had not been forgotten. Still his love was with Israel in bondage. He longed for Israel's deliverance. He prayed for it from day to day. But Moses himself no longer figured in these visions of deliverance. What could he possibly do, a mere sinner? It was a work that only God could perform. The dreams of his youth were but folly. The most for which he dared hope was that, if he lived, he might join himself to the people of God in their deliverance. If the grace of God would allow, he longed to go with Israel to the promised land.

We look back over the ages, and at first glance we too are apt to dismiss the years in Midian as of little account, a marking of time, a mere waiting for the proper time. Yet for Moses those years were the most important of all. In Egypt he was taught by man, and that had its importance and value. But in Midian he was taught by God. Moses learned to know himself as a sinner. He learned patience and complete reliance upon God.

Chapter 6

THE CALLING OF MOSES

23. And the children of Israel sighed by reason of the bondage, and they cried, and their cry came up unto God by reason of the bondage.

4. God called unto him out of the midst of the bush, and said, Moses, Moses. And he said, Here am I.

7. And the LORD said, I have surely seen the affliction of my people which are in Egypt, and have heard their cry by reason of their taskmasters; for I know their sorrows.

10. Come now therefore, and I will send thee unto Pharaoh, that thou mayest bring forth my people the children of Israel out of Egypt. (Exodus 2:23; 3:4, 7, 10)

Moses had been rejected by the children of Israel. They had refused to receive him as a brother in the faith. They did not want him as a prince and ruler to lead them out of the bondage of Egypt. For many generations they had been living in the land of Egypt. The riches of Egypt were many, and the Israelites had enjoyed them to the full. They had learned to love the bounties that could always be obtained, the fish, the onions and melons, the garlic and leeks. At the same time, the land of Canaan had lost its attraction for them. It seemed distant and far away. They seldom thought of it anymore. That their fathers had come from that land no longer seemed very important. The thought that they someday might return to Canaan gave them little joy.

Indeed, in recent years the situation in Egypt had been changing. The former kindness of the Egyptians had turned to hatred.

The joys of Egypt had been curtailed by oppression and persecution. Bitter bondage was now their part, with arduous labor in brick, and in mortar, and in all manner of service in the field. The very lives of their newborn children had been threatened again and again. But still their hope endured. Maybe something would happen to mollify the hatred of Pharaoh. If the Egyptians could be soothed, then the Israelites could settle down to enjoy once again the luxuries of Egypt that they had learned to love. When Moses appeared and slew an Egyptian, thereby clearly offering to lead them in rebellion against their masters, it left them cold and even angry. They did not want trouble and fighting; they wanted peace. They wanted to soothe their masters, not incite them. With harsh words and scornful looks they drove Moses away. Dutifully they reported his misdeed to the overseers. Moses was forced to flee for his life toward the wilderness of Midian, soon to be forgotten by all but a few.

The years passed by. The children of Israel looked for Pharaoh's anger to abate, but it did not. They tried to pacify him but could not. The future continued to look only darker. Finally, Pharaoh died, and the hopes of the Israelites revived. Perhaps the new Pharaoh would be different; maybe he would be more kind. But alas, all of their fondest dreams were dashed. Grievous oppression continued to be their part, and if anything, it was heavier than before. At last Israel's confidence in Egypt and its people began to waver and die. Anticipation gave way to despair, and there arose from their hearts a bitter sigh. Only then did they think to remember the true source of their strength in the past. They were a wretched people. Nearly eighty years of oppression had passed, during which time Israel had pinned her hopes on the world and its men. Only when all had failed did they remember to turn to their God. It was a wonder of divine grace that "God heard their groaning, and God remembered his covenant with Abraham, with Isaac, and with Jacob. And God looked upon the children of Israel, and God had respect unto them" (Ex. 2:24–25).

It was a lone shepherd who led his small flock to the backside of the wilderness of Midian. The way had been rough and barren, but here on the slopes of Horeb green pastures were sure to be found. The sheep were in good hands. The man's words were few, and his appearance was crude, but his actions were gentle, and his eyes reflected a heart that had found peace. To look at him one could hardly imagine that once his feet had trod the royal courts of Egypt, that his feats of learning had won great acclaim by his teachers, that his mind had devised plans of great and impressive works, that his dreams had been to lead a great nation hundreds of thousands strong. That had been long ago, and the way of life he had now learned was quite different. True, the dreams and ambitions of youth had died slowly, and often painfully, but die they had. The mannerisms of the court had disappeared, and in their place had come the simpler virtues of gentleness, kindness, patience, meekness, and childlike trust in his God. The one great joy that remained to him was simply to pray and worship the Lord and to meditate upon his word.

What good was it all? What was this man accomplishing alone in this barren wilderness? What was becoming of all his preparation and education? Where was his challenge? What was he doing for God? The world could hardly be expected to recognize it, the man hardly realized it himself, but through those years in the wilderness he had grown immensely in stature before God. The day would come when divine inspiration would cause it to be written that "the man Moses was very meek, above all the men which were upon the face of the earth" (Num. 12:3). What greater virtue could be ascribed to a child of God? The lesson of Midian exceeded by far all that he had learned in the greatest schools of the world.

As the shepherd made his way up the slopes of Horeb, there was a purpose guiding his life of which he was quite unaware. The invisible hand of God's providence was leading him toward a certain bush that grew there among the mountain crags. Then he saw it. There stood before him a bush, a bush enveloped in flames, a bush filled with fire but not consumed. His curiosity aroused, he turned to examine the bush more closely. And then from the bush there came the voice, "Moses, Moses," and with faltering lips he answered back, "Here am I" (Ex. 3:4). The bush was chosen as a symbol of Israel in her lowly state of bondage. In the bush was the fire of God's presence, purging his people through suffering, but not consuming them. This Moses did not yet realize, but the voice went on to instruct him. "Draw not nigh hither: put off thy shoes from off thy feet, for the place whereon thou standest is holy ground....I am the God of thy father, the God of Abraham, the God of Isaac, and the God of Jacob" (vv. 5–6). Awed and afraid, Moses hid his face. Who was he to look upon God?

The voice continued:

7. I have surely seen the affliction of my people which are in Egypt, and have heard their cry by reason of their taskmasters; for I know their sorrows;

8. And I am come down to deliver them out of the hand of the Egyptians, and to bring them up out of that land unto a good land and a large, unto a land flowing with milk and honey; unto the place of the Canaanites, and the Hittites, and the Amorites, and the Perizzites, and the Hivites, and the Jebusites.

9. Now therefore, behold, the cry of the children of Israel is come unto me: and I have also seen the oppression wherewith the Egyptians oppress them.

10. Come now therefore, and I will send thee unto Pharaoh, that thou mayest bring forth my people the children of Israel out of Egypt. (Ex. 3:7–10)

Can we begin to imagine with what depth of feeling these words must have stirred the heart of Moses? Here was the hope and longing of all his life promised by the very voice of the angel of God's presence. Already as a child sitting upon his mother's knee he had heard of God's promise that Israel would be delivered from the bondage of Egypt, and he had looked forward to it with childlike eagerness and anticipation. All during his youth, as he had applied himself with diligence to study and learning, it had been in the expectation that what he learned could be used in the service of God's people in their deliverance and settling in the promised land. Through the emerging discretion of his young adulthood, his every thought and ambition had been dominated by the determination to work for the deliverance of the people of God. Even during the forty long years of his banishment in Midian, he had ceased not to pray in the confidence that God would be faithful to his promises. Now the voice of God's angel was telling him that the time had come.

And there was more. Not only would Moses witness and take part in the deliverance, he would be the one through whom God would work to bring it to pass. Did not all of the old dreams and ambitions, which only after a hard and painful struggle had subsided from his mind, suddenly surge up again within him? He was to stand upon the foreground. All of his years of training and preparation were not without purpose after all. The dreams of his youth were to be realized. Yet, somehow, these old dreams and ambitions did not seem to have the appeal for him that they had had in former years. Was it perhaps because of the memories that came back so forcibly to him along with these thoughts of the past? He remembered the time that he had tried. The bitter words, the hate-filled looks, the foolishness of having tried to establish himself by his own words and works—these memories were painful for Moses even to recall. How could he ever go and try again? But even more, his whole outlook on life had changed. Before he had thought himself capable; now he knew that he was not. Moses rejoiced at God's promise of deliverance for Israel, but his joy was mingled with dismay at the very suggestion that it was through him that it was to be wrought. He answered back, "Who am I, that I should go unto Pharaoh, and that I should bring forth the children of Israel out of Egypt?" (Ex. 3:11).

God's answer to Moses was kind and gentle. "Certainly I will be with thee; and this shall be a token unto thee, that I have sent thee:

When thou hast brought forth the people out of Egypt, ye shall serve God upon this mountain" (Ex. 3:12). It was this that would make all of the difference. Before, Moses had tried to become the leader over Israel by acting on his own. Thus he had been bound to fail. By working apart from the command of God he had been opposing the cause of the Lord and not aiding it. But now God would be with him. God would give to him strength and authority. There was no longer any real reason why Moses should be afraid.

But the fear of Moses was set very deep, and it was not easily dismissed. Through the long years in the wilderness, he had learned to repudiate all of his dreams of leadership. Only with flushes of shame did he remember his former efforts. It hurt and pained him to remember those cutting words of rejection, "Who made thee a prince and judge over us?" How could he ever present himself to Israel again? Moses voiced his objection. "Behold, when I come unto the children of Israel, and shall say unto them, The God of your fathers hath sent me unto you; and they shall say to me, What is his name? what shall I say unto them?" (Ex. 3:13). To what could he possibly appeal to prove to them that his act was not again mere presumption?

The answer of God to Moses must rank among the greatest of the self-revelations that God has made to his people in time. "I AM THAT I AM...Thus shalt thou say unto the children of Israel, I AM hath sent me unto you...Thus shalt thou say unto the children of Israel, the LORD God of your fathers, the God of Abraham, the God of Isaac, and the God of Jacob, hath sent me unto you: this is my name for ever, and this is my memorial unto all generations" (3:14–15). I Am That I Am—this is God's name in a most unique sense of the word. No one else can possibly have this name, for everyone else is only that which God has determined him to be. Only God is the absolutely self-determining one. He alone determines what he shall be at every moment of time and throughout all eternity. He alone does only and always what he himself has determined that he shall do. Thus he can be and is ever faithful to his promises, to the promises given to Abraham, Isaac, and Jacob and to all of their spiritual seed. This absolutely independent faithfulness of the covenant God would become perfectly evident through the work that Moses was being sent to perform. This name of God would be established as a memorial of faithfulness to his people forevermore. It would prove beyond doubt that God is the I Am That I Am.

Chapter 7

MOSES AND "I AM"

14. And God said unto Moses, I AM THAT I AM: and he said, Thus shalt thou say unto the children of Israel, I AM hath sent me unto you.
15. This is my name for ever, and this is my memorial unto all generations. (Exodus 3:14–15)

I Am That I Am—this is a most profound and glorious name. It is to this name that the heart of every man aspires. No desire is more dear to man than to be able to say, "I am that which I have determined myself to be." Was not this the dream that filled the heart of Eve when she rejected the word of God for the promise of the devil, "ye shall be as gods, knowing good and evil" (Gen. 3:5)? It is a deep-set urge to be self-sufficient, to be self-determining, to be self-providing, and, could it be, self-existent. But, in spite of all this longing and even trying, it cannot be. Man is what he is made to be by his heredity and by his environment, by the constant flow of influences that press in upon his life, by his friends and foes, by riches and poverty, by prosperity and adversity, by wars and peace. Pride tells man he should be self-made. Reality is that countless determining factors mold him from without. If he is honest, man must say, "I am what God has determined that I should be."

He before whom Moses stood said, "I AM THAT I AM," and he said it in truth. He was Jehovah God, and he is the same even now. He is the source of his own being, his own life, his own existence. There is nothing that forms or molds or influences him from without. He has determined what he shall be, and even so he is. There is none over him; there is none next to him; there is no one to whom he must adapt. Nothing can change him; nothing can degrade him or raise him up; nothing can make him be different. This is even more wonderful when we consider that within his being there is a counsel concerning all things that take place in time. He does not exist alone, in isolation from all of the vicissitudes of time. His being stands in immediate contact with them all. But still he remains the I Am That I Am. He influences all the circumstances of time but is himself influenced by none. He determines all things but is himself determined by none. He sustains all things but is himself sustained by none. He creates all things but is himself created by none. He is the greatest of all, the only I Am That I Am; he is Jehovah God.

"The Lord God of your fathers, the God of Abraham, the God of Isaac, and the God of Jacob" spoke unto Moses, applying unto himself that name. This made his presence so eminently important. The same who called himself I Am identified himself as the God of the covenant. He had given to Abraham, Isaac, and Jacob the promises: that he would be a God unto them, that he would bless them, that he would give the land of Canaan to them and to their seed forever. His very name implied faithfulness to these promises. He would not change, no one could force him to change; he was able to bring it to pass. Israel would be brought from the bondage of Egypt unto the land of covenant promise. This would be his memorial unto all generations; God's people would surely be saved.

In the presence of God, Moses trembled and quaked. He was so very small. For forty years in the wilderness he had been pondering this fact. He had learned to recognize and acknowledge the folly of his youth when he had thought to do something for God. He had learned the wickedness of his impatience when he had not waited for a calling and an authoritative name in which he could act. He had learned to know his sin. Through the years of wandering in the wilderness he had become ever smaller in his own esteem. But now he stood in the presence of God, and he was not yet small enough. Quickly he shed his shoes, but the dust and sin of the ways he had trod still seemed to cleave to his feet. He covered his face for shame, but still the uncleanness of his face and lips seemed openly exposed. He was afraid, and at the sound of that voice he trembled. He was so very small, and he stood in the presence of God.

Then God spoke, "I have surely seen the affliction of my people....Come now therefore, and I will send thee unto Pharaoh, that thou mayest bring forth my people the children of Israel out of Egypt" (Ex. 3:7, 10). Moses heard these words with amazement. At this moment he felt his own nothingness as never before, and at the same moment God was telling him that he must go to deliver Israel from Egypt. This was to his mind impossible. Forty years before he would have welcomed the opportunity but not now. He had learned to know himself too well. He was not the man to do a work like that. "Who am I," he answered back, "that I should go unto Pharaoh, and that I should bring forth the children of Israel out of Egypt?" (v. 11).

God spoke again: "Certainly I will be with thee; and this shall be a token unto thee, that I have sent thee: When thou hast brought forth the people out of Egypt, ye shall serve God upon this mountain" (Ex. 3:12). Moses need not fear his own inability. God would be with him. That he was nothing in himself did not matter. God would be there to supply all that he lacked. God would even give to him a token of his calling, a promise that they would come to worship at the very mountain where he now stood.

But Moses was not afraid just of himself. He feared the people. What would they say? Would they receive him as a leader? He remembered so well those taunting jeers from the past: "Who made thee a ruler and a judge over us?" How could he possibly make them understand? How could he convince them that this time it was different? What would be the proof of his authority? To Moses it appeared to be hopeless, and he feared even to try. He dared not return to those who had rejected him before. "Behold, when I come unto the children of Israel, and shall say unto them, The God of your fathers hath sent me unto you; and they shall say to me, What is his name? what shall I say unto them?" (Ex. 3:13).

It was then that God answered, "I AM THAT I AM...Thus shalt

thou say unto the children of Israel, I AM hath sent me unto you" (Ex. 3:14). With that name Moses could go forth in boldness to speak to anyone, it mattered not who. He could speak to the people of Israel; he could speak to the elders of Israel; he could speak to Pharaoh himself. That which he would announce in the name of the I Am did not depend upon their response. Moses need not go trying to convince or persuade those to whom he spoke as though the desire of God depended upon them. God is self-determining and able to perform his own will. This was of utmost importance for Moses to understand. Because he was going in the name of I Am, he need have no fear for what the outcome would be. He could be confident that, regardless of what men might do, God's purpose and promise would be realized. God told him beforehand what he should say to Pharaoh: "Say unto him, The LORD God of the Hebrews hath met with us: and now let us go, we beseech thee, three days' journey into the wilderness, that we may sacrifice to the LORD our God" (v. 18). Even more, God warned him beforehand that, although that command to Pharaoh would be minimal, Pharaoh would not listen: "And I am sure that the king of Egypt will not let you go, no, not by a mighty hand" (v. 19). But this mattered not; God told Moses beforehand what the end result would be:

20. And I will stretch out my hand, and smite Egypt with all my wonders which I will do in the midst thereof: and after that he will let you go.
21. And I will give this people favour in the sight of the Egyptians: and it shall come to pass, that, when ye go, ye shall not go empty." (vv. 20–21)

God's will would surely be performed.

Still Moses hesitated. He feared the people, for he knew how obstinate they could be. Mere words would not be enough for them, even though they were the people of God:

1. Behold, they will not believe me, nor hearken to my voice: for they will say, The LORD hath not appeared unto thee.

2. And the LORD said unto him, What is that in thine hand? And he said, A rod.

3. And he said, Cast it on the ground. And he cast it on the ground, and it became a serpent; and Moses fled from before it.

4. And the LORD said unto Moses, Put forth thine hand, and take it by the tail. And he put forth his hand, and caught it, and it became a rod in his hand. (Ex. 4:1–4)

The rod had served to identify Moses as a shepherd in the land of Midian. Henceforth it would serve to identify him as the shepherd of God's chosen people. Through that rod marvelous works would be performed. The power of Moses' calling would be made clearly manifest. Even now as he cast the rod to the ground it was changed into a serpent. Moses knew the significance of a serpent. As a child upon his parents' knees he had been told of the use to which the serpent had been subjected in the garden of Eden. He remembered the word of God to the serpent as it had been passed down for many generations, "Because thou hast done this, thou art cursed above all cattle, and above every beast of the field; upon thy belly shalt thou go, and dust shalt thou eat all the days of thy life" (Gen. 3:14). The serpent was a symbol of Satan and his wicked power. In revulsion and fear Moses drew back. But according to the command of God, he reached forth his hand to grasp the serpent by the tail, and it was transformed to a rod again. Thus would Moses' rod have complete control over the power of Satan to release it and control it according to the power of God.

Again, God spoke unto him. "Put now thine hand into thy bosom. And he put his hand into his bosom: and when he took it out, behold, his hand was leprous as snow" (Ex. 4:6). This reflected upon Moses himself. Leprosy is a horrible disease with which the body very literally rots away. In the old dispensation this disease was considered a symbol of the corruption of sin. When one had this disease, it could be seen that his body was literally dying, even as sin is always killing the soul. Now, suddenly, Moses found himself to have contracted that terrible disease. It was as though all at once the sin that he knew was within him had come to the surface. To Moses it was as though he was being exposed and condemned before the justice of God. But again God spoke, "Put thine hand into thy bosom again. And he put his hand into his bosom again; and plucked it out of his bosom, and, behold, it was turned again as his other flesh" (v. 7) Here again was the power of the I Am, symbolically presented, a power able even to wash away the corruption of sin.

Still there was more. God continued to speak. "And it shall come to pass, if they will not believe also these two signs, neither hearken unto thy voice, that thou shalt take of the water of the river, and pour it upon the dry land: and the water which thou takest out of the river shall become blood upon the dry land" (4:9). This was to be the first of the ten great plagues that would come in judgment upon Egypt. Each in its own way would demonstrate the power of the I Am, whose will none can resist.

Moses did not want to go back to Egypt. He was afraid—afraid of Pharaoh, afraid of the children of Israel, afraid of himself. Almost as a move of desperation he presented one more excuse. "O my Lord, I am not eloquent, neither heretofore, nor since thou hast spoken unto thy servant; but I am slow of speech, and of a slow tongue" (Ex. 4:10). Through the years of lonely wandering in the desert his tongue had grown thick, and his words were slow and halting. But what was this before the Lord. "Who hath made man's mouth? or who maketh the dumb, or deaf, or the seeing, or the blind? have not I the LORD?" (v. 11). In fact, when Moses continued to object, the Lord told him with a tone of anger that preparations already had been made.

14. Is not Aaron the Levite thy brother? I know that he can speak well. And also, behold, he cometh forth to meet thee: and when he seeth thee, he will be glad in his heart.

15. And thou shalt speak unto him, and put words in his mouth: and I will be with thy mouth, and with his mouth, and will teach you what ye shall do.

16. And he shall be thy spokesman unto the people: and he shall be, even he shall be to thee instead of a mouth, and thou shalt be to him instead of God.
17. And thou shalt take this rod in thine hand, wherewith thou shalt do signs. (vv. 14–17)

Moses himself was the first to learn that it was impossible to resist the I Am. "And Moses went" (Ex. 4:18).

Chapter 8

MOSES' RETURN TO EGYPT

> 19. And the LORD said unto Moses in Midian, Go, return into Egypt: for all the men are dead which sought thy life.
> 20. And Moses took his wife and his sons, and set them upon an ass, and he returned to the land of Egypt: and Moses took the rod of God in his hand. (Exodus 4:19–20)

With mixed feelings Moses saw the fire of God's presence fade from the bush on Horeb, looked at the gentle sheep quietly grazing about him, gathered them together, and began his journey back to the camp of his father-in-law Jethro (Reuel). He had stood in the presence of the Most High God, and with awesome wonder he pondered the fact. He had heard that Israel was soon to be delivered, and he rejoiced exceedingly, for he had ever hoped for such deliverance to come. He had been commanded to go forth and lead the children of Israel, and he trembled at the thought, for through the years he had learned to know his own weakness and sin. But Moses went. He had no choice. The Lord his God had commanded him.

Upon returning to the camp of Jethro, he went immediately to his father-in-law. When he had joined himself to the household of Jethro, he had placed himself under Jethro's rule. Now that the time had come for him to leave, it would not do for him to ignore the rights of this man. Respectfully he spoke, "Let me go, I pray thee, and return unto my brethren which are in Egypt, and see whether they be yet alive" (Ex. 4:18). Only in the most general terms did Moses intimate his real reason for returning to Egypt. He had learned through the years that Jethro, although undoubtedly a child of God, had no real understanding of or concern for the need of Israel being delivered from Egypt. Jethro was of the sons of Keturah. Through the years, they had lost much of the feeling for the importance of Israel in bringing to pass the promised redemption of God. Thus, Moses did not deem it wise to share with his father-in-law's family the deep, spiritual experience and revelation through which he had just passed. Nonetheless, Jethro was satisfied with Moses' request and answered, "Go in peace" (v. 18).

Still Moses did not leave the land of Midian immediately. Was it perhaps fear of the task that lay before him that made him linger unnecessarily long in the home of Jethro? But God was watching Moses, and with him there was no allowance for such procrastination. He came and spoke to Moses to urge him on and to assure him against all unnecessary fears. "Go, return into Egypt: for all the men are dead which sought thy life" (Ex. 4:19). God had waited over four hundred years to bring Israel forth out of Egypt, but now that the time was come, there was no room for delay. Moses must learn to respond promptly to the commands of the Lord. It was not for him to linger.

There was solemnity in the occasion when that small group of people set forth from the house of Jethro. Upon a beast of burden sat a woman with two small children; before them walked the man with a shepherd's crook in his hand. The children were young and did not yet realize what was taking place. The woman was clearly troubled. She too did not understand, and she felt no desire to leave her father's home for the alien land of Egypt. She was going only because her husband said it was necessary. The man was lost deep in thought. He pondered the duties and responsibilities that were lying before him. In his hand he held the shepherd's crook, but not carelessly as he had in former years. This rod had taken on a new and special significance for him. It had been appointed of God as a symbol of his newly acquired power and authority. With an awe approaching reverence he held his staff as they traveled.

They had not gone very far before the Lord came once more to Moses. Moses had been called to a very special position as the prophet of God. It was to become a very frequent and at times almost daily experience for him to receive special revelations from God. This intimate communion with God was to characterize his life more than that of any other man. It would be written of him, "And there arose not a prophet since in Israel like unto Moses, whom the LORD knew face to face" (Deut. 34:10). Through these repeated revelations God gave to Moses constant guidance and assurance in the tremendous task. In this particular revelation he instructed Moses with a general outline of the working out of the gospel as he would experience it in the immediate future.

First God said to Moses, "When thou goest to return into Egypt, see that thou do all those wonders before Pharaoh, which I have put in thine hand" (Ex. 4:21). These works would be of utmost importance in establishing Moses as the prophet of God and in setting forth the truth that Moses was sent to proclaim. God would reveal himself in Egypt as the I Am That I Am, the Almighty God who always performs what he wills. Moses would come as God's prophet, with the rod as a symbol of God's power in his hand. Each work performed in the name of God would be unmistakably adapted to show forth the greatness and the power of God. Only the blind would refuse to acknowledge the God of Moses to be the I Am That I Am, whose will cannot be withstood.

But to this, God added a warning concerning Pharaoh's response to these works: "I will harden his heart, that he shall not let the people go" (Ex. 4:21). Pharaoh was among the blind of the world who have eyes but will not see, who have ears but will not hear, who have hearts too hard to understand. God had raised him up and set him upon the throne of Egypt exactly in order to reveal the immense perversity of the human heart. With the truth so clearly set before him, in unquestionable signs and wonders, he would deny that it was real. He would not acknowledge it to himself or to anyone else. He would suppress the truth and hold it under in unrighteousness. In utter folly he would, in the face of the truth, uphold the lie. But let no one think that by so doing he would be successfully resisting the will of

God. This, indeed, Pharaoh would try to do. His boast would ever be that he did not need to recognize the Lord, that he could withstand the God of Israel; but that very fact would be the highest illustration of the absolute sovereignty of the almighty power of God. Behind the hardened heart of Pharaoh was the eternal counsel of God, which had ordained that it should be so. God made this clear to Moses by telling him before it ever happened, "I will harden his heart, that he shall not let the people go."

Finally, God added these instructions: "And thou shalt say unto Pharaoh, Thus saith the LORD, Israel is my son, even my firstborn: and I say unto thee, Let my son go, that he may serve me: and if thou refuse to let him go, I will slay thy son, even thy firstborn" (Ex. 4:22–23). This was the ultimate meaning of the truth that God would reveal through Moses. The expression of God's love would not be without purpose and direction. It would be directed in fatherly love and affection to his son. Israel as a nation was dear to him. In the seed of Abraham it was chosen and adopted to belong to him. It had been so from eternity; it was and would be so in time. When Pharaoh persecuted Israel, he persecuted the object of God's love. When he would refuse to let Israel go, he would be seeking to deprive God of the rightful service of his own son. In righteous judgment, God would strike back. With many infallible proofs he would show his love for his chosen. He would show his power over Pharaoh by depriving Pharaoh of his son.

In this way God was preparing Moses for the conflict that was to come. The powers of evil were already arrayed for battle. In the days to come they would exert themselves to the utmost. But the outcome was sure. The power of God's love would be made known. The lines of battle were before ordained in the divine counsel. Unto Moses it was made known what they would be, in order that in due and proper time the glory might be only unto God.

While pondering all this, Moses stopped for the evening at an inn on the road to Egypt. His mind was still full of all that he had heard, and therefore it was quite unexpected that the Lord came to meet him again at the inn. But this appearance of God was quite different. This appearance was not to Moses individually but to Zipporah his wife as well. Moreover, this appearance was not primarily concerned with Moses' future work, but with his present personal life. The Lord appeared and sought to kill Moses.

Moses had entered into married life while dwelling in the house of Jethro. There true faith in God was maintained, for Jethro was a descendant of Abraham through Keturah. However, in certain matters of faith, this household had become weak and wavering. One of their most grievous shortcomings was the failure to maintain the rite of circumcision. It was a bloody ritual that they considered too painful to observe, so they failed to maintain the outward sign of the covenant that inwardly they still kept. Thus, when Moses' two sons were born, Zipporah had opposed the subjecting of her children to this painful operation, and Moses had submitted. This had been his sin.

But now Moses was returning again to the children of Israel to lead and instruct them in the will of the Lord. One of the things that he would have to teach the people was the necessity of circumcision. But how could he insist that others observe what he had not observed himself? One primary requirement of effective leadership is that a man do his utmost to observe himself what he would require of others. This Moses had not done. In the most forceful terms, God pointed this out to Moses. He told Moses and Zipporah that if Moses would not strive to live blamelessly before the ordinances of God, he would be of no use to him at all as a leader and redeemer of the chosen people. In fact, if Moses in his household did not keep the commandments of God, he would die.

Zipporah had no choice. When the Lord threatened the life of her husband, she took a sharp stone and performed the required operation. But in her heart she held only resentment and bitterness. Among her people this bloody practice had not been observed for many years. She could not understand the need of it, and she detested the thought of subjecting her own children to such a painful practice. Her inner feelings boiled in rebellion. She had not wanted to leave her father's home, and now she was required to treat her own children with cruelty. The Lord withdrew his threatening hand from her husband, but her bitterness remained. She cast the bloody foreskins at Moses' feet and said, "Surely a bloody husband art thou to me..., because of the circumcision" (Ex. 4:25–26).

To Moses it became evident that he could not go on in this way. A wife who resented the high duties of his calling could only interfere and not help. Sadly, he returned to the home of Jethro with his wife and children, there to leave them until his work had been completed. He could not allow even his own wife to stand in the way of the calling that he had received from God. Again he left for Egypt, this time alone.

God saw the loneliness of Moses' heart and made provision for him. He appeared to Aaron, Moses' brother, in Egypt and said, "Go into the wilderness to meet Moses" (Ex. 4:27). There on the way the two brothers, separated for so many years, met. With joy they kissed each other and went on together. As they went, Moses related to his brother all that he had learned of the Lord, and Aaron encouraged Moses in his calling. With his brother by his side, Moses would have the courage to stand in the great and wonderful calling that was his.

Chapter 9

THE WORD OF JEHOVAH IN EGYPT

29. And Moses and Aaron went and gathered together all the elders of the children of Israel:
30. And Aaron spake all the words which the Lord had spoken unto Moses, and did the signs in the sight of the people.
31. And the people believed: and when they heard that the Lord had visited the children of Israel, and that he had looked upon their affliction, then they bowed their heads and worshipped.

1. And afterward Moses and Aaron went in, and told Pharaoh, Thus saith the Lord God of Israel, Let my people go, that they may hold a feast unto me in the wilderness.
2. And Pharaoh said, Who is the Lord, that I should obey his voice to let Israel go? I know not the Lord, neither will I let Israel go. (Exodus 4:29–5:2)

With the burden of God's word resting upon their hearts, the two brothers, Moses and Aaron, entered the land of Egypt. After four hundred years of silence, God had revealed himself again. During that time, he had not changed: his promises of former years were still faithful and true. Soon God's love for his chosen Israel would be unquestionably demonstrated in Egypt. That truth would determine the great events soon to take place in the land of bondage. So immense were these events to be that even Moses and Aaron could not as yet imagine it. With signs and wonders God would deliver his people from the cruel clutches of sin. Let all who would oppose him beware!

Upon entering the land, Moses and Aaron gathered together the elders of Israel. To them first they made known the will of the Lord. How different it was from the first time that Moses had sought to establish himself in Israel. Then his whole concern had been with proving himself. His whole effort had been to show himself able and willing to be for them a leader and savior. In doing so he had failed. But now he came and, without one reference to himself, spoke the word of the Lord. In humble silence the people listened. They heard again the promises of grace that had been received by their covenant fathers, Abraham, Isaac, and Jacob. They were told that God looked upon them in their affliction and would come as the I Am to save them with a mighty hand. They gazed in wonderment upon the signs—the rod changed to a serpent and the leprous hand that was cleansed. Having heard and seen it all, they believed. They were the children of God within whom was the beginning of faith. In humble thanksgiving they bowed their heads and worshiped. Surely great and wondrous things were soon to be done. The I Am had promised it.

Encouraged by the reception they received from the Israelites, Moses and Aaron proceeded immediately to the court of Pharaoh. The message that they bore was simple and direct: "Thus saith the LORD God of Israel, Let my people go, that they may hold a feast unto me in the wilderness" (Ex. 5:1). This was no mere suggestion. Nor was it in any sense a request. It was very clearly a direct command. It was this that aroused Pharaoh's anger and moved him to retort, "Who is the LORD, that I should obey his voice to let Israel go? I know not the LORD, neither will I let Israel go" (v. 2). Pharaoh was not one accustomed to receiving orders or commands. He was the king of Egypt, the most powerful sovereign in all the earth. The very thought that anyone should think to command him, whether Moses or Aaron or even their God, only made him furious.

To some it would seem that this reaction of Pharaoh was quite natural, almost to the point of being excusable. After all, what did he know about the God of Israel? As far as he knew, what Moses and Aaron spoke were just words. There had been as yet no proof that their God was real and worthy of being listened to. Furthermore, the words of Aaron were notedly without tact. Two men burst into his presence and, claiming to speak in the name of their God, demanded, "Let my people go!" There was no recognition of his position and authority as king of Egypt. There was no allowance for the fact that he had his own gods that he worshiped. There was no acknowledgment of his superior power and might over Israel. With blunt and uncompromising terms they simply issued a demand. They treated Pharaoh as a mere ordinary man. Was it then surprising that he reacted so sharply?

Such speculation, however, is superficial. Pharaoh was not as ignorant of the God of Israel as at first it might seem. Had not he and his predecessors been trying now for many years to break the power of Israel as a nation? Yet their greatest efforts had proved to be of no avail because the God of Israel sustained them. Again, did he not know the history of his own nation and the great power that had been demonstrated among them in the days of Joseph? Even besides this, Pharaoh had but to look to the heavens to see the glory of God or to the firmament to see his handiwork. Had he the least bit of discernment or honesty he would have known that this was not the work of his gods, idols of wood and of stone. Moreover, if Moses and Aaron represented the true God, as they said they did, how could they possibly come in any other manner than they did? God, if he be God in truth, cannot come to man merely requesting or suggesting, offering, begging, or pleading. Such would in effect place him down on the level of man, an abrogation of his right to divinity. There is only one way that God can come to any man, even though the man be a king, and that is with the authority of a direct command.

The history that was shortly to follow would demonstrate clearly what was the real reason for Pharaoh's response. It was pride. Pharaoh had determined long before that he would be the supreme authority in his own life. It was the working of sin such as is found naturally in the heart of every man. He wanted to be as God. He recognized the gods of Egypt only because they were of wood and stone, so he could use them as he would. When, therefore, Moses and Aaron came in the name of a God with an authority greater than his, he met it as a personal challenge. It was not the fact that Pharaoh did not know whether the God confessed by Moses and Aaron was real that kept him from acceding to their demand. It was not even a fear lest he should lose the advantage of part or all of Israel's service. It was the principle of the thing. An authority had appeared that claimed to be greater than his own. His pride would not allow this to go unchallenged. The more that the power of Israel's God would become evident, the more he would set himself to prove that it was not greater than his. It was not because of ignorance that Pharaoh refused; it was because the very word of another authority set his heart in rebellion. The more he would learn, the greater this rebellion would become. This was the hardness of heart of which God had spoken. It had begun at Pharaoh's birth. It would continue until his final destruction. The word of God only hastened it on its way. God was setting up Pharaoh as an example to all ages of the rebellious working of sin. It was the same hardening that is found in the heart of every natural man. It is the hardening that only the grace of God can break. But for Pharaoh no such grace existed.

Moses and Aaron proceeded to explain themselves further. "The God of the Hebrews hath met with us: Let us go, we pray thee, three days' journey into the desert, and sacrifice unto the LORD our God; lest he fall upon us with pestilence, or with the sword" (5:3). They set before Pharaoh a minimal requirement. Moses knew that God's intent was to deliver Israel completely from the land of Egypt. He knew that in the end it would be so. However, it was first to be demonstrated that Pharaoh would not accede to the least demand, no matter how small it might be.

The requirement was perfectly sensible. Israel's God had a right to the service of his people. Moreover, it was quite impossible that such service should be rendered amid the alien religions of Egypt. That would be a mockery to Israel's God. And the Egyptians themselves would not stand for it. Thus, the thing to do was to remove themselves from the borders of the land. Surely if Israel did not render due worship to her God, that God could be expected to turn upon her in judgment. Pharaoh could easily understand that this was so.

It is quite futile for us to speculate at this point as to whether, if Pharaoh would have granted this request, God would have returned Israel afterward to Egypt. It was ordained not to be so. The mind of Pharaoh was not to be changed. He had set his course, and from it he would not waver. He would not even recognize Moses and Aaron as messengers of God, but only as mere peasants negligent in their labors. "Wherefore do ye, Moses and Aaron, let the people from their works? get you unto your burdens… Behold, the people of the land now are many, and ye make them rest from their burdens" (Ex. 5:4–5). Moreover, Pharaoh was a man of action. No sooner were Moses and Aaron dismissed from his presence than he summoned his subordinates who were in charge of the taskmasters of Israel, saying,

7. Ye shall no more give the people straw to make brick, as heretofore: let them go and gather straw for themselves.
8. And the tale of the bricks, which they did make heretofore, ye shall lay upon them; ye shall not diminish ought thereof: for they be idle; therefore they cry, saying, Let us go and sacrifice to our God.
9. Let there more work be laid upon the men, that they may labor therein; and let them not regard vain words. (vv. 7–9)

Life for the children of Israel soon became even more bitter than before. In the making of bricks that was required of them they had to mix straw or stubble to give the bricks strength. Formerly the Egyptians had supplied the large quantities of straw that they needed, but now they were told to gather their own material where they could find it, while producing the same number of bricks as before. This was an impossible task. The Israelites had always been diligent in their work, and, when many of them were taken from actual production to go out and gather stubble for the work, it became impossible to maintain their former quotas. But the Egyptians were unrelenting. Bending over them with whips, the Egyptians exclaimed, "Fulfill your works, your daily tasks, as when there was straw…wherefore have ye not fulfilled your task in making brick both yesterday and to day, as heretofore?" (Ex. 5:13–14). The Israelites were forced to labor as never before, but all to no avail. They could not make enough bricks.

The children of Israel had believed when Moses and Aaron had brought to them the Word of God, but as yet their faith was weak and wavering. Almost immediately, under this new affliction, they disowned the leadership of Moses. They sent new leaders to Pharaoh to try to make peace with him. These leaders presented their case, "Wherefore dealest thou thus with thy servants? There is no straw given unto thy servants, and they say to us, Make brick: and, behold, thy servants are beaten; but the fault is in thine own people" (Ex. 5:15–16). But Pharaoh's wrath was not so easily soothed. He answered back, "Ye are idle, ye are idle: therefore ye say, Let us go and do sacrifice to the LORD. Go therefore now, and work; for there shall no straw be given you, yet shall ye deliver the tale of bricks" (vv. 17–18).

In bitterness the children of Israel turned upon Moses and Aaron. Angrily they accused them, "The LORD look upon you, and judge; because ye have made our savour to be abhorred in the eyes of Pharaoh, and in the eyes of his servants, to put a sword in their hand to slay us" (Ex. 5:21). They were yet far from the position of strength where they would be able to follow the way of the Lord unto deliverance.

Even the strength of Moses was not yet fully developed. In despair he turned to the Lord and asked, "LORD, wherefore hast thou so evil entreated this people? why is it that thou hast sent me? For since I came to Pharaoh to speak in thy name, he hath done evil to this people; neither hast thou delivered thy people at all" (Ex. 5:22–23). Moses, like the children of Israel, had yet to learn that the way of God's people is never easy upon this earth. Slowly the Lord was teaching them.

Chapter 10

THE HARDENING
OF PHARAOH'S HEART

1. Then the LORD said unto Moses, Now shalt thou see what I
    will do to Pharaoh: for with a strong hand shall he let them
    go, and with a strong hand shall he drive them out of his
    land.
2. And God spake unto Moses, and said unto him, I am the
    LORD:
3. And I appeared unto Abraham, unto Isaac, and unto Jacob,
    by the name of God Almighty, but by my name JEHO-
    VAH was I not known to them.
4. And I have also established my covenant with them, to
    give them the land of Canaan, the land of their pilgrimage,
    wherein they were strangers.
5. And I have also heard the groaning of the children of Israel,
    whom the Egyptians keep in bondage; and I have remem-
    bered my covenant. (Exodus 6:1–5)

In Egypt, the land of Pharaoh, on the River Nile, the scene was
set for one of the greatest revelations of all times. God had determined to manifest his greatness and his power in such a way that it
would be declared throughout all the earth. For this purpose, the
providence of God had been preparing the situation in Egypt for
many years.

First there was Pharaoh. A reprobate and therefore unregenerate
man, he had been set upon the throne of the great and powerful
nation of Egypt. Already he had revealed the wickedness of his heart.
When first upon the throne he had followed the example of his

predecessors in persecuting the children of Israel with hard labor and other grievous afflictions. It was more than a merely utilitarian move to gain the fruits of their labor; it arose out of a deep-seated hatred for the people of God. Thus, when Moses and Aaron had come to him to demand that Israel be allowed to go and worship their God, he had answered back in anger. He refused to recognize the very existence of Israel's God. He refused to allow Israel to go and worship her God. As though to prove the superiority of his own authority and power, he commanded that Israel's already unbearable burden should be made many times the greater. Pharaoh was a wicked man. When presented with the word of God, he had only one desire—to prove that it was false.

Then there were the children of Israel. Their fathers had been brought into the land of Egypt by Joseph four hundred years before. For many years they had lived peacefully in Egypt and had learned to love its prosperity. But in recent years this had been changed by the ever-increasing burden of persecution. At last, groaning under their affliction, they had cried to their God for deliverance. With joy they had listened to the message of Moses and Aaron assuring them that God had heard their prayers and the time of deliverance was drawing near. With believing hearts they bowed and worshiped. But when instead of deliverance they found that the anger of Pharaoh was aroused and their burden of labor was increased, their faith faltered and was well-nigh gone. They disowned the leadership of Moses and refused to listen anymore to his words.

Finally, there was Moses himself. Through forty years in the wilderness of Midian he had learned to know himself as a sinner, dependent completely upon his God. But with humility had come a calling and a command to go and lead the children of Israel out of bondage. He had not wanted to go, but because he feared God he had obeyed. His only confidence had been based on the power of the word of God. Now he had spoken this word both to Israel and to Pharaoh. That did not bring deliverance. It had only aroused the anger of Pharaoh and increased the burden of Israel. Moses found himself rejected by all. Discouraged, he turned to God and complained, "Lord, wherefore hast thou so evil entreated this people? why is it that thou hast sent me? For since I came to Pharaoh to speak in thy name, he hath done evil to this people; neither hast thou delivered thy people at all" (Ex. 5:22–23).

This was the situation that God had prepared to show forth his glory. There was none who expected that deliverance for Israel was possible. Pharaoh was determined to use all of his power to prevent it. Israel in weakness of faith had faltered and desired only to appease the anger of Pharaoh. Even Moses had faltered when Israel was not immediately saved, and he found himself rejected by all. For what was soon to happen no man would ever be able to take the credit. It would be a work founded solely upon the faithfulness of Jehovah to his covenant.

Having heard the complaint of Moses, God came to him and spoke. "Now shalt thou see what I will do to Pharaoh: for with a strong hand shall he let them go, and with a strong hand shall he drive them out of his land" (Ex. 6:1). In spite of all appearances, God's promise remained sure and true. He had promised to deliver his people, and regardless of how impossible it appeared to Moses and Israel, he would do it. Moreover, he went on to instruct Moses how and why this could be so. He said,

2. I am the Lord [Jehovah];
3. And I appeared unto Abraham, unto Isaac, and unto Jacob, by the name of God Almighty, but by my name JEHOVAH was I not known to them.
4. And I have also established my covenant with them, to give them the land of Canaan, the land of their pilgrimage, wherein they were strangers.
5. And I have also heard the groaning of the children of Israel, whom the Egyptians keep in bondage; and I have remembered my covenant.
6. Wherefore say unto the children of Israel, I am the Lord [Jehovah], and I will bring you out from under the burdens

of the Egyptians, and I will rid you out of their bondage, and I will redeem you with a stretched out arm, and with great judgments:

7. And I will take you to me for a people, and I will be to you a God: and ye shall know that I am the LORD [Jehovah] your God, which bringeth you out from under the burdens of the Egyptians.

8. And I will bring you in unto the land concerning the which I did swear to give to Abraham, to Isaac, and to Jacob; and I will give it you for an heritage: I am the LORD [Jehovah]." (vv. 2–8)

Central in the whole work of God whereby he delivered his people from the bondage of Egypt was the name Jehovah. By giving this name preeminence in his revelation, God was introducing a new phase of covenant dealings with his people. This name had been known by Abraham, Isaac, and Jacob, but not as the principal name of God. In their day he had revealed himself as God Almighty, who, because of his great power, was able to establish his covenant and take them to be his covenant friends. Now it was no longer necessary to stress the establishment of the covenant and the ability of God to do it. Now it was necessary to reveal his faithfulness to the covenant long before established with the fathers. This faithfulness was implied in the name Jehovah. It was equivalent to the name I Am That I Am, with which God had first appeared to Moses in the burning bush. It implied that God would continue to perform the works promised to the fathers many years before. He had heard the groanings of Israel and would restore them to the land of promise. It implied, as God said to Moses, "I have remembered my covenant" (Ex. 6:5).

Revived by this word from God, Moses went again to speak to the children of Israel. But the people had tasted of the cruelty of Pharaoh and would not be encouraged by anything that might arouse his fury the more. In anguish of spirit they rejected the word of Moses.

Again God appeared unto Moses and said, "Go in, speak unto Pharaoh king of Egypt, that he let the children of Israel go out of his land" (Ex. 6:11). To Moses this appeared a hopeless command. He felt as though he had come up against a wall past which he could not proceed. The people of his own nation, who had at first received him with joy, would no longer listen to him. For this he felt guilty and responsible. Was it not perhaps the crudeness and vileness of his own lips that had offended them and brought the matter to such an evil state? If he could not maintain his influence over the Israelites who were essentially sympathetic, how could he ever do anything with Pharaoh who hated him? He brought his objection to God, "Behold, the children of Israel have not hearkened unto me; how then shall Pharaoh hear me, who am of uncircumcised lips?" (Ex. 6:12).

Patiently the Lord explained to Moses,

1. See, I have made thee a god to Pharaoh: and Aaron thy brother shall be thy prophet.
2. Thou shalt speak all that I command thee: and Aaron thy brother shall speak unto Pharaoh, that he send the children of Israel out of his land.
3. And I will harden Pharaoh's heart, and multiply my signs and my wonders in the land of Egypt.
4. But Pharaoh shall not hearken unto you, that I may lay my hand upon Egypt, and bring forth mine armies, and my people the children of Israel, out of the land of Egypt by great judgments.
5. And the Egyptians shall know that I am the LORD, when I stretch forth mine hand upon Egypt, and bring out the children of Israel from among them." (Ex. 7:1–5)

It was not the inability of Moses to speak well that had aroused the anger of Pharaoh; it was the normal reaction of a wicked heart to the word of God. Moses stood as the representative of God, and it was that which provoked the anger of Pharaoh. This was, as God had ordained, the way in which he would reveal his own greatness as Jehovah. Not Moses, but God, was hardening Pharaoh's heart.

It was at that time also that God instructed Moses, saying, "When Pharaoh shall speak unto you, saying, Shew a miracle for you: then thou shalt say unto Aaron, Take thy rod, and cast it before Pharaoh, and it shall become a serpent" (Ex. 7:9).

Encouraged again by this revelation from God, Moses and Aaron went forth into the court of Pharaoh. Boldly they repeated the command of God that Israel should be released to serve God in the wilderness. As God had foretold, Pharaoh was ready to challenge them by demanding of them a sign of power, a miracle. At the command of Moses, Aaron cast down Moses' rod and it became a serpent.

This was a significant miracle. The rod was a symbol of the authority that had been entrusted to Moses at the burning bush, the office of shepherd to God's chosen people and representative of God. The serpent, on the other hand, had been, since the fall of man, a symbol of Satan and the power of sin. Rather significantly, the Egyptians of that time had taken it also as the chief symbol of their gods. The act of Moses revealed symbolically that the powers of evil can go forth as determined only by the act and authority of Jehovah, the God of Israel.

To Pharaoh, however, this miracle was not very impressive. His wise men were experienced in the works of sorcery, which included the charming and manipulation of snakes. Summoned by Pharaoh, they with their enchantments soon put on the appearance of duplicating the act of Moses.

It was then that the truly significant thing happened. The serpent that came forth from Moses' rod swallowed those that the Egyptian magicians had cast down. This was a warning to which Pharaoh might well have taken heed. The evil deeds of Pharaoh and his magicians and his gods, represented in the serpents, would never be able to escape the determinate power of Israel's God. The power represented by Moses' rod would swallow them up and bring them to naught. Moses had but to catch the tail of the remaining serpent and it was restored again into his rod, destroying forever the works of the wise men of Pharaoh.

This was the first outward demonstration of the power of Jehovah in Egypt. All that was to follow would serve only to substantiate its truth. In faithfulness to his covenant, God was determined to deliver his people. All the powers of sin that sought to oppose him could only do so in subjection to his determination and power. In doing so they would be swallowed up and destroyed. God was showing directly to Pharaoh what soon would happen to him. But this revelation served only to harden the heart of Pharaoh the more. In the stubbornness of his wicked pride, he refused to hearken unto the word of God, even as God had said.

Chapter 11

THE BEGINNING OF JEHOVAH'S JUDGMENT ON EGYPT

1. And the LORD said unto Moses, See, I have made thee a god to Pharaoh: and Aaron thy brother shall be thy prophet.
2. Thou shalt speak all that I command thee: and Aaron thy brother shall speak unto Pharaoh, that he send the children of Israel out of his land.
3. And I will harden Pharaoh's heart, and multiply my signs and my wonders in the land of Egypt. (Exodus 7:1–3)

God had said to Pharaoh through Moses and Aaron, "Thus saith the LORD, Israel is my son, even my firstborn: and I say unto thee, Let my son go, that he may serve me: and if thou refuse to let him go, behold, I will slay thy son, even thy firstborn" (Ex. 4:22–23). It was an affirmation of Jehovah's eternal love, a love for his only begotten Son Jesus Christ, an affirmation of love for all those who were chosen eternally in his Son, even Israel. Because it was Jehovah who spoke, this affirmation would not and could not change. This love would be realized, and if Pharaoh or anyone else sought to change this, he would do so only unto his own ruin.

Pharaoh had answered to this, "Who is the LORD, that I should obey his voice to let Israel go? I know not the LORD, neither will I let Israel go" (Ex. 5:2). Pharaoh was the king of Egypt and the world's most powerful potentate. Moreover, he was a man of great pride and ambition, determined to maintain his place of greatest power and influence in the earth. Words brought by this mere pair of shepherds, Moses and Aaron, were not going to sway him. He was not going to cower before the God of a nation that served as his slaves.

The mere suggestion that he should do so made him indignant. He would prove himself to be the potentate that he was. He would take on the challenge of this Jehovah, even if he were a God.

Thus, there was drawn up in Egypt the great battle line of all times. On the one side there was Pharaoh, determined to prove himself self-sufficient and able to withstand even the power of God. On the other side was Jehovah, eternally resolved to realize his love. The ensuing conflict was ordained to reveal the power and glory of God as a witness unto all times. All that was to follow would serve to witness to the faithfulness of Jehovah's love even to the ruin of his enemies. It would be a witness so clear that only the blind would be so foolish as to deny.

First, there was a sign from God. Moses' rod, a symbol of his office appointed by God, was cast to the ground and transformed into a serpent, a symbol of Satan and the sin of Egypt. But Jannes and Jambres, the magicians of Pharaoh, were able to imitate this with their incantations, and Pharaoh remained unimpressed. The fact that Moses' serpent swallowed those of the magicians and then was restored to a rod foreboded no good for Pharaoh. But Pharaoh was in no mood to tremble before a mere sign. His heart was only hardened in its sinful resolve.

Then, early one morning, as Pharaoh was engaged in his daily worship of the Nile River, Moses and Aaron were sent to begin a series of works that would manifest the unwavering determination of Jehovah's love and judgment beyond dispute. The rod of Moses would become like a rod of iron, breaking into shards the pretense of Pharaoh like a potter's vessel.

The Nile was very really the lifeline of Egypt. Without the Nile, Egypt as a nation could not have existed. The Nile was Egypt's only real source of water. From it the fields were irrigated, and its waters filtered through the soil to fill their wells. Its surface provided channels for shipping and communication; its depths furnished fish and such food to eat. It was the very source of the land itself, for the sediment deposited by its floods formed the rich fields from which

Egypt lived. Quite naturally the Egyptians worshiped the river. Not only did this satisfy the religious inclinations of their nature, but it furnished them with an impersonal god that would not interfere with their sins. Willingly the Egyptians served the creature rather than the Creator.

Moses and Aaron were standing on the bank of the river that morning when Pharaoh came to offer his daily sacrifice to the Nile. He knew them well by this time and the cause that they represented. He despised them from the depths of his heart. That they should think to interfere with his morning worship he undoubtedly found distasteful. But they did not allow him time either to speak to them or to order that they should be removed. They bore a message from Jehovah, and immediately they spoke,

16. The LORD God of the Hebrews hath sent me unto thee, saying, Let my people go, that they may serve me in the wilderness: and, behold, hitherto thou wouldest not hear.
17. Thus saith the LORD, In this thou shalt know that I am the LORD: behold, I will smite with the rod that is in mine hand upon the waters which are in the river, and they shall be turned to blood.
18. And the fish that is in the river shall die, and the river shall stink; and the Egyptians shall lothe to drink of the water of the river. (Ex. 7:16–18)

Thereupon Aaron lifted the rod of Moses, and just as they had said, it was done.

As Pharaoh watched, the waters of the Nile took on a deep red hue as of blood. It was not as though this color in itself was too astounding, for the Nile customarily at certain seasons was red in appearance; but this was different. This coloring of the waters did not come gradually, but all of a sudden at the wave of Moses' rod. Moreover, there was a stench that arose from the river's surface. Soon dead fish were to be seen floating upon the water, and the water was unpalatable to the taste. It filled the river and its tributaries, the ponds and pools and wells, even the water sitting in open vessels of wood and of stone. Every exposed surface was corrupted. Still, it was not all this that troubled Pharaoh. The only question to which he gave thought was whether this great demonstration of power could be matched by his magicians. Quickly Jannes and Jambres were again summoned, and soon with their enchantments they had performed a small imitation of the wonder wrought by Moses' rod. True, they did not and could not relieve the plague that was upon them. At best, they only made it worse. But Pharaoh was relieved and satisfied. Heady with pride and hard of heart he turned and went up into his house.

It remained for the Egyptian people to taste the torment of what had happened. In all the land there was no water for them to drink. Quickly new wells had to be dug down to water that had not been corrupted. But even then the stench remained, a constant reminder that the river that they worshiped had been turned into a curse. Seven days passed by while the people suffered, until at last the plague was lifted.

The respite for the Egyptians was not long. Soon Moses and Aaron appeared again before Pharaoh to announce a new manifestation of the power and judgment of Jehovah. Again their words were bold:

1. Thus saith the LORD, Let my people go, that they may serve me.
2. And if thou refuse to let them go, behold, I will smite all thy borders with frogs:
3. And the river shall bring forth frogs abundantly, which shall go up and come into thine house, and into thy bedchamber, and upon thy bed, and into the house of thy servants, and upon thy people, and into thy ovens, and into thy kneadingtroughs:
4. And the frogs shall come up both on thee, and upon thy people, and upon all thy servants. (Ex. 8:1–4)

Immediately thereupon the rod was stretched forth again, and even as it had been said, frogs came up from the waters and filled the land.

Once again, the first thought of Pharaoh was whether this work could be matched, and Jannes and Jambres did not fail him. They succeeded again in creating an imitation of Moses' act. Yet, this time the work of the magicians did not give Pharaoh the satisfaction that he had felt before. The fact was that the plague of frogs was there, and it persisted. Jannes and Jambres could bring forth more frogs, at least in appearance, but they could do nothing to drive the frogs from the land. The situation was much more grave than he had anticipated. The frogs were becoming a burden. Everywhere he went they were present, a constant reminder of the power of Moses' God. Something had to be done to relieve the land, and the only thing he could think of was to use subterfuge with Moses. He called Moses and Aaron and said, "Intreat the LORD, that he may take away the frogs from me, and from my people; and I will let the people go, that they may do sacrifice unto the LORD" (Ex. 8:8). He had no intention of doing this, but at least it was a way to relieve them of the frogs.

Moses was pleased to think that at last Pharaoh was going to yield to the power of Jehovah. He said to Pharaoh, "Glory over me: when shall I entreat for thee, and for thy servants, and for the people, to destroy the frogs from thee and thy houses, that they may remain in the river only?" (Ex. 8:9). So that Pharaoh might appreciate the power of Jehovah the more, he would be allowed the glory or privilege of determining when the plague should cease.

Pharaoh answered, "To morrow."

And Moses replied, "Be it according to thy word: that thou mayest know that there is none like unto the LORD our God. And the frogs shall depart from thee, and from thy houses, and from thy servants, and from thy people; they shall remain in the river only" (Ex. 8:10).

On the morrow, Moses prayed to God and the frogs died throughout the land. All that remained were the heaps of stinking carcasses that the people gathered together, a reminder of the curse that had visited their land. Pharaoh was relieved. As soon as he saw that the plague of frogs had ceased, he informed Moses that his promise would not be kept.

But the relief of Pharaoh was short lived. God commanded, and Aaron smote the dust of the ground with the rod. The dust was changed into lice that lighted on man and beast. It crawled into the eyes and ears and nose and penetrated under the skin.

This plague had come unannounced, but Pharaoh knew well enough from whence it was. As before, he immediately summoned his magicians, if only to satisfy himself that this work also could be matched. But this time it was to no avail. Their incantation could not go so far as to even appear to bring forth such lice. Rather, as though to add to Pharaoh's consternation, they turned and solemnly confessed, "This is the finger of God" (Ex. 8:19).

Now Pharaoh knew mere subterfuge would not work. It might relieve one plague, but it would be followed immediately by another just as bad and maybe even worse. In his heart he was determined. He would withstand Israel's God. But he knew not how. In moody silence he sat and pondered.

Meanwhile in Goshen, the children of Israel also had been feeling the hand of their God. They had rejected his promises out of fear of Pharaoh, and now they too were made to suffer. But the very same demonstrations of power and judgment that were making the heart of Pharaoh progressively harder were having on them an entirely different effect. They were being reminded of the folly of their doubts and sins. They were being turned in repentance. They were being brought to acknowledge as never before the greatness of their God.

Chapter 12

JEHOVAH'S POWER REVEALED IN PHARAOH

13. And the LORD said unto Moses, Rise up early in the morning, and stand before Pharaoh, and say unto him...

16. And in very deed for this cause have I raised thee up, for to shew in thee my power; and that my name may be declared throughout all the earth. (Exodus 9:13, 16)

Each day it was becoming more clearly evident in Egypt that the God of Moses spoke truth. He is Jehovah, the I Am That I Am, the covenant God and defender of his chosen people Israel. Each plague testified to that anew.

But Pharaoh was far from an objective judge of what was happening. The more clearly the truth was revealed before him, the more he was determined to oppose it. He was caught up in a personal passion for power. His pride would not allow him to acknowledge that there was anyone greater than himself. Every new demonstration of power only made him more determined to prove that his power exceeded that of Israel's God. Step by step he was being hardened in the way of sin. It was the normal reaction of a wicked heart to God's truth.

These same demonstrations of Jehovah's power that hardened the heart of Pharaoh were felt also by the children of Israel. At first under the threats of Pharaoh they had lost confidence in the promises of Jehovah and had renounced the leadership of Moses. But now under the hand of the Lord in the first three plagues, they saw the folly of this sin. They saw clearly what Pharaoh refused to acknowledge, that Jehovah was much greater than all the kings of the earth. Faith revived, and Israel repented from her sin. The seed of Abraham once more began to look unto its God and to wait for the promised salvation. The same word that was hardening the heart of Pharaoh was restoring the people of God.

God heard Israel's cries of repentance, and he forgave. With the announcement of the next plague to Pharaoh, he told Moses to say, "I will put a division between my people and thy people" (Ex. 8:23). Henceforth a new aspect of the name Jehovah would be made known. Not only is Jehovah a God of all power, able to control all of nature to the consternation and punishment of the wicked, he is also a God who is faithful to reward the righteous and to show favor to them that love him. Throughout the rest of the plagues the favor of God to his chosen people would be clearly seen.

A second series of three plagues was soon to begin, and once more God told Moses to rise up early in the morning and meet Pharaoh as he went to engage in his daily worship at the Nile's brink. He was to say unto him,

20. Thus saith the LORD, Let my people go, that they may serve me.

21. Else, if thou wilt not let my people go, behold, I will send swarms of flies upon thee, and upon thy servants, and upon thy people, and into thy houses: and the houses of the Egyptians shall be full of swarms of flies, and also the ground whereon they are.

22. And I will sever in that day the land of Goshen, in which my people dwell, that no swarms of flies shall be there; to the end thou mayest know that I am the LORD in the midst of the earth.

23. And I will put a division between my people and thy people: to morrow shall this sign be. (Ex. 8:20–23)

The morrow came and, just as Moses had said, swarms of flies settled down upon the land. They were mean, biting flies that lighted on a man's body with a piercing sting. There was no escaping them, for they covered the land and filled the houses. Every surface was covered with flies, and they corrupted everything: the water, the food, the land. Once more Pharaoh found himself surrounded by the misery of another plague. Jannes and Jambres were powerless. There was nothing they could do. Gradually there emerged in the mind of Pharaoh the conviction that perhaps it would be best if he would seek a compromise. He would allow the children of Israel to sacrifice in his own land. It was a foolish idea. The sacrifice of animals, such as the Israelites practiced, was an abomination to the Egyptians. His people would become enraged if they saw the Israelites conducting such sacrifices in their land. But it was not this that concerned Pharaoh. He had to prove himself capable of influencing the God of Israel, and, if nothing else would do it, a compromise would suffice.

He summoned Moses and Aaron and said, "Go ye, sacrifice to your God in the land" (Ex. 8:25). To this, Moses responded by exposing the folly of Pharaoh's proposition: "It is not meet so to do; for we shall sacrifice the abomination of the Egyptians to the LORD our God: lo, shall we sacrifice the abomination of the Egyptians before their eyes, and will they not stone us? We will go three days' journey into the wilderness, and sacrifice to the LORD our God, as he shall command us" (vv. 26–27).

The reasoning of Moses was only too evident, and Pharaoh knew not what to reply. All he could think of was to resort once again to subterfuge, to promise that which he had no intention of doing. The flies had to be taken away. He said with feigned humility, "I will let you go, that ye may sacrifice to the LORD your God in the wilderness; only ye shall not go very far away: intreat for me" (Ex. 8:28).

Moses was beginning to recognize the duplicity of Pharaoh's heart. Carefully he warned Pharaoh, "Behold, I go out from thee, and I will intreat the LORD that the swarms of flies may depart from Pharaoh, from his servants, and from his people, to morrow: but let not Pharaoh deal deceitfully any more in not letting the people go to sacrifice to the LORD" (Ex. 8:29).

On the morrow the flies were taken away, just as Moses had said, but the heart of Pharaoh was hard as always, and he would not let the people go.

Again the Lord sent Moses to Pharaoh to say,

1. Thus saith the LORD God of the Hebrews, Let my people go, that they may serve me.
2. For if thou refuse to let them go, and wilt hold them still,
3. Behold, the hand of the LORD is upon thy cattle which is in the field, upon the horses, upon the asses, upon the camels, upon the oxen, and upon the sheep: there shall be a very grievous murrain.
4. And the LORD shall sever between the cattle of Israel and the cattle of Egypt: and there shall nothing die of all that is the children's of Israel.
5. …To morrow the LORD shall so this thing in the land. (Ex. 9:1–5)

For a fifth time the land of Egypt was beset by a plague from Jehovah. Step by step every different aspect of life was being touched by the hand of God. Jehovah was proving with many indisputable proofs that his power extended over all the earth; nothing can withstand his will. Pharaoh felt himself being driven to distraction. He had tried Jannes and Jambres, and they had bolstered his pride for a while. Now even they were helpless. He had tried subterfuge, and he had tried compromise. Each time the hand of Jehovah descended to smite him again; each plague seemed heavier than the one before. What was he to do? If only he could find one thing that could withstand, or limit, or in the least bit mitigate the power of Jehovah's hand, then he could maintain his pride. Desperately he sent to Goshen to find out whether Israel was actually being spared; but even that was so. It seemed that only one possibility remained. If he could wait out this plague and maybe another, perhaps the God of Israel would withdraw. So with a hardened heart Pharaoh waited until this plague subsided.

But it was not long before Pharaoh felt the hand of Jehovah yet again. This time it came unannounced. The Lord commanded Moses to take of the ashes of the furnace, to sprinkle it toward heaven in the sight of Pharaoh. Without one word to the king, Moses did so, and when the dust descended upon Pharaoh's skin it brought forth boils. Quickly it spread throughout the land, affecting man and beast. As always, Pharaoh called for his magicians, hoping that they would be able to do something again, but this time they could not come because of the boils that had already broken forth on their bodies. Nevertheless, Pharaoh was firm in his resolve. He would wait it out. Perhaps the God of Israel would tire and withdraw his hand. So, with hardened heart he waited until also this, the sixth plague, subsided.

The second series of three plagues was ended. They had demonstrated more clearly than ever before the great power that belonged to the God of Israel. It was a power that included every phase of life. Water and land, animals and man, all were subject to his will. Pharaoh saw it all but would not believe. God was preparing him for the end. Yet three more plagues, and then the final judgment would come.

The third series of plagues, as the first two, was preceded by a special explanation of the intent of God. Pharaoh would never be able to say that God had not explained to him what was taking place. Each time it was explained more clearly than before. Before the first plague God had said, "In this thou shalt know that I am [Jehovah]" (Ex. 7:17). That gave to Pharaoh the general significance of all the plagues. They proved that God is Jehovah, as he said. Before the fourth plague God had said to Pharaoh, "And I will put a division between my people and thy people" (8:23). The power and judgment of Jehovah will show mercy upon his people even at the very time that it goes forth in consuming wrath upon the wicked. Now, before the seventh plague, God would say to Pharaoh,

14. For I will at this time send all my plagues upon thine heart, and upon thy servants, and upon thy people; that thou mayest know that there is none like me in all the earth.

15. For now I will stretch out my hand, that I may smite thee and thy people with pestilence; and thou shalt be cut off from the earth.

16. And in very deed for this cause have I raised thee up, for to shew in thee my power; and that my name may be declared throughout all the earth. (9:14–16)

In this word of God to Pharaoh we have one of scripture's clearest statements of the place of the reprobate in God's creation: they are there for the purpose of God. So it was, very explicitly, with Pharaoh. He was not a wicked and rebellious man who just happened to be upon the throne at the time, resisting the grace of God. He was not a king whom God would have liked to save, but who, because he would not believe, had to be destroyed. Many would like to say this, but the very clear teaching of scripture is otherwise. God knew long beforehand what Pharaoh would be like. God according to his own determinate counsel raised Pharaoh up. God had for Pharaoh a very definite purpose. That purpose was that Pharaoh's heart should be hardened in sin, that Pharaoh and his people might be justly smitten by Jehovah's hand and destroyed, and thus that the power of God might be revealed in him. Unto all generations Pharaoh remains the perfect example of the man who hardens his heart against the evident truth of God's word to his own destruction and to the glory of God's name.

One marvels at the obduracy of Pharaoh's heart. Before this very explicit revelation of God, it was made so very clear what a terrible place he was making for himself in history. When all was made so plain, how could he keep himself from falling to his knees in repentance and tears? But no, Pharaoh only hardened his heart the more. God had ordained it so. No matter how clear it would be, he would resist the word of God. He would do it unto the end.

Chapter 13

THAT YE MAY KNOW THAT
I AM THE LORD

1. And the LORD said unto Moses, Go in unto Pharaoh: for I have hardened his heart, and the heart of his servants, that I might shew these my signs before him:
2. And that thou mayest tell in the ears of thy son, and of thy son's son, what things I have wrought in Egypt, and my signs which I have done among them; that ye may know that I am the LORD. (Exodus 10:1–2)

The land of Egypt lay desolate, the people were dismayed, the servants of the palace were apprehensive, and Pharaoh was distraught. Six times devastation had swept through the country, and everyone knew in his heart that there was more yet to come. War had been declared against Egypt by Israel's God. In pride Pharaoh had said, "I know not Jehovah." Now he was being shown; and the more Pharaoh saw, the more he rebelled.

A third series of three plagues was beginning, and God said again unto Moses,

13. Rise up early in the morning, and stand before Pharaoh, and say unto him, Thus saith the LORD God of the Hebrews, Let my people go, that they may serve me.
14. For I will at this time send all my plagues upon thine heart, and upon thy servants, and upon thy people; that thou mayest know that there is none like me in all the earth.
15. For now I will stretch out my hand, that I may smite thee and thy people with pestilence; and thou shalt be cut off from the earth.

16. And in very deed for this cause have I raised thee up, for to shew in thee my power; and that my name may be declared throughout all the earth.

17. As yet exaltest thou thyself against my people, that thou wilt not let them go?

18. Behold, to morrow about this time I will cause it to rain a very grievous hail, such as hath not been in Egypt since the foundation thereof even until now.

19. Send therefore now, and gather thy cattle, and all that thou hast in the field; for upon every man and beast which shall be found in the field, and shall not be brought home, the hail shall come down upon them, and they shall die." (Ex. 9:13–19)

Once more, as Pharaoh stood by the riverbank vainly offering oblations to his god, Moses appeared and brought the message of Jehovah. Pharaoh knew by now that the God of Moses was a terrible enemy. He had learned to hate and even fear these visits from Moses. Never had an enemy behaved like this. He announced to Pharaoh each step of the way just exactly what he was going to do; he told Pharaoh why he was doing it; and he warned him what the results would be. This very fact infuriated Pharaoh. The God of Israel was treating him as a potter might treat his clay. The fact that he was the king of Egypt seemed to make no difference at all. And yet a new feeling was beginning to find its way into his life. Even as Moses said, these plagues were beginning to touch his *heart;* his courage was beginning to waver; he, Pharaoh, was becoming afraid. Both to maintain his pride and to hide his fear, Pharaoh did not so much as answer Moses. In stubborn determination he would not take his cattle from the field, even though within his heart he knew that it was best. In all of Egypt there were but a few who would listen to the warning of Moses, because they had learned to fear the word of Israel's God.

Again Moses raised his rod, this time toward the heavens. On the horizon the storm clouds gathered, strangely foreboding in a land of few storms. Swiftly they advanced to overshadow the land, and the earth shook with the roll of their thunder. Lightning like fire lashed forth from the clouds, running across the ground and striking out this way and that, much too swiftly for any to escape. And then came the hail, large like rocks, able to bruise, able to hurt, able to kill—and they did. Animals and men lay dead in the fields, trees and plants hung broken and limp, stripped of their vegetation, but none dared go out to investigate. Only in the land of Goshen, where the children of Israel were, did the land and the people remain untouched.

In the palace, even Pharaoh crouched and trembled while the hail drummed on the ground and on the roofs like the hoof beats of thousands of horses. He was beginning to know what it was to taste fear. How was he to resist this power? In desperation he called for Moses, and Moses came through the midst of the storm unscathed, as though overshadowed by the hand of the Lord. While anxiety contorted his face, Pharaoh blurted out, "I have sinned this time; the LORD is righteous, and I and my people are wicked" (Ex. 9:27). Were these the words of Pharaoh? What was it that he wanted? Forgiveness? Salvation? Peace with God? No: "Intreat the LORD... that there be no more mighty thunderings and hail; and I will let you go, and ye shall stay no longer" (v. 28). That the thunder and hail should stop—that was all he wanted.

Calmly Moses answered,

29. As soon as I am gone out of the city, I will spread abroad my hands unto the LORD; and the thunder shall cease, neither shall there be any more hail; that thou mayest know how that the earth is LORD's.
30. But as for thee and thy servants, I know that ye will not yet fear the LORD God. (Ex. 9:29–30)

Soon all was silent again; the thunder and hail had ceased; even the rain no longer fell. With a sigh of relief, Pharaoh returned to his normal self. He dared ask of himself the old question again, "Who is Jehovah that I should let Israel go?" With boldness he issued the order that the Israelites should continue their work.

It was then that God came to Moses and said,

1. Go in unto Pharaoh: for I have hardened his heart, and the heart of his servants, that I might shew these my signs before him:
2. And that thou mayest tell in the ears of thy son, and of thy son's son, what things I have wrought in Egypt, and my signs which I have done among them; that ye may know how that I am the LORD. (Ex. 10:1–2)

This gave the basic reason for the plagues. They were a means of revealing the power of God; they were a means of hardening the heart of Pharaoh and thus revealing the power of God; they were a means of bringing about the deliverance of Israel from Egypt; but, more than anything else, they were a testimony of God's righteousness and mercy that would work in the hearts of his people through all generations.

Again Moses appeared before Pharaoh and said,

3. Thus saith the LORD God of the Hebrews, How long wilt thou refuse to humble thyself before me? let my people go, that they may serve me.
4. Else, if thou refuse to let my people go, behold, to morrow will I bring the locusts into thy coast:
5. And they shall cover the face of the earth, that one cannot be able to see the earth: and they shall eat the residue of that which is escaped, which remaineth unto you from the hail, and shall eat every tree which groweth for you out of the field:
6. And they shall fill thy houses, and the houses of thy servants, and the houses of all the Egyptians; which neither thy fathers, nor thy fathers' fathers have seen, since the day that they were upon the earth unto this day. (Ex. 10:3–6)

Furious with indignation, Pharaoh remained sullenly silent until Moses turned and left. It was in the servants that stood by that the misgivings arose. Could their country endure any more destruction? Carefully formulating their words so as not to offend, they said to Pharaoh, "How long shall this man be a snare unto us? let the men go, that they may serve the LORD their God: knowest thou not yet that Egypt is destroyed?" (Ex. 10:7). Bitterly they laid all of the blame at the feet of Moses; but the fact remains that they were *afraid*.

In light of those concerns, Pharaoh decided to try again to negotiate with Moses another compromise. Quickly he commanded that Moses and Aaron should be called back into his presence. Almost triumphantly he spoke as soon as they entered, "Go, serve the LORD your God: but who are they that shall go?" (Ex. 10:8).

Sensing the deception that hung heavy upon Pharaoh's words, Moses answered positively and with care. "We will go with our young and with our old, with our sons and with our daughters, with our flocks and with our herds will we go; for we must hold a feast unto the LORD" (Ex. 10:9).

Taken aback by the finality of Moses' answer, Pharaoh nonetheless could not resist expressing the compromise that would be acceptable to him. "Let the LORD be so with you, as I will let you go, and your little ones: look to it; for evil is before you. Not so: go now ye that are men, and serve the LORD; for that ye did desire" (Ex. 10:10–11). Israel might go, but only on Pharaoh's terms. As though concerned for the women and children, he would not allow them to go out into the evils of the wilderness. Only the men might go. But this was quite unacceptable to Moses and Aaron, and in rage Pharaoh drove them from his presence.

Moses raised his rod, and immediately a strong wind sprang up from the east. The next day the locusts appeared. As a black cloud they came in the east, blotting out the rays of the morning sun. Their approaching wings beat a deafening roar until they settled like a smothering blanket over the earth. Soon all that could be heard was the crunching of thousands of jaws consuming the land. No piece of green vegetation was safe; they devoured it all. Even the roofs of the palace afforded no sanctuary from this. The locusts poured in upon Pharaoh in his privacy until once again he knew the choking grip of fear even stronger than before. No matter where he fled, the grizzled faces of the insects were there to remind him of his sin. To them, his pride could no longer provide an answer.

At last in haste he sent for Moses and Aaron, and he fairly shouted at them when they appeared, "I have sinned against the LORD your God, and against you. Now therefore forgive, I pray thee, my sin only this once, and intreat the LORD your God, that he may take away from me this death only" (Ex. 10:16–17). Even the colossal pride of Pharaoh was being bowed before the judgment of God. Not that there was any repentance. The similar prayer of a few weeks earlier was already forgotten. But even a heart of solid wickedness could no longer deny the power of Israel's God. It was not really the forgiveness that he wanted; it was deliverance from those insect jaws of death.

Without so much as honoring this hypocritical prayer with an answer, Moses went out again. Soon there came a west wind to cast the locusts into the sea. But Pharaoh's pride was still there. With resilience, it sprang back as soon as the plague was lifted. He would not let Israel go. The answer of the Lord was swift. He commanded Moses, "Stretch out thine hand toward heaven, that there may be darkness over the land of Egypt, even darkness which may be felt" (Ex. 10:21).

Without warning to Pharaoh it came, but he knew full well from whence. Such darkness had never been known before. It was more than an absence of light. In this darkness a fire was of no use, and a lamp could not penetrate its depths. This darkness could be felt. For three days not an Egyptian dared stir from his place. The land was shrouded in an earthly figure of their obdurate hearts. Torn between fear and resentment, Pharaoh decided to make one more attempt to negotiate with Israel's God. He called Moses to him and spoke through the darkness, "Go ye, serve the LORD; only let your flocks and your herds be stayed: let your little ones also go with you" (Ex. 10:24).

Patiently Moses answered, "Thou must give us also sacrifices and burnt offerings, that we may sacrifice unto the LORD our God. Our cattle also shall go with us; there shall not an hoof be left behind; for thereof must we take to serve the LORD our God; and we know not with what we must serve the LORD until we come hither" (Ex. 10:25–26). He demanded of Pharaoh a complete surrender.

It was too much. Pharaoh's pride would not surrender. Screaming with fury he cried out, "Get thee from me, take heed to thyself, see my face no more; for in that day thou seest my face thou shalt die" (Ex. 10:28).

There was somber warning in Moses' answer: "Thou hast spoken well, I will see thy face again no more" (Ex. 10:29)

Chapter 14

PREPARING THE PASSOVER

And when I see the blood, I will pass over you. (Exodus 12:13)

The last meeting between Moses and Pharaoh had taken place. It had been a tense, troubled affair. How Pharaoh had learned to hate these visits from Moses! Moses represented the God of Israel, who now for many months had been ravaging his land. In Moses' presence Pharaoh was torn between pride and fear; but pride had won out. Vainly he had sought a compromise, finally offering that all of Israel might go to worship Jehovah except for the cattle and sheep. But the God of Moses would not compromise. He demanded absolute obedience to his command. This, Pharaoh would not give, in spite of his inward fear. His pride had broken forth in anger until he fairly shouted at Moses, "Get thee from me, take heed to thyself, see my face no more; for in that day thou seest my face thou shalt die" (Ex. 10:28).

Moses answered, "Thou hast spoken well, I will see thy face again no more" (Ex. 10:29).

It was as Moses was turning to leave that God came and spoke to him. He said, "Yet will I bring one plague more upon Pharaoh, and upon Egypt; afterwards he will let you go hence: when he shall let you go, he shall surely thrust you out hence altogether" (Ex. 11:1).

Turning once again to Pharaoh, Moses spoke his parting message.

4. Thus saith the Lord, About midnight will I go out into the midst of Egypt:
5. And all the firstborn in the land of Egypt shall die, from the first born of Pharaoh that sitteth upon his throne, even

unto the firstborn of the maidservant that is behind the mill; and all the firstborn of beasts.

6. And there shall be a great cry throughout all the land of Egypt, such as there was none like it, nor shall be like it any more.

7. But against any of the children of Israel shall not a dog move his tongue, against man or beast: that ye may know how that the LORD doth put a difference between the Egyptians and Israel.

8. And all these thy servants shall come down unto me, and bow down themselves unto me, saying, Get thee out, and all the people that follow thee: and after that I will go out. (Ex. 11:4–8)

While anger still contorted the face of Pharaoh, fear laid its cold grip upon his heart. Through bitter experience he had learned that the warnings of Moses were not to be taken lightly. The firstborn of Egypt were the strength of the land, and now their death had been foretold. He had tried to break the strength of Israel, and now that very destruction had turned back upon himself. But Pharaoh's pride would not allow him to submit. His hatred for Jehovah would carry him with hardened heart to the very end. For a moment the two men stared at each other in bitter anger until Moses at last turned and went.

Leaving the palace of Pharaoh, Moses went immediately to speak to the children of Israel. With humble fear and wonderment, they received the news. The time for deliverance had come. They were to leave the land of their affliction, not just for three days as might have been expected, but forever. Pharaoh would thrust them out and tell them never to return. Nor would their departure be in poverty. They were to demand (not just "borrow") everyone jewels of silver and gold from their Egyptian neighbors in payment for the labor that they as free sons of Abraham had expended. In that hour the Egyptians, humbled by the judgment of Jehovah, would be more than willing to comply. The children of Israel would go forth in power and glory on the tide of Jehovah's strength. In the name of their God, they would conquer.

Yet, such was the word of God unto Israel that not one reason was left for anyone to become lifted up with personal pride or boasting. Israel was to be delivered indeed, but this deliverance was to be through judgment. The angel of God's judgment would visit the land, and not one household that was yet guilty of sin would be spared. The firstborn, the strength of every such household, would be destroyed. Could anyone of Israel forget that in the first three plagues of Egypt they had not been spared? Could anyone honestly say that his household was free from all sin and guilt? Could anyone be sure that in this final day of visitation his household would be worthy of being spared?

With careful attention the children of Israel listened as Moses explained to them the way of deliverance. This was not going to be merely a national emigration, nor only the conquest of one nation over another. The Lord God of heaven and earth was going to visit the land, and the things that would transpire would be of importance for the well-being of their souls. His presence would work judgment upon all who were not found dwelling in his favor.

"In the tenth day of this month," said Moses, "take…every man a lamb, according to the house of their fathers, a lamb for an house" (Ex. 12:3). The children of Israel knew well what was the meaning of the lamb. From the time that the Protevangel had been spoken in paradise, it had been known. The lamb was a sign of the promised seed of the woman that would crush the head of the serpent; it was a sign of the seed of Abraham in which they and their children would be blessed; it was a sign of the seed of Judah from whom the scepters would never depart; it was a sign of the promised Redeemer that would save his people from the guilt and curse of their sin. Every time a lamb was brought to the altar by a believing child of God's covenant, it was thereby confessed that this believer looked in faith to the promise of God as the only redemption from his sin.

Now as Moses proceeded with his instructions, it became evident to every believer that this long familiar type of revelation was taking on a new dimension of meaning. The judgment of God was impending in Egypt, and, though in itself also only a figure and type, only through a confession of faith would anyone escape. As this way of redemption was unfolded, it brought new depth of understanding to those who trusted in the promise of God.

The lamb that was taken should be without blemish. Although this had also been known in the past, it emphasized for Israel again that redemption could come only through one that was perfect. The lamb to be slain must bear the believer's sins, and thus it could not be marred and in itself unworthy to live. The lamb in its earthly perfection must serve to foreshadow the promised seed, who alone, in being perfect before the sight of God, could be a substitute for Israel's sin.

It was the blood of that lamb that would be of utmost importance to the children of Israel in the midst of the judgment of Egypt. The blood was to be struck upon the two side posts and on the upper post of every door behind which dwelt the believing children of God. It was an open sign for all to see that this household felt a need of a covering for its sins; it was a public confession of guilt in the presence of man and of God. When God in judgment drew nigh, his promise would be faithful and true: "When I see the blood, I will pass over you, and the plague shall not be upon you to destroy you, when I smite the land of Egypt" (Ex. 12:13).

Furthermore, the lamb whose blood would serve as an atonement to turn aside the judgment of God from the households of Israel was to be taken and roasted in the fire. It was not to be left raw, nor even boiled in water; the very body of the lamb had to pass through the fire. And this was to be done while the body was yet whole, unmutilated with a knife, and while the bones were yet unbroken. The fire symbolized the righteousness and justice of God through which the lamb of atonement had to pass. It did this in the stead of the sinners for whom it was offered. The lamb had to pass through the fire of God's justice, and it had to do this, as closely as was possible in mere symbolism, while still whole and unmutilated, in the strength of its being. Only in this way could it fulfill the demands of substitution for sin.

It was at this point that this new form of atoning sacrifice took on an even richer and deeper meaning. The body of the lamb that was slain was given to the people of God for food. Through the events of the approaching judgment, Israel was to be saved to the uttermost. Not only were the children of God to be saved negatively from the stroke of the angel of judgment, they were also to be led forth out of the land of bondage into the Canaan of promise. As Israel went forth, the very body of the lamb whose blood had redeemed her would supply the nourishment and strength in which she would go. The flesh of the lamb was a heavenly meal instituted and given by God. In the lamb that was slain was the fullness of Israel's redemption. This lamb was to be eaten completely, and should any of it be left over, it was to be burned. The nourishment of its body was only for those who were covered by the atonement, and none might be left for those to whom it did not belong. The benefits of salvation are only for the children of God.

The meal surrounding the lamb was full of rich significance. It was to be eaten with unleavened bread and bitter herbs. Leaven was the old dough that was kept from one baking to another; a small bit of it used in a new baking of bread would serve to make the new bread rise. Because it was saved from week to week and because but a small bit of it would permeate a whole loaf of bread to make it rise, leaven served well to symbolize the old way of life that in the redemption from Egypt had to be left behind. Only a small bit of the old life of Egypt taken along could corrupt the whole life of Israel. The bitter herbs reminded Israel that the way of redemption would not be pleasant for the flesh. The way of God's people must pass through bitter hardships.

Finally, even the manner in which this meal was to be eaten was prescribed with careful instructions. "Thus shall ye eat it," Jehovah commanded, "with your loins girded, your shoes on your feet, and your staff in your hand; and ye shall eat it in haste: it is the LORD's passover" (Ex. 12:11). Israel must be ready to go, prepared to leave the land of bondage and sin. Even more, Israel must be willing and eager. There should be no desire to loiter. It was to be the deliverance of the Lord; it should fill the whole will and desire of his people.

Great and unusual was the activity that filled the land of Goshen. The atmosphere was filled with the feelings of eager anticipation. With great fear and reverence, the children of Israel went about their preparations. As they looked upon the ceremonial preparations, it was almost as though they looked directly into the face of God. The true believing Israelite, though only vaguely through type and shadow, looked ahead through the ages and saw the promised Redeemer offering himself as the Lamb on Calvary's hill, that at the sign of his blood the people of God might be redeemed.

The Egyptians, too, could not help but note the great activity in Goshen. The plague of darkness had departed, but its shadows still seemed to cling to their hearts. They saw the lambs being gathered and slain, and it was an abomination to their eyes. They saw the preparations for journey, and hateful anger burned within their hearts. But none dared to try to make the Israelites stop. They had tasted the power of Israel's God; it had ruined their land. Bitterly they watched the Hebrews work. Paralyzed with fear, they dared not interfere.

Chapter 15

JUDGMENT AND DELIVERANCE

29. And it came to pass, that at midnight the Lord smote all the firstborn in the land of Egypt...

30. And Pharaoh rose up in the night, he, and all his servants, and all the Egyptians; and there was a great cry in Egypt; for there was not a house where there was not one dead.

31. And he called for Moses and Aaron by night, and said, Rise up, and get you forth from among my people, both ye and the children of Israel; and go, serve the Lord, as ye have said.

32. Also take your flocks and your herds, as ye have said, and be gone; and bless me also. (Exodus 12:29–32)

The sun set that night on a land divided within itself. There were the slaves of the land, Hebrews all, busily engaged in most unusual activities—the sacrificing of choice young lambs, the painting of their door posts with blood, and the preparation of the bodies of the sacrificed lambs into a unique meal with bitter herbs and bread that had not been leavened. The atmosphere over Goshen was tinged with feelings of deep reverence and wonderment, eager anticipation, and inner confidence and joy. There were also the freemen of the land, the Egyptians, who looked on the activity of the Hebrews with haughty contempt, although none dared to interfere. Stoically they went about their regular activities while inwardly their hearts were gripped with qualms of apprehension. The fear of Jehovah hung over Egypt, and it divided the land in two.

Gradually all activity began to cease among the Egyptians, and the lights were put out. They were determined not to show any sign of concern. As usual they retired, but few were able to find sleep.

Had they not heard of the warning of Moses, "Thus saith the LORD, About midnight will I go out into the midst of Egypt: and all the firstborn in the land of Egypt shall die" (Ex. 11:4–5)? They had suffered so grievously already, could they doubt the ability of Jehovah to smite them again even unto all of the firstborn of the land?

It is hard for us to understand the importance of the firstborn child in those ancient days. Today, of course, parents love their firstborn, but not a great deal more than those that follow. It is because our society is individualistic, while then it was almost completely centered in the family. The population of the world was much more sparse, and the well-being of the individual was dependent upon the family to which he belonged. In these family units the firstborn child, especially if a son, took on the greatest importance. The parents looked upon the firstborn as the assurance that they would be cared for in their old age, their security and enduring strength, the one through whom their name would endure. He was named immediately as the heir. Each succeeding child soon learned that the oldest brother would be head of the family after the death of the father. In his strength they would prosper, or in his weakness they would be weak. In that day the firstborn child was the sign of strength and promise. There could be no greater threat to Egypt than that all of its firstborn would die. It was exactly under that threat that every household in Egypt became silent that night.

Meanwhile, in Goshen the activity continued. No one showed any intention of sleeping. As the night progressed, the activities actually seemed to increase, or at least the feelings of the Israelites became more strongly charged with anticipation. All remained fully dressed as though preparing for a journey. All portable possessions were carefully being arranged and packed so that they might be carried away. With reverence but with evident haste each family gathered about the meal that centered in the flesh of the sacrificial lamb. The Israelites anticipated too, even more strongly than the Egyptians, the final visitation of Jehovah upon the land. In them the fear of dreads had given way to the spiritual fear of reverent awe, filling their hearts with joy and hope. They had looked upon the shed blood of the lamb and believed the promise that was symbolized therein. At the sign of the blood, the angel of Jehovah would pass over them. Even more: by the judgment of Egypt, they would be saved.

The hour was approaching midnight and Egypt was tossing in the sleepless silence of apprehension when suddenly, as though at one moment, there burst forth a great cry. There were the moans of men and the painful sobs of women, the wails of little children and even the bleat of animals in distress. Quickly every household was aroused to gather around the bedside of its firstborn and to gaze helplessly on as the strength and hope of every family writhed on a bed of pain. Even the household of Pharaoh was not spared. With fear gripping his heart, the king hastened to the chamber of the young prince. There lay the child he had so carefully groomed with a father's love to sit upon his throne, groaning with pain. There lay the pride and hope of the nation. There lay the joy of a father's love. And what could Pharaoh do? He could send for the physicians of Egypt; he could send for the magicians and priests; but what were they against the terrible power of Israel's God? Pharaoh knew in his heart it was vain. What a fool Pharaoh had been. What good was the great nation he ruled, what good were his armies and riches, what good was his endless battle of pride with Jehovah, if his own son must perish in the end? The angel of Jehovah had passed through the land. The pestilence had followed in his wake. All of Egypt stood helplessly by as all of its firstborn children breathed forth their last breath in pain and died.

A moment of silence, and then the cries of pain from the dying were replaced with the wails of the mourners. There went up a great cry throughout all of Egypt. Seldom has the world known such extreme and great despair. Natural love had been deprived of the object in which it rejoiced. Here a father, there a brother, and there a son had been loved and now was gone. Even the beasts of the field gazed dumbly on the carcasses of their dead. It was cause enough for the great cry that went up. But there was even more. A great and strong nation had been brought to ruin. Egypt was renowned among the nations. Its armies were the strongest, its wealth was the richest, its learning the profoundest, its works the greatest of any civilization that had ever been. It had learned to hold itself proudly aloof among all people. And now it was ruined. In a matter of months the whole of the land of Egypt had been laid desolate by nine different plagues in succession. But that had not been the worst. After each one of them, they had been able to say like Ephraim in a later day, "The bricks are fallen down, but we will build with hewn stones: the sycomores are cut down, but we will change them into cedars" (Isa. 9:10). But now the tenth plague had struck, and what were they to say? All of the firstborn of Egypt, the strength and hope of the nation, were dead, smitten by the God of Israel. It was especially that which hurt. Had it been a mere chance happening of circumstances, they might have stoically endured it. Had it been another nation that had conquered them by reason of their greater might, they might have borne it. But now it was the God of the Hebrews, a people whom they counted as mere servants. It was Jehovah against whom they were not able to raise so much as a sword. It was he whom they despised and hated above all others. It outraged the Egyptians' pride, even as they groaned for the death that surrounded them on every side and trembled for fear of their own lives. The cries that went up that night in Egypt formed perhaps the clearest figure this world shall ever see of the cries that shall go up eternally from the pit of fire that is called Hell.

In the palace Pharaoh felt the piercing pain of defeat more than anyone else. With his monumental pride, he had led the hateful rebellion against God. By each pronouncement of Jehovah, his heart had been made the harder, until now, before the dead body of his son, even he could not deny the sovereign power of Israel's God. In utter terror and dismay, he had to bow. Only one wish remained in his heart, to be rid of his oppressor. In the desperation of terror, he sent the message to Moses, "Rise up, and get you forth from among my people, both ye and the children of Israel; and go, serve the LORD, as ye have said. Also take your flocks and your herds, as ye have said, and be gone; and bless me also" (Ex. 12:31–32).

The perfect faithfulness of Jehovah God was beyond doubt to every Israelite when they heard this message repeated. For years it had appeared as if deliverance from the tyranny of Egypt was utterly impossible. It had seemed even more so when under one plague after another Pharaoh still would not relent. But now even this most hardened of wicked men had been made to bow. There was no resisting of the power of their God. It was a warning to all men everywhere of the futility of resisting Jehovah God—but a warning that wicked men will never heed, until they like Pharaoh are brought unto the pangs of Hell.

The Israelites were ready for Pharaoh's relenting command. Already they were wearing clothes suited for travel. They had eaten the flesh of the sacrificial lamb for nourishment to bear them forth in their journey. Their possessions were packed ready for travel. Bread without leaven had been baked. And, more important than anything else, they had seen and trusted in the promise of God typified in the shed blood of the lamb. In that faith they would go forth as conquerors. Quickly they gathered for the journey.

For the Egyptians looking on in terror, this all was not done quickly enough. Distraught with fear they could not wait for Israel to depart. Their firstborn were already dead, and might not the pestilence soon destroy them all? They urged and pleaded with the Israelites to make haste, to be gone and not to wait. Hysterically they muttered to themselves, "We be all dead men" (Ex. 12:33), over and over again. The fearful dread of Jehovah was upon them, and with utter impatience they urged that Jehovah's will, which they had so long resisted, should now without delay be done. Israel suddenly found those who had ruled over her with cold-blooded tyranny pleading with her through anxious tears. The Israelites, even as their God had commanded them, turned to their former taskmasters to demand payment for their labors in jewels of silver and gold. Even at this, the Egyptians did not balk. With reckless abandonment they took all of their wealth and urged the Israelites on their way if only it would serve to hasten them. So after four hundred and thirty years Israel departed out of Egypt, leaving a land smitten and spoiled behind them. In the name of her God she had conquered, and she traveled from Rameses to Succoth.

Yet, in their departing, one more warning would God give to his people, "Sanctify unto me all the firstborn, whatsoever openeth the womb among the children of Israel, both of man and of beast: it is mine" (Ex. 13:2). In the very hour of victory, he would have no one of Israel forget to whom their victory belonged. Had it not been for the gracious promise of God, their firstborn too would have perished with the Egyptians' firstborn, and they too would all have been as dead men. Their victory was not due to any excellence of their own, but only to the sacrificial blood instituted by their God. They in their victory belonged unto him. They must needs acknowledge this fact, and henceforth the strength and hope of their nation, all of the first-born children, must be sanctified unto him. Thus would they ever confess that they were not their own; they belonged to the faithful God who had saved them.

Chapter 16

THROUGH THE SEA ON DRY GROUND

15. And the LORD said unto Moses, Wherefore criest thou unto
    me? speak unto the children of Israel, that they go forward:
16. But lift thou up thy rod, and stretch out thine hand over the
    sea, and divide it: and the children of Israel shall go on dry
    ground through the midst of the sea. (Exodus 14:15–16)

As a great tidal wave of humanity, the children of Israel gathered
themselves together and moved toward the borders of Egypt.
They numbered in the millions: 600,000 men plus women and children. An aura of joy and confidence shone from their faces. From
bondage they had been delivered by the power of their God. They
were bound for the promised land, the covenant inheritance of their
fathers. Behind they left their cruel task masters, terror-stricken and
silent. The dominion of Egypt over Israel was broken.

The children of Israel brought with them what was a great,
although silent, testimony of the faith in which they went. They carried the bones of Joseph. It was he who had brought the children of
Israel into Egypt to save them from the famine in Canaan; but always
his testimony had been that to Canaan they must return. Even in
his death he had assured them, "God will surely visit you; and ye
shall carry up my bones away hence with you" (Ex. 13:19). Over four
hundred years had passed, and still his bones remained waiting, a testimony of faith that Israel belonged in Canaan. Now finally the bones
of Joseph were being carried to their final resting place.

From Rameses to Succoth the Israelites traveled and then on to
Etham at the edge of the wilderness. It was as they made this journey
that a marvelous reality appeared. Against the azure sky there loomed

a great white cloud, stretched as a pillar from heaven to earth. As the people moved, the cloud went before them, guiding them on the way. When darkness fell, the cloud was transformed and began to glisten with the radiance of a heavenly light. In the cloud was Jehovah, or, more specifically, the Angel of Jehovah. Through it Jesus Christ functioned in his old dispensation form. The Shekinah, as the pillar of cloud has come to be called, was to be the constant manifestation of Jehovah's presence to the children of Israel throughout their wilderness journey. It was to be the source of continual blessings. Not only did it serve to guide Israel through the trackless wastes of the wilderness and provide her with light in the dark hours of the night, but it would serve as a shield to protect her from her enemies and a shade to shelter her from the burning rays of the desert sun. Before it the believing children of Israel would learn to know the blessedness of dwelling in the presence of their God. Only through the power of God in the cloud would Israel be able to endure the hardships of the journey in the months and years to come.

It was after the departure from Etham that Jehovah commanded a very surprising thing. He commanded Moses to turn from the road leading to Canaan and travel to the south. At another time many of Israel might have objected to this move, but faith in Jehovah was high and, without murmuring, the people followed the guidance of the cloud. Little did the people realize the hardships that this would entail. The route on which they were being taken was long, and it led through hot and barren deserts. Months and years would pass in which they would find nothing on which to survive except the sustaining power of their God. Complete trust and confidence in Jehovah would be the only source of strength. That was exactly the divine wisdom of this way. Jehovah was not misled by the apparent enthusiasm of the moment. He knew the hearts of men and was able to discern the weaknesses of Israel. Only by passing through the hardships of the wilderness could the children of God grow sufficiently in faith to inherit the promised land. Only by tasting of the barrenness of this earth and of their own strength could they come to rely solely upon their God. The way of hardship was for them the way of grace.

Besides this, there was also another reason why the Lord led Israel in the way he did. Yet one more judgment was to be brought upon the Egyptians. As Israel was starting on her journey, Egypt was just beginning to recover from the stunning effects of the last plague. Egypt had been humbled, but it had not been brought to repentance. It had acknowledged the greatness of Jehovah God, but it had not come to conversion of heart. In fear Pharaoh had pleaded for a blessing, but he despised the very God of whom he asked it. No sooner did Pharaoh hear of the strange, southerly route that Israel followed, than he eagerly laid hold upon it as proof that the wisdom of Israel's God was foolishness. Ignoring the humiliating defeats of the past, his pride was only too ready to believe again that it could gain a final victory over Israel's God. With arrogant glee Pharaoh concluded of this latest move, "They are entangled in the land, the wilderness hath shut them in… Why have we done this, that we have let Israel go from serving us?" (Ex. 14:3, 5). With bitter enthusiasm Pharaoh prepared his chariots to follow after Israel, determined to justify himself of his greatest enemy. It was of the Lord. Finally and fatally he had hardened Pharaoh's heart. Not Pharaoh but Jehovah was to be conclusively vindicated.

Only gradually did the implications of the route they were traveling dawn upon the children of Israel. At first, they were perplexed, but this soon turned to dismay. As they proceeded, there emerged on the left the shores of the Red Sea, and as they looked ahead, they saw the looming peaks of an impassable mountain range reaching out also to cut them off on the right. It was then that they turned their heads and saw to their astonishment the distant glint of sunlight on steel. Soon they were able to discern the chariots of Pharaoh coming upon them in hot pursuit. In a matter of moments all of the former enthusiasm had died. Conviction and confidence gave way to the same carnal reasoning that had tempted Pharaoh. The cloud of God's presence continued to proceed steadily on the way, but the people were confused and troubled, refusing to follow. In a faithless prayer of complaint, they began to cry out unto the Lord, but the heavens remained unmoved and silent. Finally, they turned to Moses, laying upon him all of the blame. "Is not this the word that we did tell thee in Egypt, saying, Let us alone, that we may serve the Egyptians? For it had been better for us to serve the Egyptians, than that we should die in the wilderness" (Ex. 14:12). Here it was suddenly manifested how strong Israel really was. On the tide of victory, the people had counted themselves strong, exclaiming the praises of their God. But now in the face of difficulty, where only faith could conquer, they revealed how weak they still were. They were willing to exchange the way of faith for the former bondage of sin. No wonder they could not go directly to Canaan. Israel had yet much to learn.

Even Moses had begun to waver. He had only one duty to perform: to lead the people on, following the cloud. Distracted by the complaints of the people, he had yielded and stopped. The cloud went on alone until it hovered over the sea. This was the way of salvation, a way impossible to the eyes of the flesh, a way that only the strongest faith could follow. But even Moses did not have that. Rather, he turned to the people and said, "Fear ye not, stand still, and see the salvation of the LORD, which he will shew to you to day: for the Egyptians whom ye have seen to day, ye shall see them again no more for ever. The LORD shall fight for you, and ye shall hold your peace" (Ex. 14:13–14). Words of faith? At certain times and in certain places they might have been. Moses was correct in that he looked to Jehovah for deliverance, but one thing he neglected—he forgot the guidance of the Lord in the cloud. The answer of God was a reprimand, "Wherefore criest thou unto me? speak unto the children of Israel, that they go forward" (v. 15).

This was the way of salvation: to follow the guidance of the Lord even when it led into the very depths of the sea. The Lord would provide salvation for his people, but only through the way that he had determined, not by bringing them along an easy road, which was the carnal expectation of many in Israel, not by engaging the Egyptians in open battle as Moses had evidently expected, but by leading them through the depths of the sea. That way, we are told in the New Testament, was a symbol of baptism in the blood of Jesus Christ (1 Cor. 10:1–2). In the cloud was the Angel of Jehovah, Jesus Christ in his Old Testament form. Israel must follow the cloud in faith, and following it must pass under it even by passing through the depths of the sea, which sea was a symbol of death. The gospel was being unfolded, that the believing children of Israel might see and learn of the only way of salvation. Although in the shadow of Old Testament type, the chosen people of God had to learn the same truth that was later set forth by the apostle Paul when he said,

3. Know ye not, that so many of us as were baptized into Jesus Christ were baptized into his death?
4. Therefore we are buried with him by baptism into death: that like as Christ was raised up from the dead by the glory of the Father, even so we also should walk in newness of life.
5. For if we have been planted together in the likeness of his death, we shall be also in the likeness of his resurrection. (Rom. 6:3–5)

That Moses and the people might more clearly understand, God commanded Moses, "Lift thou up thy rod, and stretch out thine hand over the sea, and divide it: and the children of Israel shall go on dry ground through the midst of the sea" (Ex. 14:16). This Moses did, and immediately there arose a strong east wind forcing back the waters of the sea and making the ground underneath dry. With walls of water on each side, a dry path was made through the bottom of the sea. Meanwhile the Angel of Jehovah in the cloud "removed and went behind" the camp of Israel dividing them from the armies of Egypt (v. 19).

Night was falling as the people of Israel began to pass through the depths of the sea. The enemy was close behind them, yet could not approach because the cloud was to the Egyptians an impassable wall of darkness. The sky grew dark above Israel, but the very cloud that was darkness to the Egyptians was to the Israelites a glowing column of light shining behind and above them to guide their feet so that not one foot was made to stumble. There was humble wonderment in the hearts of the children of God as they made this amazing passage in their journey. They had marveled at the power of God as he had revealed himself in Egypt, and now even more wonderful works than those they were experiencing. They had doubted the possibility of salvation as they stood by the shore of the sea, and now they knew how foolish they had been, for nothing could withstand the hand of the Lord. As Israel passed through the sea, they worshiped.

Through the hours of the night, only the Egyptians were apprehensive. Did they perhaps hear through the darkness the sounds of Israel's passage? Anxiously they sought to pierce the blackness with their eyes. Not until morning dawned and all of Israel had left the shore did God lift the cloud and allow them to see. In complete amazement they beheld the last of the Israelites passing between the waters. But God had hardened Pharaoh's heart, and he would not hesitate in his determination even at the sight of so evident a miracle. With reckless abandonment he led his army into the depths of the sea in pursuit of his enemy. It was when the last Israelite had reached the shore and the Egyptians were pursuing wildly through the depths of the sea that God commanded Moses again to stretch forth his hand. The wind subsided, and slowly the waters began to settle again into their place. Before the eyes of all Israel the chariots were stopped, the horses were covered, and all of the host of Pharaoh was devoured by the closing sea. Finally and forever Jehovah was vindicated of a nation that before his very presence had hardened its heart.

Chapter 17

THE SONG OF MOSES

> Then sang Moses and the children of Israel this song unto
> the LORD. (Exodus 15:1)

U nder the full light of the morning sun, Israel found herself in
the quiet stillness of the wilderness. The air hung in hushed
silence except for the gentle sound of the waves lapping rhythmically
upon the seashore. The expanses of the desert stretched out before
them in peaceful serenity.

And then reality began to sink in. Overwhelming it must have
been. Suddenly they knew themselves to be free men. All of their
lives they had lived in the bondage of Egypt. They were used to rising wearily every morning to the call of their Egyptian masters. They
were used to spending their days at the sole command of others.
They were used to bending their backs to the cry of cruel taskmasters. They were used to ending their days in utter fatigue without one
thought or consideration to their own personal desires. Now suddenly they were free; free to live their lives according to the wishes of
their own hearts; free to return to a land that they themselves could
possess; free to labor for their own benefit and that of their families;
free, above all, to worship Jehovah their God in liberty after the manner that they ought. The newness of this feeling, the exuberance of
spirit it aroused in their hearts, the very joy with which it filled their
souls was almost more than their minds could begin to comprehend.

And then there was the torrent of memories that surged again
and again through their hearts; the memory of Jehovah coming to
them through Moses to take their part against the enemy and to
strike the Egyptians with judgments nine and ten times over again;

the memory of that final midnight hour when the angel of Jehovah passed through the land smiting with pestilence and death the first-born of every house that was not covered by the sign of the redeeming blood; the memory of that last symbolic meal composed of the flesh of the lamb with bitter herbs and unleavened bread, eaten in haste while fully dressed and ready for travel, because it was to serve as a source of physical and spiritual strength to carry them on to the promised land; the memory of their triumphal departure, urged on by the trembling Egyptians who willingly pressed into their hands jewels of silver and gold, an unexpected payment for all of their years of labor; the memory of that strange and mysterious journey that brought them to their freedom; the joy of those first few days of travel when the cloud of Jehovah appeared to lead them toward the south; the feelings of consternation and dismay when they found themselves closed in on every side by the sea and the mountains and Pharaoh's army, so that even the bondage of Egypt seemed better to them than their expected end; the hovering cloud of Jehovah urging them to go onward into the very depths of the sea and swinging around behind them to separate them from Pharaoh's army, only after Moses had raised his rod to divide the sea asunder; the singular nighttime passage through the deep with the winds of heaven holding the tempestuous waters in walls beside them while lightning and thunder flashed and rumbled overhead, and the glow of the pillar of fire gave light to guide their feet; the ascent from the sea as though from the very bosom of death to stand finally upon land that was free; the final justification of Jehovah over his enemies as he brought the walls of water flowing in upon the Egyptians in their rash and foolish pursuit through the sea.

All these memories pressed upon them as they stood amid the quiet stillness of the wilderness, basked in the rays of morning light. Only the bodies of the Egyptian army, washed up on the shore by the waves, were to be seen as a reminder of all that had transpired through the hours of the night. That morning as never before, the Israelites understood the greatness of Jehovah their God. Even as his name implied, he had been faithful to his covenant. For all that had taken place, they could take none of the credit. They had proved hesitant and even rebellious, but Jehovah had gone forth in his love to punish their enemies, to bring them out of bondage, and with many miraculous works to carry them on their way victoriously. Their hearts swelled within them at the greatness of their God.

At last there burst forth from the lips of Moses and of Israel a song of adoration to their God. After an opening refrain expressing the theme of praise, three glorious verses followed. Each verse opened with an expression of praise to Jehovah, after which the first and second verses recounted his victory over Pharaoh, and the third gave expression of their faith in the promises yet to come. So they sang:

Sing will I to the Lord, for highly exalted is He,
Horse and his rider He hath thrown into the sea.
My strength and song is JAH [Jehovah],
He became my salvation;
He is my God, whom I extol,
My father's God, whom I exalt.
For he became salvation to me,
Granted me deliverance and salvation:
The God of my father:
Jehovah is a man of war:
Jehovah is His name:
Pharaoh's chariots and his might He cast into the sea,
And the choice of his knights were drowned in the Red Sea.
Floods cover them;
They go down into the deep like stone.
Thy right hand, Jehovah, glorified in power,
Thy right hand dashes in pieces the enemy.
In the fulness of Thy majesty Thou pullest down Thine
    opponents.
Thou lettest out Thy burning heat, it devours them like stubble.
And by the breath of Thy nostrils the waters heaped them-
    selves up;

The flowing ones stood like a heap.
The waves congealed in the heart of the sea:
The enemy said: I pursue, overtake, divide spoil,
My soul becomes full of them;
I draw my sword, my hand will root them out.
Thou didst blow with Thy breath:
The sea covered them,
They sank as lead in the mighty waters.
Who is like unto Thee among the gods, O Jehovah?
Who is like unto Thee, glorified in holiness?
Fearful for praises, doing wonders,
Thou stretchest out Thy hand, the earth swallows them.
Thou leadest through Thy mercy the people whom Thou
    redeemest;
Thou guidest them through Thy might to Thy holy habitation.
People hear, they are afraid;
Trembling seizes the inhabitants of Philistia.
Then are the princes of Edom confounded;
The mighty men of Moab, trembling seizes them;
All the inhabitants of Canaan despair.
Fear and dread fall upon them; for the greatness of Thine arm;
They are dumb as stones, till Thy people pass through,
Jehovah, till the people which Thou hast purchased pass through.
Thou wilt bring and plant them in the mountain of Thine
    inheritance,
The place which Thou hast made for Thy dwelling-place,
    Jehovah,
For the sanctuary, Lord, which Thy hands prepared.
Jehovah will be King for ever and ever.[1]

The voices of the men of Israel resounded from the mountains of
the wilderness and reechoed across the waters of the sea. The sound

---

1   This translation of the song of Moses is taken from Carl Friedrich Kiel and
    Franz Delitzsch "Commentary on Exodus 15:4." https://www.studylight.org
    /commentaries/kdo/exodus-15.html (accessed December 17, 2020).

of victory literally filled the air. Even as they sang, the women of Israel, with Miriam at their head, took up the opening refrain. With timbrel and dance, they responded again and again, "Sing ye to the LORD, for he hath triumphed gloriously; the horse and his rider hath he thrown into the sea" (Ex. 15:21). To the church of all ages the joy of the children of Israel expressed in this song stands as a picture and a type of the triumphal rejoicing of the saints in New Jerusalem when they in like manner shall sing the song of Moses and of the Lamb (Rev. 15:3). In that day all glory was given to God. Could this nation ever doubt his power again?

When at last they resumed their journey, there was confidence in every step. Here and there among the throng there could still be heard the verses of Moses' song coming from the lips of those who, even as they walked, continued to sing. The conversation flowed freely as friends walked and talked together on the way. Only gradually did the people begin to notice how different the land was from that which they had left. Gone were the fertile valleys of Egypt with their ever-flowing fountains and springs. Gone was the rich vegetation of trees, vegetables, and grain. All that was to be seen were the barren expanses of desert with only the thinnest covering of wilted grass. Dominating the scene was only the glaring blast of the mid-day sun with its burning, oppressive heat. But this was not a day in which to worry. They had tasted the joy of victory through the power of their God.

It was not until the second and third day afterward that the feelings of the people began to waver. Their joy they still remembered, but the monotony was beginning to tell. Everywhere they looked there were the glaring rays of the sun reflected from barren wastes. True, they did not suffer, for the cloud of Jehovah sheltered them from the greatest heat of the daytime sun, but it was oppressive just the same. And then there was the complete lack of fresh water. That which they carried in their skins had become warm and uninviting to the taste, and even that was about gone. Conversation began to lag, and the song of Moses was no longer heard; the joy of the nation so soon was changed into morbid silence.

It was on the third day that the crisis came. The word was passed through the camp that water had been seen in the distance. The strongest hastened ahead so as to be the first to receive its refreshment. They stooped to drink deeply, only to rise spewing it out and crying, "Marah!" The water was bitter. One after another they tried it, but the result was always the same. The water was too bitter to drink. A tide of anger quickly passed through the people until they turned to Moses and said, "What shall we drink?" (Ex. 15:24).

It was Moses who went in prayer to God. He was shown a tree that, when it was cut down and cast into the water, made the waters became sweet. The people were able to drink.

But something had happened at Marah. By the Red Sea there had been a joy and confidence that they thought would never end. But now it was known that weakness still remained. The Song of Moses they knew in principle; but only in the life to come would they be able to sing it with such confidence again.

Chapter 18

BREAD FROM HEAVEN

14. And when the dew that lay was gone up, behold, upon the face of the wilderness there lay a small round thing, as small as the hoar frost on the ground.
15. And when the children of Israel saw it, they said one to another, It is manna: for they wist not what it was. And Moses said unto them, This is the bread which the Lord hath given you to eat. (Exodus 16:14–15)

Marah laid the pattern for the life of the nation of Israel that would prevail throughout the wilderness journey. There the people first began to murmur because of the rigor of the life they were called to lead. There God clearly demonstrated that he was perfectly able to provide for them in all of their need. There God set forth his statute and ordinance to prove them, saying, "If thou wilt diligently hearken to the voice of the Lord thy God, and wilt do that which is right in his sight, and wilt give ear to his commandments, and keep all his statutes, I will put none of these diseases upon thee, which I have brought upon the Egyptians: for I am the Lord that healeth thee" (Ex. 15:26).

From Marah Israel moved to Elam. There they camped. It was a pleasant place to be, with its seventy palm trees and twelve wells of water. During the stay at Elam the camp was quiet; but underneath there was a deep-seated division that had developed. There were those who remembered the marvelous works of Jehovah their God and trusted in his abiding love. For them the Song of Moses still reechoed in their hearts. They looked forward in faith, confident in the promises of God. But there were also the others. They too had sung the Song of Moses on the shore of the Red Sea; but already it was forgotten. They were discovering that the way of the wilderness was to be hard, and doubts were creeping in. They wanted material prosperity, and, as long as it did not come, they would object. Henceforth this division would become ever more evident in the life of the nation. The two elements would be constantly vying together for control of the nation. The latter group, being by far the more numerous, would surely have overcome were it not for the repeated intervention of Jehovah.

Elam provided a peaceful camp. Under the shade of its palms, the people found rest. But it could not last. The cloud of Jehovah would lead them onward. Soon the tents were packed, and Israel set forth again to the rigor of the wilderness way. A few days of travel passed, and again the discontents had a reason to speak. This time it was food. The supply was getting low, and, looking about in the wilderness, they saw none that was to be had. First there were just sullen faces with mutterings under the breath; but before long, there were animated and angry conversations. Men circulated through the camp spreading the flames of rebellion. What were they going to do for food? Soon what they had would be gone, and they would all be left without. This was not what they had been promised. It was not right. It was not fair. Some became outspoken and united themselves into a crowd. With flushed faces they made their way to Moses and Aaron. Their voices were angry and loud. "Would to God we had died by the hand of the LORD in the land of Egypt, when we sat by the flesh pots, and when we did eat bread to the full; for ye have brought us forth into the wilderness, to kill this whole assembly with hunger" (Ex. 16:3).

To them Moses and Aaron would not answer. Moses and Aaron would not meet anger with anger, heated words with heated words. The implication was very clear. They, Moses and Aaron, were being blamed for the fear of the people. The people accused them because they were men. The people dared not lay the blame to God. Silently Moses and Aaron turned to do the only thing they could. They went in prayer to God. As they prayed, God came to Moses and spoke. "Behold, I will rain bread from heaven for you; and the people shall go out and gather a certain rate every day, that I may prove them, whether they will walk in my law, or no" (Ex. 16:4). Meanwhile, as the people waited, a hushed silence fell over the camp. Tension was drawn to the point of breaking. One short month had passed since their departure from Egypt, and already the third crisis had come. The trouble was in the route they had been made to take. They never knew what was coming next. Every day anew the way ahead looked impossible. It made them uncertain and afraid. Why could they not travel an easier road? Then they would not feel so much like rebelling. Still, there were some whose discernment went deeper than this. They had an underlying awareness of guilt. As yet, they realized, they had never really lacked what they needed. The presence of Jehovah was before them in the cloud, and he had always provided for them in time. It was just that they had to trust so exclusively in him. There was never anything tangible upon which they could rely. That made it so hard.

Finally Moses and Aaron returned. First they went to the waiting group of leaders. With stern words of reprimand, they spoke.

6. At even, then ye shall know that the LORD hath brought you out from the land of Egypt:

7. And in the morning, then ye shall see the glory of the LORD; for that he heareth your murmurings against the LORD: and what are we, that ye murmur against us?

8. …This shall be, when the LORD shall give you in the evening flesh to eat, and in the morning bread to the full; for that the LORD heareth your murmurings which ye murmur against him: and what are we? your murmurings are not against us, but against the LORD. (Ex. 16:6–8)

Next, all of the congregation was called together. The people gathered at the edge of the camp, and Aaron stood before them. Tensely the people waited for him to speak, but at the same time, there was an awareness of the cloud of Jehovah that hovered at a distance in the wilderness. Aaron's pronouncement was short. "Come near before the LORD: for he hath heard your murmurings" (Ex. 16:9), and with that he pointed them toward the cloud. Before their eyes the cloud began to glow. Brighter and brighter it shone until the glory, the beauty, the awful light of God's presence blinded their eyes. While the people stood trembling, Moses was commanded to speak to them again: "At even ye shall eat flesh, and in the morning ye shall be filled with bread; and ye shall know that I am the LORD your God" (v. 12).

Slowly the people returned to their tents and waited. They had seen the glory of Jehovah and heard the messages of Aaron and Moses. A feeling of anxious anticipation filled the camp. They could try to go about their usual activities, but their minds would only reflect again on what they had seen and heard. They had been told that they would eat flesh, but from where? They had been told that they would have bread, but how? It all seemed again so utterly impossible; yet they could not dismiss it from their minds. In groups or alone, they waited. And then, there arose an excited cry. A dark cloud had been sighted on the horizon. For a moment their hearts beat faster. Was it an approaching storm of judgment such as they had seen roll repeatedly over Egypt? They knew that they had displeased Jehovah by their complaining. But no, it approached too swiftly for that. Closer and closer it came, vibrating as though with life and with the sound of many thrashing wings. It was a flock of birds covering the sky, quails without number. The birds came; they hovered over the camp; and then they settled down. In sheer amazement the people hesitated; but then they reached out and captured the birds with bare hands, as many as they wanted.

Countless fires burned brightly that night in the camp of Israel. The people had fresh meat to eat. They had thought it to be impossible, but Jehovah had brought it to pass. To the faithful it was an occasion of greatest joy. They were assured of the faithfulness of their God and of his abiding love. Repenting from their murmuring, they had peace in their souls. But there were also the others. In their mouths the meat was tasteless, and bitter in their stomachs. They would have almost preferred not to have seen the quails, even if many had starved. Then they would have been justified in their complaints. Now they stood condemned. And still there was more to come.

Early the next morning another excited cry went up. The earliest risers, awaking in the morning's dawn, found the ground covered with white like snow. Quickly the people turned out to examine this new thing that they saw. Small, white kernels, like coriander seeds, covered the ground as far as the eye could see. The people looked and cried, "Manna? (What is it?)" It was a substance such as human eyes had never before seen. They stooped and sifted it through their fingers. They lifted it to their lips and found it sweet to the taste like honey. It was a miraculous substance perfectly adapted for food. It could provide all of the nourishment needed by the human body even amid the rigorous life of the wilderness. Moses stood before the people and explained. "This is the bread which the LORD hath given you to eat. This is the thing which the LORD hath commanded, Gather of it every man according to his eating, an omer for every man, according to the number of your persons; take ye every man for them which are in his tents" (Ex. 16:15–16).

A feeling of festivity filled the camp as the people hastened to find containers. They found this new kind of food exciting. It was a delicious food, and an omer (perhaps about five pints), was sufficient for every man's daily need. Soon they discovered that not only could it be eaten raw, but it could be seethed or baked as they chose. The manna was an indisputable testimony that Jehovah their God was fully capable of supplying their every need, and he did even when they were unthankful and wicked. But the manna was also a means by which they were being proved. Some there were who followed Moses' command exactly, gathering only enough for one day. They understood that God would supply more food every morning and believed that it was so. But there were others who would take no chance. They gathered as much manna as they could until under the heat of the sun it melted away. They wanted to be sure that they would have food for the morrow regardless of what Moses said. The next morning a putrid stench hung over the camp, for worms had invaded the pots where this extra manna was kept. With angry words Moses admonished them.

With the sixth day of the week a new command was given by the Lord. Moses brought it to the people. "This is that which the LORD hath said, To morrow is the rest of the holy sabbath unto the LORD: bake that which ye will bake today, and seethe that ye will seethe; and that which remaineth over lay up for you to be kept until the morning" (Ex. 16:23). Again there were some who obeyed. They trusted the word of the Lord. But there were others who feared the stench. They preferred to gather in the morning even if it were the sabbath. But in the morning there was none, and it remained for them to go hungry. Again Moses spoke, "How long refuse ye to keep my commandments and my laws? See, for that the LORD hath given you the sabbath, therefore he giveth you on the sixth day the bread of two days; abide ye every man in his place, let no man go out of his place on the seventh day" (vv. 28–29). Jehovah was teaching Israel an important lesson. She could exist as a nation only through complete dependence upon him. It was the truth set forth by Moses and later quoted by Jesus: "Man doth not live by bread only, but by every word that proceedeth out of the mouth of the LORD doth man live" (Deut. 8:3; Matt. 4:4). It was as though they heard beforehand the words of Jesus: "Take no thought for your life, what ye shall eat, or what ye shall drink; nor yet for your body, what ye shall put on. Is not the life more than meat, and the body more than raiment? But seek ye first the kingdom of God, and his righteousness; and all these things shall be added unto you" (Matt. 6:25, 33).

Chapter 19

WATER FROM THE ROCK

1. Moreover, brethren, I would not that ye should be ignorant, how that all our fathers...

4. Did all drink the same spiritual drink: for they drank of that spiritual Rock that followed them: and that Rock was Christ. (1 Corinthians 10:1, 4)

Daily the people of Israel arose from their sleep to gaze upon the bread from heaven that in the morning light covered the floor of the desert. It was a beautiful sight, glistening white under the rising sun. They gathered of it until they had plenty to eat. They ate of it until they were satisfied. The taste of it was sweet, giving the people much joy. It reminded them again and again of the great and all-comprehensive power of Israel's God. To those who were spiritual in Israel, the truth that the manna brought was even richer. Eating of it to nourish their bodies, they were reminded every time again that they must also find the nourishment for their souls in God. His grace had to uphold their spiritual life. They were being told "that man doth not live by bread only, but by every word that proceedeth out of the mouth of the LORD doth man live" (Deut. 8:3). In the dim outline of Old Testament shadow, they saw the promise of the living bread that was yet to come from heaven, so that if any man would eat of it, he would live forever. To those who had eyes to see, the manna of the wilderness testified of the promise of the gospel. But there were others. They saw in the manna nothing more than a form of food that was pleasant to the taste and satisfying to the body. For a time, they too marveled at the daily replenishment of this wonderful food, but before long they began to take it completely for granted. They became tired of the constant repetition of manna. They ate of it only because there was nothing different, but the pleasure of eating had departed. There was a rift in the camp of Israel, and constantly it was growing deeper.

Every day they were being led deeper into the wilderness by the cloud of Jehovah, and once more the difficulty that preceded their arrival at Marah began to reappear. Their water bags were becoming empty, and they found no springs or fountains upon the way to refill them. Again the tension of fear and disappointment began to build. What good was their daily supply of manna without water to drink? Carefully what water they had was meted out; but no one received quite enough to satisfy. Every mile along which they were led appeared to be drier than the one before. Why did they have to travel such a dismal route? They needed fresh supplies of water if they were to live. Why was it not supplied? More and more bitter their thoughts became until at last in anger they turned again to Moses. "Give us water," they demanded, "that we may drink" (Ex. 17:2).

In this the children of Israel revealed an evil that is often typical of sin. The people were rebelling against God. They were dissatisfied with the way in which the Lord was leading them. In their hearts they were thinking that they could have found a better route. It would have been better to take a shorter way with an abundant supply of food and water, they thought. The road upon which they traveled now was foolish and ill advised. But at the same time, they lacked the honesty to acknowledge that they were questioning the wisdom of God. Instead they would lay the blame at the feet of another mere man. The fact that Moses did nothing more than to follow the cloud of Jehovah, they would ignore. The fact that he led them as he did by direct instruction from God, they would forget. They would speak to Moses as though he were the responsible party. In that way the wickedness of their rebellion did not appear quite so evident. This Moses pointed out when he answered, "Why chide ye with me? wherefore do ye tempt the LORD?" (17:2).

Well might the people have stopped at this. It was a grievous error to become guilty of tempting the Lord their God. They made themselves worthy of being destroyed even as the Egyptians were. But the angry minds of the Israelites were much too heated to stop at this. It made them even more angry to think that in the present situation they should be accused of sin. With accusing voices and threatening gestures, they answered Moses, "Wherefore is this that thou hast brought us up out of Egypt, to kill us and our children and our cattle with thirst?" (17:3).

Gradually Moses was learning how deep the roots of sin were still implanted in the nation of Israel. He could lead them in the way that the Lord had ordained, but he could not make them willing to follow. He could admonish them for their rebellion, but he could not make them repent. He could speak to them the truth, but he could not give them ears that would hear and hearts that would believe. Rather, it was becoming ever more evident that many were offended by the word of God. They wanted nothing more than the things of this earth. When these things were supplied, they were satisfied and would even put on the appearance of thankfulness. But when the word of God came to them without the material things they wanted, it made them angry and rebellious. They would not place their trust in God alone, and the very suggestion that they should do so was offensive. Each time the murmuring of the people was becoming more violent. They were even beginning to threaten his life. Overwhelmed with a feeling of helplessness, he cried unto the Lord in prayer, "What shall I do unto this people? they be almost ready to stone me" (17:4). With God he found a calm but firm answer. Obediently Moses set himself to obey.

First Moses gathered together the elders of the people. They were the leaders of the nation. Many of them were the most outspoken in the repeated murmurings of the wilderness journey. Now they stood before Moses and there was tension in the air. Antagonism was dividing the nation that before had been so closely united. They looked upon each other as enemies.

With firm authority Moses began to lead the men out of the camp toward the wilderness. Within the minds and hearts of the elders a feeling of uneasiness began to stir. They had defied the living God, and the bearing of Moses told them that the time of reckoning was drawing near. The uncertainty of sin began to trouble them within. Only a few weeks before, at Marah, the word of God had come to them saying, "If thou wilt diligently hearken to the voice of the LORD thy God, and wilt do that which is right in his sight, and wilt give ear to his commandments, and keep all his statutes, I will put none of these diseases upon thee, which I have brought upon the Egyptians: for I am the LORD that healeth thee" (15:26). Now, as they walked behind Moses, their memories echoed these words again and again. In their murmuring and rebellion, they had refused to keep the commandments of Jehovah and his statutes; they had rejected the voice of the Lord, and what would their end now be? Looking ahead they saw in the hand of Moses the rod that had come to symbolize his God-appointed office. This was the rod that had brought the plagues and diseases of the Egyptians upon them. It was that rod, indeed, that had opened up the Red Sea for Israel's deliverance; but that same rod had closed the sea again to the destruction of the wicked. It was a rod of judgment. Now, they had made themselves guilty. Would it turn upon them?

On into the wilderness they went until they saw before them a great rock cliff of towering granite. In its shadow they stood, and how small it made them feel. In pride they had thought themselves great, but the feeling melted before the elevated rock that God had made. They had thought themselves strong, but before the vast, immovableness of the granite cliffs the feeling could not endure. In number they were many, but here they seemed as nothing. And then, lifting up their eyes, they saw the cloud. It stood before them and the rock. It was the cloud of Jehovah radiating with purity and righteousness from above, and it was as though the rock and the cloud were merged into one. The holy brilliance of the cloud seemed to cover the face of the rock; and the vast immovableness of the rock belonged also to the cloud. The people stood small and insignificant in the presence of Jehovah God.

There was fear in their hearts when they turned again to look at Moses. And then they trembled, for he had lifted up above his head the rod given him by Jehovah. They had sinned. Now they had to admit it. What right did they have to question the way of the Lord? What right did they have to doubt that he was able and willing to fulfill his promises and supply their every need? What right did they have to murmur and complain when things did not go as they wanted? And yet they had done it over and over again. Now the time of judgment had come. There was the cloud, glimmering with the holy glory of God. There was the cliff of rock, typifying his immovableness. There was the rod, which before their eyes had brought down judgments on countless wicked before. What was their end to be? Would fire and brimstone be called down from on high repeating the judgment of Sodom? Would the rock fall upon them and grind them to powder? Would they be cast into hell?

Through the stillness of the desert air sounded the weight of a heavy stroke. Moses had brought down the rod once and again on the rock. Punishment was being meted out, not on them, but on the rock, on the rock where the cloud of Jehovah stood, on the rock where the Angel of Jehovah was. The punishment of their sins was being laid on the Angel of God.

And that was not all. As the astonished people watched, there burst forth from the foot of the rock a stream of water—clear, cool, and pure. It brought refreshment to their dry and thirsty lips. It was the proof that God could and would provide the needs of Israel.

It was a beautiful scene to behold as the people gathered to drink of the waters that poured mysteriously forth from the rock. But there was also a tinge of sadness, for the division in the camp had become more deep.

There were those who drank of the water and found nothing more in it than refreshment for their burning lips. When they left the waters, they would forget them. They would be ready to murmur again.

But there were also the others, who drank the water with a sense of spiritual reverence. They could not forget the way in which it was brought forth. They remembered how unworthy they were. They remembered that they had sinned. They remembered that they had been worthy of judgment. They remembered that their judgment had been laid upon the Angel of Jehovah that stood on the rock, and then the waters came forth. It was as though they heard already the voice of the prophet many ages away saying, "But he was wounded for our transgressions, he was bruised for our iniquities: the chastisement of our peace was upon him; and with his stripes we are healed" (Isa. 53:5). As they stooped to drink of the waters, the glorious refreshment of the waters of life poured in to quicken their souls. Through faith they drank of the spiritual Rock, which was Christ.

Chapter 20

MOSES' INTERCESSION AND ISRAEL'S VICTORY AT REPHIDIM

11. And it came to pass, when Moses held up his hand, that Israel prevailed: and when he let down his hand, Amalek prevailed.
12. But Moses' hands were heavy; and they took a stone, and put it under him and he sat thereon; and Aaron and Hur stayed up his hands, the one on the one side, and the other on the other slide; and his hands were steady until the going down of the sun.
13. And Joshua discomfited Amalek and his people with the edge of the sword. (Exodus 17:11–13)

At Rephidim, Israel was given water from the rock. According to the command of Jehovah, Moses had struck the rock over which hung the cloud of God's presence. The people drank; their thirst was quenched; and they were satisfied. The spiritual among Israel received from that event even more. By it they were instructed in the truth of the gospel. The rod that should have descended upon them because of their rebellion against God had been turned upon the rock where the Angel of Jehovah stood in the cloud. The rock had borne their burden, and from it had come forth for them a blessing: water to quench their thirst. It was a picture of the salvation that would be theirs when finally the promise would be fulfilled.

Over and over again Israel was experiencing the amazing power and love of Jehovah. From the first he had given her his word as the ever-faithful God who would surely keep all of his promises. At every occasion this was proving to be so—in the plagues and the deliverance from Egypt, in the passage through the Red Sea, in the sweetened water of Marah, in the quails and manna in the wilderness of Sin, and then in the water from the rock at Rephidim. Moreover, each one of these miracles reflected a deeper spiritual reality that would be given her in the realization of the promised Messiah. As these miraculous signs progressed, Moses was beginning to stand more and more upon the foreground. At first Aaron had been his spokesman. Aaron would speak publicly the word of God, and Moses often retreated almost timidly into the background. But as time went on, Moses was becoming more bold. No longer was the agency of Aaron needed. It was becoming ever more evident that Moses alone was the prophet appointed by God. Aaron was still there to assist him, but Moses was the one to whom Israel had to look for deliverance. He was her typical redeemer. Moses was being set forth by God as a picture of the Messiah who was to come. In his life and official functions, he was an embodiment of the gospel. By his works Israel was being saved.

The truth of this was becoming evident even from the reactions of the people. To the spiritual Israel in her strength, Moses was a very rich blessing. Just by looking upon him in his God-appointed works, they were being edified. They were learning to appreciate the more the wonderful grace of Jehovah God. But to Israel in its weakness, and especially to those who were carnal, Moses was becoming increasingly a cause for offense. While, if for nothing more than appearance's sake, the people hesitated to speak directly against God, the more Moses became identified with the way of the Lord, the more they found occasion to rebel. Upon him they dared lay all the blame. Against him they would murmur. To him they would ascribe all kinds of evil motives. Him they dared threaten to kill. All this they could do under the pretense of having nothing against God.

This is the very reaction that men always have to the gospel of Jesus Christ. To the elect in their strength, he is precious; but to men in their weakness and to the reprobate, he is a cause for offense. Moses aroused these same reactions because he was a type of Christ.

Soon after Israel drank the water from the rock at Rephidim, another event took place that revealed the greatness of Moses. Amalek made war upon Israel.

The Amalekites were a wild, roaming tribe of the wilderness. Apparently they were the descendants of Amalek, Esau's grandson (Gen. 36:12). For some time now they had been following the Israelites in their wilderness journey and harassing them by attacking those who wandered too far from the camp or who straggled behind when they traveled. They hated Israel as an intruder upon their wilderness domain but also as the ancient enemy of Esau their father. They hated even more Israel's God because he had rejected their father. They were a reprobate nation; there was no fear of God in their hearts.

It was at Rephidim that the Amalekites finally decided that they were capable of doing battle with the nation of Israel as a whole. Perhaps they had witnessed the dissension in the camp of Israel and concluded that the nation could never put up a united front in battle. They began to prepare their forces for battle in the hills surrounding Rephidim. The report of this was soon brought to Moses.

Once again the nation of Israel found herself in a crisis. They were the chosen people of God and the objects of his favor. But they were learning that because of this they should never expect that their way in life would be easy. In their deliverance from Egypt, they had left one great enemy behind. Now but a few months on their way another enemy has appeared. This would always be their experience wherever they went: God's people are strangers in this world, and all of mankind is their enemy. Nor could they expect that, as in Egypt, God would destroy these enemies before them while they stood by and watched. There would come times when they themselves would be required to go out and fight. Indeed, when they walked in faith, God would be on their side. He would give them strength. He would discomfit the enemy. He alone would provide the victory. But often it would only be when they went out with weapons in their hands and entered the very thick of battle. Trusting in God, they would have to engage in many actual wars. So it was also that day with the Amalekites.

Following the command of God, Moses called to him a young man of Israel named Joshua. Already he had distinguished himself as a spiritual man in Israel even amid the murmuring rebellions of the many. He stood firm in the fear of the Lord. Now he was being singled out to lead the forces of God into battle. Accordingly, Moses instructed him, "Choose us out men, and go out, fight with Amalek: to morrow I will stand on the top of the hill with the rod of God in mine hand" (Ex. 17:9).

It was a difficult task that had fallen to Joshua. Israel had never been a warring nation. Few, if any, had any acquaintance with weapons. Even the weapons they had on hand could hardly be considered sufficient to engage in a real battle. It would take men of great courage who would go forth to risk their lives against such odds, for the enemy was a wild tribe of men with much experience in fighting the battles of the wilderness. There was only one factor that Israel had in her favor: God was on their side. He was the God of heaven and earth, with a power far surpassing that possessed by the greatest of men. But for this to make any difference, the army that went into battle had to be composed of spiritual men. Joshua had to search out men who were not merely strong in physical development, but were strong also in the convictions of faith. The miraculous power of God would not supply them with swords and spears that were sharp. It would not provide shields that were sturdy and strong. He would not give them in a moment the experience for battle that they lacked. He would provide only a spiritual bulwark for their souls.

Early on the morning of the day chosen for the battle, Joshua gathered his forces together. It hardly resembled an army. There were no horses such as the Amalekites rode. There were no chariots such as Pharaoh had had when he had pursued them into the sea. There was only a crowd of men with a minimum number of weapons and a willingness to give their lives for the cause of the church of God. Many were the apprehensive glances that went out from the people that were gathered around to watch. Could this army gain a victory? For a moment there was a surge of hope when Moses came from his tent with the rod of Jehovah in his hand. This was a weapon with which the people were familiar. They had seen its power over Egypt. But Moses did not join himself to the gathering army. He would not march at its head with the rod of Jehovah in his hand. Rather, with Aaron and Hur, he began to climb a nearby hill overlooking the proposed field of battle. The army that was to engage in battle was left by him far below.

Slowly the forces with Joshua began to move and make their way toward the battlefield. It was then that they began to understand why Moses had gone where he did. Looking up they saw him standing on the nearby hill with the rod of Jehovah in his hand, held in a gesture with which by now they were familiar. It was the gesture with which he had called down the plagues upon Egypt. It was the gesture with which the Red Sea had been opened up before them and closed again upon Pharaoh. It was a gesture of prayer and intercession by which the prophet called forth the power of God's grace to reveal itself on behalf of Israel. Just to look upon the prophet with believing eyes brought a new surge of confidence to the warriors' hearts. They knew that they had a mediator presenting their cause before the throne of God. They saw in a figure the Mediator, Jesus Christ, who one day would be taken up to heaven to stand eternally lifting up his hand to the throne of God in intercession for his people.

The Amalekites too saw Moses. And though they had never seen him before, they understood full well what he was doing. He was beseeching the help of the God of Israel, whom they after the manner of their father Esau did not fear but hated. Sneers stood out on their faces, and mockery was bantered between them. They became even more determined to have for themselves the battle. They became heady in their anger. But still within, they felt strangely discomfited. They were beginning to realize that their battle was not against men but against God.

Forcefully the two opposing armies met, and already in the early moments the outcome of the battle seemed apparent. The forces of Israel were confident and sure. The experienced warriors of Amalek were strangely confused and uncertain. Glance after glance was hastily thrown from the battlefield toward Moses. Somehow all felt that it was there that the outcome was being determined. But Moses, though a type of Christ, was only a man. There was a limit to his endurance. His arms became tired, and the rod of Jehovah drooped. Each time the rod was lowered, the battle would change to the favor of Amalek. Again and again he tried to keep the rod held aloft, but it was more than he could do. Finally it was Aaron and Hur who came to his assistance. While Moses sat on a stone between them, they held his arms up high. Beneath, the battle surged forth finally and conclusively in Israel's favor, until Amalek and his people were scattered. Through the intercession of Moses, victory was secured.

It was in solemn assembly that Israel gathered that night upon the battlefield. At the command of Moses, an altar of thanksgiving was erected. By proclamation it was named Jehovah-nissi, meaning "Jehovah my Banner." Amalek stood as a representative of the reprobate world seeking to destroy the church. But the true Intercessor is ever lifting up his hands unto the throne of the Lord in behalf of his people. Therefore, God will ever do battle against Amalek from generation to generation until the remembrance of them is utterly blotted out from under the heavens. That altar was a symbol and a promise of God's unwavering love.

Chapter 21

JETHRO'S WISE COUNSEL TO MOSES

5. And Jethro, Moses' father in law, came with his sons and his
    wife unto Moses into the wilderness, where he encamped
    at the mount of God...

8. And Moses told his father in law all that the LORD had
    done unto Pharaoh and to the Egyptians for Israel's sake,
    and all the travail that had come upon them by the way,
    and how the LORD delivered them.

9. And Jethro rejoiced for all the goodness which the LORD
    had done to Israel, whom he had delivered out of the hand
    of the Egyptians. (Exodus 18:5, 8–9)

Many months had passed by since Moses had made his departure
from the home of his father-in-law, Jethro, in the wilderness
of Midian. So many events had taken place that it seemed like years.
First there had been the daring approach to Pharaoh with the demand
that he should let the children of Israel go to serve Jehovah in the
wilderness. When Pharaoh had emphatically refused, there were the
judgments of the plagues, proving that Jehovah was God and that
he did have the right and authority to demand of Pharaoh what he
did. But Pharaoh, in the face of these plagues, had only hardened his
heart the more, until they reached their culmination in the pestilence
of death upon the firstborn of the land at the very time when Israel
was partaking of the paschal feast in preparation for her promised
departure. With a high hand Israel had left the land, and by a miracle
of salvation she had passed through the depths of the Red Sea, while
the Egyptians, attempting to follow her, had been drowned. Now for

several months, the Israelites had been making their way through the wilderness, still experiencing again and again the gracious and miraculous powers of their God in the repeated wonders that supplied their food and drink. All of these things had so completely occupied the time and attention of Moses that he hardly had opportunity to dwell on the absence of his wife and children.

For forty years Moses had lived in the house of Jethro. God had graciously brought him there, for Jethro was a God-fearing man. He was of the sons of Abraham through Keturah and had carried on the faith as a prophet and priest in his family. With him Moses had experienced the communion of saints, and of his daughters, Moses had taken Zipporah to wife. Two sons were born to them, Gershom and Eliezer.

In one thing, however, Moses' communion with Jethro fell short. Neither Jethro nor Zipporah could appreciate the predominant position that the children of Israel held in the covenant of God. After all, the Israelites were nothing more than slaves to the Egyptians, while the sons of Keturah were free men. Why should the children of Jacob hold a more important position in the covenant than that which was held by them? They considered it nothing more than self-centeredness on Moses' part to consider his own family and tribe to be especially precious in the sight of God. This difference of opinion between them had eventually developed into a great breach. Especially when Moses returned from Horeb with the conviction that he should go to Egypt because the time of Israel's salvation was drawing near, they found it hard to consider it as anything more than the working of his own imagination. First Zipporah intended to go with him, but when she was forced to circumcise her sons, it was more than she could take. Wisdom dictated that it would be best for her to return to her father with the children while Moses went on alone.

But Moses' return to Egypt had been an act of faith, and the true basis for its hope soon was completely manifested. Israel was precious unto God, and a great and glorious salvation from bondage was realized for them. God poured forth upon them blessings such as the world had never before seen. It became perfectly clear to all that the Lord of heaven and earth was their God. This was established beyond dispute. The reports of this did not take long in coming to Jethro and Zipporah. At first, they were quite amazed, for this they had not anticipated. But soon they began to realize that Moses had been right after all. Being children of God, they did not continue futilely to defend their original conviction. They acknowledged their error, and in the works that God wrought through Moses they found occasion to give glory to God.

Then it was heard by Jethro that Moses and the children of Israel had come to Horeb, not a great distance from where Jethro was making his home. He took with him Zipporah and Moses' two sons and made the journey to the camp of Israel. It was an occasion of great joy. A messenger was sent ahead to Moses with the announcement, "I thy father in law Jethro am come unto thee, and thy wife, and her two sons with her" (Ex. 18:6). With due oriental formality, Moses went out to meet them. First, he bowed before Jethro, and then he arose to kiss him. He asked of their welfare and then brought them into his tent.

With a new basis of understanding, there was much for them to discuss. Carefully Moses recounted all that had transpired in the months gone by. The events in themselves were wonderful, defying human imagination, and Moses possessed a spiritual understanding of their real significance far surpassing that of any other. There was enthusiasm in Moses' voice; there was richness in his description. Moses clearly loved the truth of that which he expressed. Slowly he unfolded the account of all that had taken place, not just as amazing events, but as revelations of the greatness of Jehovah in his infinite love for his people. Attentively Jethro listened. He was already an old man, full of years and experience, but he listened with the attention of a learning child. He was the pupil being instructed by the prophet of God. He felt a new depth of understanding flooding his heart, a new warmth of feeling overwhelming his soul. In all that had transpired, the truth of the gospel was contained in Old Testament type and shadow. All of this was undoubtedly expounded by Moses until Jethro broke forth in the joyful expression, "Blessed be the LORD, who hath delivered you out of the hand of the Egyptians, and out of the hand of Pharaoh, who hath delivered the people from under the hand of the Egyptians. Now I know that the LORD is greater than all gods: for in the thing wherein they dealt proudly he was above them" (18:10–11). Solemnly they went forth from the tent. Aaron and all of the elders of Israel were summoned to a great feast, at which Jethro, a priest in his own right, offered a sacrifice of burnt offerings unto the Lord.

In the days that followed, Jethro went throughout the camp of Israel to make his acquaintance with the people and with their situation in the wilderness. Immediately he saw with what complete dedication Moses was giving his life to those whom he led. He was the authority in almost everything that took place in the camp. He had to instruct the people. He had to give instructions for all of the affairs of the nation. He had to judge the people in every disagreement that arose, both big and small. It was especially this latter that consumed his time. From morning to evening people were coming to him for the purpose of airing all of their grievances. Many of these troubles were petty, yet they took time to relate and immeasurable wisdom to settle. Patiently Moses had to explain to each party the way of godly life in which they should walk with their individual problems. Day after day this went on without end, for in a nation so large there were always countless occasions for trouble. For a time Jethro stood by watching and listening to all that was taking place. He could hardly help but admire Moses' dedication and concern. For a man who had been so impetuous in his youth, such patience was marvelous. There was love in the patience with which he listened. There was gentleness even in his rebukes. Moses was a shepherd, willing to do all for the welfare of his sheep. Still, Jethro was displeased.

Finally he spoke. "What is this thing that thou doest to the people? why sittest thou thyself alone, and all the people stand by thee from morning unto even?" (Ex. 18:14).

To Moses the answer was perfectly evident. He answered, "Because the people come unto me to enquire of God: when they have a matter, they come unto me; and I judge between one and another, and I do make them know the statutes of God, and his law" (Ex. 18:15–16).

But Jethro was a man of experience, and the answer of Moses did not satisfy him. He knew the limitations of a man who would serve as a leader and a ruler among men. Carefully he answered again,

17. The thing that thou doest is not good.

18. Thou wilt surely wear away, both thou, and this people that is with thee: for this thing is too heavy for thee; thou art not able to perform it thyself alone.

19. Hearken now unto my voice, I will give thee counsel, and God shall be with thee: Be thou for the people to God-ward, that thou mayest bring the causes unto God:

20. And thou shalt teach them ordinances and laws, and shalt shew them the way wherein they must walk, and the work that they must do.

21. Moreover, thou shalt provide out of all the people able men, such as fear God, men of truth, hating covetousness; and place such over them, to be rulers of thousands, and rulers of hundreds, rulers of fifties, and rulers of tens:

22. And let them judge the people at all seasons: and it shall be, that every great matter they shall bring unto thee, but every small matter they shall judge: so shall it be easier for thyself, and they shall bear the burden with thee.

23. If thou shalt do this thing, and God command thee so, then thou shalt be able to endure, and all this people shall also go to their place in peace. (Ex. 18:17–23)

There was much wisdom in what Jethro said. Moses was a prophet of God. He was to be to the people God-ward, that is, his primary purpose was to bring the word of God to them and to set before them the will of the Most High. In the application of these principles to individual life, there were, of course, numerous problems that would arise. These too were spiritual problems. However,

Moses was making the mistake of completely taking over these problems for the people. In this, he had not only taken on an impossible task, but he was preventing the people from learning to handle their problems themselves. He was actually hindering their spiritual development. This is a lesson that every spiritual leader must learn. The children of God must be encouraged to understand and apply the word of God to their own lives as much as possible by themselves.

But there was also another side to Jethro's advice that was good, for there do arise problems in life that one cannot settle by himself. Thus, various wise and spiritual men were to be appointed over different groups of families in an ascending order of tens, fifties, hundreds, and thousands. The problems of life could be passed along according to their importance, and only the greatest of them would have to be heard by Moses. In this way the children of Israel would learn to share each other's burdens.

Moses wisely went with this matter to God, and he was commanded to do as Jethro said. Soon capable men were appointed, and Israel was organized into a body able to live in the practice of godly love.

We may be sure that there was sorrow in the camp of Israel, and especially in the heart of Moses, when the time came for Jethro to depart. With him Moses had experienced a spiritual communion in the love of God. As true communion should always be, it had been mutually beneficial. With a prayer of thanksgiving, Moses and his father-in-law parted, never on this earth to meet again, but with the assurance of a final reunion that would endure forevermore.

Chapter 22

GOD SPEAKS AT SINAI

16. And it came to pass on the third day in the morning, that there were thunders and lightnings, and a thick cloud upon the mount, and the voice of the trumpet exceeding loud; so that all the people that was in the camp trembled.

1. And God spake all these words... (Exodus 19:16; 20:1)

At last, the first goal of Israel's journey was reached. They had come to Sinai as Jehovah had promised Moses that they would. Two full months had been spent in travel, and it seemed much longer than that for all the events that had taken place. The last few miles had been through a mountainous valley with its granite cliffs on either side rising higher and higher as they went. Over them had hung the quiet stillness of the desert air, broken only by the tread of many feet and the muted whispers of awe-struck lips. It was as though they were passing through the long corridor of a vast, natural temple until it finally broke forth into a broad mountain plain, the inner sanctuary of the Lord. It was surrounded on every side by the hills, and there was one that rose above all the rest. That was Sinai, the mountain of their God. Its sides soared up directly from the desert floor forming, as it were, a huge altar for the service of Almighty God. Feeling their own minuteness beneath the grandeur of creation's peaks, they quietly stopped and made their camp.

Moses, more than anyone else, felt the wonder of this place. He had been here once before. Here he had met with God; he had seen him in the burning bush; he had listened to his voice. How clearly he remembered God's promise: "When thou hast brought forth this people out of Egypt, ye shall serve God upon this mountain" (Ex. 3:12). Now his heart was full with anticipation. Quickly he made his way up the mountain, perhaps to the place where he had seen the burning bush, in the hope that once again he would be met by God. And even as he hoped, it happened; God came to him there. God called to him out of the mountain with promises rich and full. He said,

3. Thus shalt thou say to the house of Jacob, and tell the children of Israel;

4. Ye have seen what I did unto the Egyptians, and how I bare you on eagles' wings, and brought you unto myself.

5. Now therefore, if ye will obey my voice indeed, and keep my covenant, then ye shall be a peculiar treasure unto me above all people: for all the earth is mine:

6. And ye shall be unto me a kingdom of priests, and an holy nation. These are the words which thou shalt speak unto the children of Israel. (Ex. 19:3–6)

Moses went down from the mountain quickly, and immediately he summoned the people together. Still they were aware of the strange, mountainous grandeur, and they felt in their hearts that in this place there was something special. They looked up again and again to the cloud of Jehovah that now had come to rest on that highest mount. The presence of God seemed closer than ever before. Attentively they listened as Moses spoke and told them exactly what God had said. As they listened, they knew in their hearts that what he said was truth. They had seen what Jehovah did in Egypt; and in very fact, he had borne them forth upon eagles' wings. Now they stood at Horeb in his presence. What could be more desired than to live in his covenant, to be a kingdom of priests, separated and dedicated to his service, a holy nation unto the Lord? There was no hesitation or question in their answer. With unanimous voice, they gave it, "All that the LORD hath spoken we will do" (Ex. 19:8).

Once more Moses ascended the mountain to meet with the Lord. The answer of the people rested upon his heart, and he was anxious to repeat it. God came to him and spoke, "Lo, I come unto thee in a thick cloud, that the people may hear when I speak with thee, and believe thee for ever" (Ex. 19:9). But this was not the thing about which Moses was concerned. He did not fear that the people would not listen. Rather, they had expressed their willingness to obey. Eagerly Moses repeated their answer, "All that the LORD hath spoken we will do."

The reply of the Lord was quite unexpected. There was no expression of appreciation for what the people had promised. It partook more of the nature of a solemn warning.

10. Go unto the people, and sanctify them to day and to morrow, and let them wash their clothes.
11. And be ready against the third day: for the third day the LORD will come down in the sight of all the people upon mount Sinai.
12. And thou shalt set bounds unto the people round about, saying, Take heed to yourselves, that ye go not up into the mount, or touch the border of it: whosoever toucheth the mount shall be surely put to death:
13. There shall not an hand touch it, but he shall surely be stoned, or shot through; whether it be beast or man, it shall not live: when the trumpet soundeth long, they shall come up to the mount. (Ex. 19:10–13)

As yet neither Moses nor the people understood completely what it was that they had promised. They might well say, "All that the LORD hath spoken we will do," but did they realize what this meant? Had they forgotten their rebellion at the Red Sea, at Marah, in the wilderness of Sin, and at Rephidim? The danger was not so much that they would fail to promise to be faithful to their God; the greater danger was that they might think that by merely giving their word they became worthy of approaching unto God. They were a sinful people, and their mere word of promise did not wash that sin away. Jehovah is a God of justice, and only the pure and perfect have a right to enter his presence. Let every Israelite beware lest he presumptuously take to himself the right of approaching the holy mountain, of touching it, or of attempting to ascend into the presence of God.

Explicit instructions were given to Moses. The people were sinful and they must know it. Definite boundaries were to be set about the mountain, and everyone was to be commanded not to presume to pass over them. Should anyone try, whether man or beast, he must be put to death. In addition, the people should be commanded to sanctify themselves. All their clothes were to be washed, and they were to keep themselves from all actions and contacts that might defile them. These were mere external actions, but they had specific, spiritual import for Israel as to her heart. In three days God will appear before the people and speak, but the people must not presume to think that they were worthy of this in their present state. They were sinful and corrupt. They were unworthy of approaching unto God. They were in need of being cleansed. As the children of Israel went through their ceremonial actions, they were reminded of the fact that they were unworthy of entering into covenant relationship with God.

The third day came, and no one had to be reminded of the import of that day for them. They awoke in the morning to the sound of mighty, rolling thunder, and, looking out of their tents, they saw the mountain of God lit by flashes of lightning and covered with a thick, dark cloud. Through this there came the piercing sound of a great trumpet, exceedingly loud and clear. The people heard; they saw; and they trembled before the great signs of a pure and holy God.

Soon the whole nation was gathered together about Moses, and, with him at their head, they advanced slowly until they stood at the very foot of the mountain. In reverent fear, they looked, and as they looked the mountain crags began to belch forth great, black clouds of billowing smoke. The fire of God's presence had descended upon it from above. The whole mountain appeared as one great, fiery furnace, and under the presence of Jehovah, the granite cliffs trembled and shook. All the while Israel watched. And did not some stop to ask how they had presumed so lightly to think that they could dwell in covenant relationship with this mighty God?

At last Moses, standing at the head of the people, heard the sound of the trumpet of God waxing louder and louder. Then he lifted up his head toward the mountain and spoke. God answered him and called to him to come up. With the gaze of the people following him, he climbed until he disappeared into the cloud. There God spoke to him and said, "Go down, charge the people, lest they break through unto the LORD to gaze, and many of them perish. And let the priests also, which come near to the LORD, sanctify themselves, lest the LORD break forth upon them" (Ex. 19:21–22).

Impatiently Moses replied, "The people cannot come up to mount Sinai: for thou chargedst us, saying, Set bounds about the mount, and sanctify it" (Ex. 19:23).

But there was reason for God's command. Even in this hour, the people must be reminded of their unworthiness to approach into the presence of their God. Curtly he said to Moses again, "Away, get thee down, and thou shalt come up, thou, and Aaron with thee: but let not the priests and the people break through to come up unto the LORD, lest he break forth upon them" (Ex. 19:24).

Moses went, and soon he stood among the people, repeating God's warning to them. Then, while this reminder of God's inapproachable holiness rested upon their hearts, God spoke.

2. I am the LORD thy God, which have brought thee out of the land of Egypt, out of the house of bondage.
3. Thou shalt have no other gods before me.
4. Thou shalt not make unto thee any graven image…
7. Thou shalt not take the name of the LORD thy God in vain…
8. Remember the sabbath day, to keep it holy…

12. Honour thy father and thy mother…
13. Thou shalt not kill.

14. Thou shalt not commit adultery.
15. Thou shalt not steal.
16. Thou shalt not bear false witness against thy neighbour.
17. Thou shalt not covet. (Ex. 20:2–17)

Now the people understood their folly. They had thought it a light thing to promise, "All that the LORD hath spoken we will do." They had not realized all that it meant. Now the voice of God had spoken his commandments in their ears, and they knew better. By each commandment anew, they stood condemned. They knew they would never be able to keep God's covenant. Now they saw the lightning and smoke with new eyes, and heard with new ears the thunder and the trumpet. This was the God who would judge them when the least of his commandments was transgressed. With fear, they turned and fled back to their tents.

It was a humbled people that came to Moses that night and said, "Speak thou with us, and we will hear: but let not God speak with us, lest we die" (Ex. 20:19). Suddenly they had come to realize that they were in need of a mediator. By themselves they could never stand in the presence of this just and mighty God. They needed one to take their place and bring their cause into the presence of God. As never before, they began to see Moses as their savior, the one who could bring their cause to God, a figure and a type of the promised Redeemer, Jesus Christ.

With humble gratitude, they heard Moses answer, "Fear not: for God is come to prove you, and that his fear may be before your faces, that ye sin not" (Ex. 20:20). With thankful awe, they stood and watched as Moses once again ascended the mountain and, with their cause on his heart, "drew near unto the thick darkness where God was" (v. 21).

Chapter 23

GOD'S COVENANT WITH ISRAEL

4. And Moses wrote all the words of the Lord, and rose up early in the morning, and builded an altar under the hill, and twelve pillars, according to the twelve tribes of Israel.

5. And he sent young men of the children of Israel, which offered burnt offerings, and sacrificed peace offerings of oxen unto the Lord.

8. And Moses took the blood, and sprinkled it on the people, and said, Behold the blood of the covenant, which the Lord hath made with you concerning all these words. (Exodus 24:4–5, 8)

Israel had heard the voice of Jehovah speaking the ten words of his law from the summit of Sinai and found it disconcerting. Before the signs of God's righteousness and justice, thundering and lightning, the sound of the trumpet, and the smoking of the mountain, the people had trembled and fled away. The Israelites were beginning to realize how impossible it was that they should ever satisfy the demands of God's law and how terrible would be the judgment of Jehovah if they did not. Boldly they had said, "All that the Lord hath spoken we will do" (Ex. 19:8), but now they were beginning to realize how presumptuous this promise had actually been. The very sound of God's voice was more than they could endure. To stand any longer in his presence they no longer felt able to do. They needed someone who could stand between, who could intercede for them, who could be a mediator between them, a sinful people, and Jehovah, the perfect and righteous God. With a new sense of humility, they came to Moses and pleaded,

"Speak thou with us, and we will hear: but let not God speak with us, lest we die" (20:19).

Moses' answer was kind and full of comfort. He said, "Fear not: for God is come to prove you, and that his fear may be before your faces, that ye sin not" (Ex. 20:20). The presentation of God at Sinai had been designed exactly to instruct them in the truth. Israel must know that God is holy and just in his every demand. The purpose was not to frighten them, but to show them the way of salvation. It was necessary that they should feel the need of a mediator. This would become even more evident in the future.

While the people watched from afar, Moses took up their cause and drew near unto the thick darkness where God was. There, on behalf of the people, he talked with God. They were chosen to be a nation of priests, but many years, even centuries, would have to pass before they would be able to function individually as such. First the perfect Mediator would have to come and implant his Spirit in their hearts. Then every true, spiritual Israelite would be able to draw nigh unto the presence of God.

There on the mountain, God spoke to Moses. He explained in greater detail the words of his law. Beginning with the most important matter of true worship, he said, "Thus thou shalt say unto the children of Israel, Ye have seen that I have talked with you from heaven. Ye shall not make with me gods of silver, neither shall ye make unto you gods of gold" (Ex. 20:22–23). And God went on to explain the true way in which he was to be worshiped, by means of an altar built of unhewn stone. God had shown clearly to them that he is far too great to be represented by any image formed by man's hand. Henceforth there would never be an excuse to worship him in a way other than he had given command. Thereupon, God went on to explain to Moses many matters pertaining to all of the commandments of the law: matters of religious festivities deriving from the fourth commandment of the law; matters pertaining to masters and servants and their duties to each other as they follow from the fifth commandment of the law; matters relating to personal injuries and the sixth commandment of the law; matters of marriage and the seventh commandment; matters of personal property and the eighth commandment; matters of truthfulness and the ninth commandment. Finally, God returned again to the primary subject of true worship; only, this time, he included with it a glorious promise.

20. Behold, I send an Angel before thee, to keep thee in the way, and to bring thee into the place which I have prepared.
21. Beware of him, and obey his voice, provoke him not; for he will not pardon your transgressions: for my name is in him.
22. But if thou shalt indeed obey his voice, and do all that I speak; then I will be an enemy unto thine enemies, and an adversary unto thine adversaries.
23. For mine Angel shall go before thee, and bring thee in unto the Amorites, and the Hittites, and the Perizzites, and the Canaanites, the Hivites, and the Jebusites: and I will cut them off.
24. Thou shalt not bow down to their gods, nor serve them, nor do after their works: but thou shalt utterly overthrow them, and quite break down their images.
25. And ye shall serve the LORD your God, and he shall bless thy bread, and thy water; and I will take sickness away from the midst of thee. (Ex. 23:20–25)

Moses returned from the mountain to the camp with these words of God resting upon his heart. The people were watching and waiting to hear what he had to say. Slowly and exactly, he repeated to them all that the Lord had said. The people remembered the wonder of the voice of Jehovah that they had heard from the mountain; but, by now, some of the fear had subsided. Still there was enthusiasm and interest in what God had to say, and they listened to Moses attentively. Boldness and confidence had returned. With a loud voice they responded, "All the words which the LORD hath said will we do" (Ex. 24:3).

That night in his tent, Moses wrote all that God had spoken to him in a book. He called it the book of the covenant.

Early the next morning, Moses arose and began to gather stones for the building of an altar. According to the command of God, he took the stones directly from nature, unhewn and unpolluted by the tools of man, twelve in number. For some time, he had been serving typically in the position of mediator between God and his people, but only through the recent events were the people beginning to realize his importance in this office. Today, however, it was to be brought even more emphatically to their attention. With his own hands, Moses built the altar, and around it he set up twelve pillars of stone representing each of the tribes in much the same pattern in which the twelve tribes later were to be encamped about the tabernacle. Then he called together a group of young men to serve as his assistants.

By the time this work was accomplished, the rest of the camp had arisen and the people were standing about watching. They realized that something of great significance was about to take place, even though Moses as yet had said nothing. As the people watched, Moses commanded the young men to gather together sacrificial animals and to offer them on the altar, first a series of burnt offerings and then a series of peace offerings of oxen unto the Lord. Moses himself brought the blood of these sacrificial victims. One half of the blood he put in basins, and the other half he sprinkled on the altar.

The children of Israel, watching, realized well what these actions meant without need of any explanation. They were used to the typical ceremonies of Old Testament times. The burnt offerings offered were atonement for sin. The peace offerings were sacrifices of thankfulness and dedication. These sacrifices were being offered by Moses, but in behalf of the people. The people, indeed, had promised, "All the words which the Lord hath said will we do," but that mere affirmation of intention did not make them worthy of the favor of God. Atonement had to be made for them. This was being provided by the sacrifices of Moses. The blood sprinkled upon the altar symbolized that the atoning sacrifice was being given unto God for the satisfaction of his justice. All was accounted for but the blood that Moses still held in the basins. Moses turned to the people and, before them, opened up the book of the covenant and read. The children of Israel, deeply impressed by the solemnity of the occasion, gave close attention, and again, with enthusiasm responded, "All that the LORD hath said will we do, and be obedient" (Ex. 24:7). Then Moses took up the basins of blood and sprinkled their contents on the people. Even as he did so, he spoke, "Behold the blood of the covenant, which the LORD hath made with you concerning all these words" (v. 8).

The symbolism of this event was beautiful. Moses as a typical mediator was demonstrating to the children of Israel the gospel of the true Mediator who was to come in fulfillment of the promise given to their fathers. Even as Moses offered the sacrifices amid the pillars of Israel's twelve tribes, so someday the true Mediator would offer himself as the perfect sacrifice in the midst of the people he loved. His blood would be shed in an offering of love to God, and the same blood would be sprinkled, as the blood of reconciliation, upon his people. In this way, and in this way alone, they would be drawn into covenant communion with God. Even more, it would be the blood of sanctification by which the children of God would be enabled to say in truth, "All that the LORD hath said will we do, and be obedient." Through the work of this Mediator the covenant of God is established.

But still the functions of that day were not finished. Moses called together Aaron and his two oldest sons, Nadab and Abihu, the future priests of God, with seventy of the elders who represented all Israel. Together they ascended the mountain, for they were now cleansed by the sacrificial blood. The covenant was now established, and even the people, represented in the elders, were enabled to draw nigh unto the presence of God. There on the mountain, they saw God. We are not told in what form God appeared. It was beautiful for sure. Not, indeed, as glorious as the vision Moses was later to see. Not, perhaps, even as great as the radiance that later would reflect from Moses' face so that the people could not endure to look. But nonetheless beautiful, so as to defy description by human lips. Now there were none of the threatening signs of judgment, the thunder and lightning and smoke. All was peaceful and serene. The very rocks in their appearance were transformed, clear and brilliant like sapphire of heavenly origin. Even the seventy elders, mere ordinary men, stood in God's presence and were not consumed; the hand of the Lord did not touch them. This was the blessedness of God's covenant. They stood before the face of God and were given to eat and to drink, to partake of a table prepared by the Lord.

There, in symbolic beauty, was realized the blessedness of life in the covenant of God's grace. For all who are in spiritual reality taken into God's fellowship, all these very same things are true. In the covenant, God reveals himself to his people. Not to all, indeed, does God reveal himself in some visible form as was seen there by the elders, and later by Moses alone, and by Isaiah, and by Ezekiel; but to all of God's people is given the much more enduring revelation of God in spirit and in truth. It is an experience peaceful and serene, as though radiating with the brilliance of sapphires from heaven. For the true covenant child, gone are the judgments, the thunder and lightning and blackness of smoke. The hand of God's anger will not touch them. They are made to eat and drink of the bread and waters of eternal life spread by the hand of the Lord. In a figure, those elders of old were made to know the blessedness of true covenant life.

Once this heavenly meal was finished, the elders were told that they, with Aaron and his sons, must tarry behind in the camp while Moses and Joshua went on farther. God was to give to Moses instructions concerning a more enduring sign of the covenant: the tabernacle that he would establish in Israel's midst.

Chapter 24

THE GOLDEN CALF

18. And Moses went into the midst of the cloud, and gat him up into the mount: and Moses was in the mount forty days and forty nights.

1. And when the people saw that Moses delayed to come down out of the mount, the people gathered themselves together unto Aaron, and said unto him, Up, make us gods, which shall go before us; for as for this Moses, the man that brought us up out of the land of Egypt, we wot not what is become of him.

7. And the Lord said unto Moses, Go, get thee down; for thy people, which thou broughtest out of the land of Egypt, have corrupted themselves:

8. They have turned aside quickly out of the way which I commanded them: they have made them a molten calf, and have worshipped it. (Exodus 24:18; 32:1, 7–8)

For six days the glory of the Lord abode upon the peaks of Mt. Sinai. The cloud of God's presence covered the mountain, and it was as a devouring fire to the eyes of the people. This marked the consummation of the beautiful and impressive ceremony by which Jehovah had ratified his covenant of grace with his chosen people. As Israel watched, Moses had built an altar and surrounded it with twelve pillars of stone, representing the various tribes of their nation. Upon the altar, Moses had offered burnt offerings and peace offerings unto Jehovah, and one half of the blood of the sacrificial victims he had sprinkled upon the altar, keeping the other half in basins. To the people, he read the book of the covenant, and, when they responded, "All that the LORD hath said will we do, and be obedient" (Ex. 24:7), he sprinkled the blood from the basins on the congregation. Thereby it was symbolized that God was united with his people through the blood of the sacrifice that Moses had offered, as Moses said, "Behold the blood of the covenant, which the LORD hath made with you concerning all these words" (v. 8). While the people watched, seventy of their elders, with Moses and Aaron and Aaron's two sons, went up unto the mountain where God was. There they beheld the glory of God and were not consumed. There they ate of a meal prepared by God and were filled. While Aaron and the elders tarried behind, Moses and Joshua went farther into the mountain. It was then that the glory of God was revealed for six days upon Sinai's peaks.

On the seventh day, God called Moses to come up into the midst of the cloud that covered the mountain. Joshua was left on the side of the mountain to wait for Moses' return while Moses met for forty days and forty nights with God. During this time he had neither food to eat nor water to drink, nor does it seem that he slept. His communion with God so filled his life that he felt no need for these earthly things, and a miracle of God sustained the life of his body through this period. It anticipated the time when Elijah would live for the same period of time without food and drink, and when Jesus would do the same. By actual experience they came to know what it meant that "man shall not live by bread alone, but by every word that proceedeth out of the mouth of God" (Matt. 4:4).

The purpose for which God had called Moses into the mountain followed naturally from the ratification of the covenant that had just taken place. God had determined to give unto Israel a visible symbol of covenant life for their instruction. Symbolically he would come to dwell among them by placing his tent, or tabernacle, in the midst of the camp. During the forty days and nights upon the mountain, Moses was given explicit instructions for the making of this tent. From the inmost sanctuary in which the ark of the covenant was set, to the Holy Place in which was placed the table of showbread, the golden candle sticks, and the altar of incense—representing the bread of life, the light of life, and the prayers of the saints—to the outer court in which was the laver of cleansing and the altar of burnt offerings through which God's people might approach unto him, all was described in detail to Moses. The priesthood, its dress, and its utensils of service were all planned by God and revealed unto Moses. The tabernacle in all of its details was important as a type and symbol of the richness of spiritual life that is imparted unto those who dwell in communion and fellowship with Jehovah. He dwells in their midst, and they are blessed.

Meanwhile, in the camp at the foot of the mountain, the children of Israel were beginning to relax after their days of intensive spiritual instruction. For a time the awe of all they had beheld continued to hang over the camp, but gradually their thoughts began to return to more earthly concerns. Now that Moses was absent from them, they no longer felt the closeness of God's presence, even though the cloud of his presence still hung low over the nearby mountain peaks. In fact, there was a certain group of men in the camp who were overjoyed with the fact that Moses was gone, even if it would be for only a little while. They formed a hardened core of reprobate men who had been dissatisfied with the leadership of Moses from the beginning. They had never been pleased with the way in which Moses led them and had never neglected an opportunity to reveal their displeasure. Whenever the way had become difficult, they had led the people to murmur and complain—at the Red Sea, at Marah, in the wilderness of Sin, and at Rephidim. But always Moses had been there with the power of God to show that the way in which the people of Israel were going was right and blessed by God. Every time their attempt at rebellion had failed, they had become more rebellious in their hearts. These were wicked men who loved the pleasures of sin and hated the way of the Lord. They hated Moses because they hated the cause for which he stood. Now that he was gone, they felt free to act as never before.

It was not long after Moses left that these men began to spread their seeds of dissension. As usual, they first made their attack on the person of Moses. Days and weeks were passing by, and Moses did not return from the mountain. How did they know what had become of him? Maybe he had been consumed by the fire of God upon the mountain. Maybe he had deserted them never to return again. Throughout the camp the dissenters circulated, spreading their venomous poison. Within the relaxed inactivity of the camp, the seed of discontent caught on fast and soon began to grow.

Underneath this all, however, there was a deeper and more vicious motive. The Israelites had grown up amid the wickedness of Egypt. Many of them had watched the Egyptians in the service of their idol gods and some had, perhaps, even taken part. In Egypt, as in almost all of the heathen nations, the service of idols was used as an occasion for licentious, sensual pleasures. It was accompanied by fornications of the most abominable sort. To those who were carnal in Israel, these things had afforded much pleasure. They had enjoyed the ways of sin to the full. But now, since they had been following Moses, it had become evident that such pleasures would never be condoned by Israel's God, and that made them seem sweeter than ever before. The uncompromising proclamations of God's law was to them an occasion for offense. It only increased their lust for the pleasures of sin. As soon as Moses was gone and the opportunity had availed itself, they began to plot how they might have their wicked pleasures after all.

A delegation of the people soon presented themselves before Aaron. "Up, make us gods, which shall go before us," they demanded, "for as for this Moses, the man that brought us up out of the land of Egypt, we wot not what is become of him" (Ex. 32:1).

Aaron, without Moses to strengthen him, was at a loss. Often Aaron appeared to be much more capable than his brother; he could talk much better. But he lacked Moses' spiritual courage and discretion. So now he thought to fall back craftily upon his own power of persuasion. He answered the men by saying, "Break off the golden earrings, which are in the ears of your wives, of your sons, and of your daughters, and bring them to me" (Ex. 32:2), perhaps expecting that this price would be more than they would be willing to pay. In this he underestimated the strength of their desires. Soon there had been brought to him more than enough gold for the making of an image.

Upon the receipt of the required gold, Aaron was committed to proceed according to the desires of the people. Accordingly, the gold was melted, formed and graven into an image of a golden heifer like unto the god Apis, which the Egyptians worshiped. Aaron's only hope was that Moses might return before the deed was done; but it was vain. No sooner was the image finished than the people began to shout. "These be thy gods, O Israel, which brought thee up out of the land of Egypt" (Ex. 32:4). A spiritual rebellion of the greatest magnitude was taking form.

Still Aaron, although he had not the courage to oppose the people outright, thought that something might be gained by working a compromise. Before the image he built an altar such as was used in the service of Jehovah. If the people must have an image, he could still urge that they use the image for the service of Jehovah. To the people he made a solemn proclamation, "To morrow is a feast to the LORD" (Ex. 32:5). For the moment it appeared to him that Israel's idolatry would not be quite so serious if only the name of Jehovah was remembered. And the people were in no mood to haggle over a name. It made little difference to them by what name their god was called as long as they could serve him in the way they chose.

It was on the morning of the fortieth day after Moses had gone up into the mountain that the camp of Israel arose to engage in their new adventure. The festivities began solemnly enough. Quietly the people gathered as burnt offerings and peace offerings were offered to their newly formed idol in the name of Jehovah. Once they were finished, all the rich food and wine that could be found in the camp was brought out, and the people sat down to eat and to drink. Finally, when their stomachs were filled with rich food and the strong drink had gone to their heads, they rose up again to play and to dance. Erotic dances they were, those which had been learned from the Egyptians. Giving themselves over to concupiscence and lust, they cast aside their outer garments until their limbs were sensually exposed. The camp of God's chosen people, Israel, echoed with the orgies of the wicked.

On the mountain, God had completed his revelation of the tabernacle to Moses. Thereupon, he turned to Moses and said,

7. Go, get thee down; for thy people, which thou broughtest out of the land of Egypt, have corrupted themselves:

8. They have turned aside quickly out of the way which I commanded them: they have made them a molten calf, and have worshipped it, and have sacrificed thereunto, and said, These be thy gods, O Israel, which have brought thee up out of the land of Egypt.

9. …I have seen this people, and, behold, it is a stiffnecked people:

10. Now therefore let me alone, that my wrath may wax hot against them, and that I may consume them: and I will make of thee a great nation. (Ex. 32:7–10)

Israel had sinned a great sin. They had proved themselves worthy of destruction. Only one thing prevented the judgment of God from striking out and consuming them: Moses the mediator, the type of Jesus Christ, stood between them and their judgment. If he would stand aside and fail to plead for them, Israel would be no more.

Chapter 25

MOSES' INTERCESSION FOR A STIFFNECKED PEOPLE

31. And Moses returned unto the LORD, and said, Oh, this people have sinned a great sin, and have made them gods of gold.
32. Yet now, if thou wilt forgive their sin—; and if not, blot me, I pray thee, out of thy book which thou hast written. (Exodus 32:31–32)

With a frightening abruptness, the tone of God's revelation to Moses on Mt. Sinai changed. He said,

7. Go, get thee down; for thy people, which thou broughtest out of the land of Egypt, have corrupted themselves:
8. They have turned aside quickly out of the way which I commanded them: they have made them a molten calf, and have worshipped it, and have sacrificed thereunto, and said, These be thy gods, O Israel, which have brought thee up out of the land of Egypt.
9. ...I have seen this people, and, behold, it is a stiffnecked people:
10. Now therefore let me alone, that my wrath may wax hot against them, and that I may consume them: and I will make of thee a great nation. (Ex. 32:7–10)

For Moses, this announcement, coming so abruptly, was almost more than his mind could grasp. For forty days he had been engaged in peaceful communion with God concerning the tabernacle, God's holy dwelling place, which was to be established in the midst of Israel's camp. It was a promise of spiritual blessings uncompared in depth of spiritual meaning and richness of spiritual implications. The glory of gospel revelation would shine forth from every portion of this holy dwelling place. And now this. Israel had proved itself unworthy. The wrath of the Lord was waxed hot. The soul of Moses was overwhelmed. How could he comprehend it? He had left Israel spiritually enraptured by the glory of God's revelation in the law and the covenant. Could the people have turned so soon to commit such gross transgression? How could Moses conceive of it? But he could not deny the word of God. There was God's wrath. For forty days Moses had heard nothing but the love of God for Israel as his chosen people. It was an unchanging love, as the whole structure of the tabernacle testified. And now, suddenly Moses stood before God's righteous indignation against this same people because they had sinned. And the word of God could not be questioned. And still there was more. God had said that if Moses would stand aside, Israel would be consumed, and a great nation would be brought forth from his own loins. How could he—the mere man that he was—stand in the way of the will of the Most High? And, if a nation were to be brought forth from him, would it be any different or better than Abraham's seed? For moments Moses stood pondering the depths of all these questions.

Finally, faintly faltering, he presumed to answer.

11. LORD, why doth thy wrath wax hot against thy people, which thou hast brought forth out of the land of Egypt with great power, and with a mighty hand?

12. Wherefore should the Egyptians speak, and say, For mischief did he bring them out, to slay them in the mountains, and to consume them from the face of the earth? Turn from thy fierce wrath, and repent of this evil against thy people.

13. Remember Abraham, Isaac, and Israel, thy servants, to whom thou swarest by thine own self, and saidst unto them, I will multiply your seed as the stars of heaven, and all this land that I have spoken of will I give unto your seed, and they shall inherit it for ever. (Ex. 32:11–13)

It was all that he could say. There had been a day when he might have forsaken the nation of Israel; in fact, he had done that very thing when he fled from Egypt to Midian. In that day he might have been enticed by the thought of becoming himself a great nation before the Lord. But that had been long ago, and much had happened since then. In Midian he had learned to know himself for what he was, a sinner unworthy of God's covenant and grace. How well he now knew that he was no better than the rest of Israel, and his seed could never be any better than Abraham's. His life was bound to Israel, not because of the excellency of the people, but because to them belonged the covenant and the promises by an unchangeable oath from God. He loved Israel and could not stand aside. He must plead for them. But what could he plead? He could not plead their virtue; in forty days they had fallen from grateful obedience into the depths of grossest sin. He could not plead their merit; the journey from Egypt had been one unending series of murmuring, complaining rebellion. There was only one thing he could plead: the unwavering faithfulness of Jehovah to his promises. God had promised to reveal his glory by bringing his people out of bondage to the richness of the land of Canaan. This promise had to be realized, in order that God's glory might shine to the ends of the earth. He had sworn to Abraham, Isaac, and Jacob to make their seed great in the land of their inheritance. This oath had to be fulfilled, lest Jehovah be found unfaithful. Humbly Moses set these truths before God, and God turned from his wrath.

Almost unconsciously Moses was being brought to fulfill the function of his office as a type of Jesus Christ. He was but a man, and had he come upon Israel engaged in this sin, totally unprepared, the very repulsiveness of their act would have turned him away from them in utter disgust. Now, before he was able to feel the full impact of Israel's terrible act, he was being brought very emphatically to understand that, regardless of Israel's deed, the faithfulness of Jehovah had to be maintained. Even more, he, being the representative of God before the people and the typical figure of the perfect Mediator to come, had to remain faithful unto the people of God in love, to admonish them for their iniquity, but also to lead them in the way of salvation.

Sadly, Moses turned to make his descent unto the people. Had he not known what he did, he would have gone down in joy. Now he went in sorrow. Still, he went quickly, feeling drawn to the people of God even in this hour of their great sin. Soon he came to the place where Joshua had throughout the forty days and nights been waiting, unaware of the glorious revelations that had been made known above and of the wretched transgression that was being perpetrated below in the valley. He saw the sorrow written on Moses' face but in proper meekness withheld himself from asking questions. Silently they descended together until the sound of the camp began to reach their ears.

Innocently, Joshua offered the only explanation he could imagine, for the noise was very great. "There is a noise of war in the camp," he suggested (Ex. 32:17).

His heart wrenched with anguished dismay, Moses answered, "It is not the voice of them that shout for mastery, neither is it the voice of them that cry for being overcome: but the noise of them that sing do I hear" (Ex. 32:18).

But it was only after they had rounded the mountain's edge and stood overlooking the camp that the full magnitude of Israel's transgression struck Moses. There in the middle of the camp, on an ornate pedestal, stood a golden calf, an idol like those kept and worshiped by all the heathen. Around it were the people whom he had so shortly before left with the promise upon their lips, "All that the LORD hath said will we do, and be obedient" (Ex. 24:7). They were engaged with the idolatrous, adulterous orgies of the wicked. They shouted and sang and danced a wild, sensuous dance. Suddenly the tables of the law that Moses unconsciously had been carrying seemed to hang like lead on his arms, a weight too heavy to carry. It seemed utterly incongruous and impossible to bear God's holy commandments to a people that had broken every one of them already. With an angry thrust he threw them from the ledge on which they stood to be dashed to pieces on the rocks below. Then, with an angry dash, he descended what remained of the mountain.

Like an arrow Moses pierced the multitude of the people, scattering them with the vehement glint of his eyes and the resolute determination of his face. Straight to the golden image he went, and by the strength of his own arms tore it, pedestal and all, into shreds. The golden metal he ground into powder, and its dust he scattered into the water, commanding the people to drink. Let them taste the bitter results of their sin with their mouths before they tasted it with the pangs of their guilty hearts.

Only then did Moses speak, a searing accusation to Aaron. "What did this people unto thee, that thou hast brought so great a sin upon them?" (Ex. 32:21).

Aaron's answer was juvenile and naïve.

22. Let not the anger of my lord wax hot: thou knowest the people, that they are set on mischief.
23. For they said unto me, Make us gods, which shall go before us: for as for this Moses, the man that brought us up out of the land of Egypt, we wot not what is become of him.
24. And I said unto them, Whosoever hath any gold, let them break it off. So they gave it me: then I cast it into the fire, and there came out this calf. (Ex. 32:22–24)

Aaron's excuse, so evidently false, only made more evident his weakness and guilt.

Dismayed at his brother's duplicity, Moses turned to the people. Most of them had fled to the privacy of their tents, afraid and ashamed before Moses' accusing gaze. But still there were some who, caught up in the pleasure of their sin, would not leave it alone even in the presence of God's servant. In bold defiance they continued to dance nakedly in the aisles between the tents. Quickly Moses took up their challenge, and, standing at the camp's gate, shouted, "Who is on the Lord's side? let him come unto me" (Ex. 32:26). Soon the men of Levi, Moses' own tribe, took courage to come and stand by his side. Moses' command was uncompromising, "Thus saith the LORD God of Israel, Put every man his sword by his side, and go in and out from gate to gate throughout the camp, and slay every man his brother, and every man his companion, and every man his neighbour" (v. 27). Israel's only hope for salvation could be through renouncing their sin and all those who continued in it without regard of persons. As Moses said, "Consecrate yourselves today to the LORD, even every man upon his son, and upon his brother; that he may bestow upon you a blessing this day" (v. 29). By nightfall three thousand men lay dead in the camp.

It was an entirely different people that gathered before Moses the next morning. The bitter pangs of guilt and shame were beginning to touch their hearts. Accordingly, Moses now spoke to them in love. "Ye have sinned a great sin: and now I will go up unto the LORD; peradventure I shall make an atonement for your sin" (Ex. 32:30).

Soon Moses stood again on the mountain in the presence of God. Though he had thought much, he hardly knew what to say. Slowly he began, "Oh, this people have sinned a great sin, and have made them gods of gold. Yet now, if thou wilt forgive their sin—" (Ex. 32:31–32). The sentence faltered and broke. It could not be finished. Had he intended to say that, if God would overlook this sin, the people would hereafter abide by his law? But he could not make that promise. Those who had sinned so greatly once would surely do so again. The only thing left was for Moses to express the only other possibility he saw. "And if not, blot me, I pray thee, out of thy book which thou hast written" (v. 32). It was a beautiful prayer, permeated with love. It anticipated the cry of Paul the apostle, "I could wish that myself were accursed from Christ for my brethren, my kinsman according to the flesh" (Rom. 9:3). It anticipated the teaching of Jesus, "Greater love hath no man than this, that a man lay down his life for his friends" (John 15:13).

But it could not be so. Moses was a mere man and could not make atonement for the sins of others. God answered him,

"Whosoever hath sinned against me, him will I blot out of my book…nevertheless in the day when I visit I will visit their sin upon them" (Ex. 32:33–34). Every sin committed would have to be paid for by another than Moses. God would visit everyone in judgment. For some in Israel, this day of visitation would be very soon, even as they proceeded on their wilderness journey, for they were not true Israel. For others, the day of visitation would be yet many years to come, when God would visit the sins of his chosen people in the visitation of Calvary.

Chapter 26

FURTHER INTERCESSION

18. And [Moses] said, I beseech thee, shew me thy glory.
19. And [God] said, I will make all my goodness pass before thee, and I will proclaim the name of the LORD before thee; and will be gracious to whom I will be gracious, and will shew mercy on whom I will shew mercy. (Exodus 33:18–19)

The festive sounds that had filled the camp of Israel had ceased. Where but one day before there had been the noise of wild heathenish orgies, silence lay like a heavy shroud. Through Moses the justice of God had smitten the people. They had tasted the water made bitter by the ground dust of gold. Three thousand of their men lay dead because they had continued to dance among the tents in base disregard of Moses' burning reprimand. The point of Moses' actions had come home. Israel huddled in its tents under the bitter conviction of sin. In trembling fear, they awaited further exactions of the justice of God.

Moses had returned to the mountain to prostrate himself there before the Lord. He had told the people in departing, "Ye have sinned a great sin: and now I will go up unto the LORD; peradventure I shall make an atonement for your sin" (Ex. 32:30). Once in the presence of God, he started to present his plea falteringly. "Oh, this people have sinned a great sin, and have made them gods of gold. Yet now, if thou wilt forgive their sin—" (vv. 31–32). But then he had stopped. He had meant to add a promise that henceforth the people would be faithful and true; but even before it was uttered, he knew that it was a promise upon which no one could ever rely. There was only one other alternative of which he could think. Sadly he continued with that: "And if not, blot me, I pray thee, out of thy book which thou hast written" (v. 32). He was ready to give his all for the salvation of the people. But God had refused. He said, "Whosoever hath sinned against me, him will I blot out of my book. Therefore now go, lead the people unto the place which I have spoken unto thee: behold, mine Angel shall go before thee: nevertheless in the day when I visit I will visit their sin upon them" (v. 33–34).

Moses trembled from what he had heard. Indeed, God had told him before that he would spare the nation and even now that they should go on to the land of Canaan and he would send his Angel before them. Still, the fact remained that the sin of Israel was yet to be visited. It could not be forgotten or overlooked by the justice of God. This became even more foreboding in what God added.

1. Depart, and go up hence, thou and the people which thou hast brought up out of the land of Egypt, unto the land which I sware unto Abraham, to Isaac, and to Jacob, saying, Unto thy seed will I give it:
2. And I will send an angel before thee; and I will drive out the Canaanite, the Amorite, and the Hittite, and the Perizzite, the Hivite, and the Jebusite:
3. Unto a land flowing with milk and honey: for I will not go up in the midst of thee; for thou art a stiffnecked people: lest I consume thee in the way. (Ex. 33:1–3)

It was this last element that worried him. So great was the sin of Israel that God could not dwell in their midst without consuming them. And what good to them was the land of Canaan if God did not dwell in their midst? They could go on, but it would be without divine revelation, without spiritual communion, and without spiritual life. Without the presence of God in their midst, the milk and honey of Canaan would be a curse and not a blessing.

The mind of Moses was in a quandary. Israel was the people of God. This he knew beyond a doubt. God had given that promise to their fathers, and he could not change. Just the day before, he had presented that plea to God, and God had repented from destroying the nation. And still, the justice of God could not be compromised either. Israel was wicked. She had sinned a great sin, and that could not be overlooked. There was good reason why God would not dwell in her midst. The very holiness of God would consume the people in their wickedness. But how could they be the people of God if he did not dwell in their midst?

With a troubled heart, Moses returned to the people to tell them what God had said. Sadly he informed them of his failure. He had not made atonement. They must be visited for their sin. To this he added God's command, "Ye are a stiffnecked people: I will come up into the midst of thee in a moment, and consume thee: therefore now put off thy ornaments from thee, that I may know what to do unto thee" (Ex. 33:5). Soon the silence of the camp gave way unto mourning. The ornaments that they had worn disappeared. Sorrow and sad repentance were evident on every side. God was leading Israel into a deeper understanding of truth. Before, the people had trembled in the presence of God's greatness, but there had also been a certain element of self-confidence. They had been bold to say, "All that the LORD hath said will we do, and be obedient" (24:7). And they had actually thought that they would be able to do this. Now they knew better. Their self-confidence was swept away. Their sin and unfaithfulness could not be denied. All they could be was repentant sinners.

Still, Moses was not satisfied. He felt the need of the revelation and guidance of God. For him it would be impossible to go on without it. However, if God would come into the camp to reveal himself, it would only lead to disaster. Moses commanded that the tent of meeting that served as his headquarters should be moved without the camp. Perhaps God would reveal himself there. The people understood the reason for moving the tent. Soon the most sincere of the children of Israel were to be seen going out to this tabernacle to express their repentance before God and to pray for his blessing. When finally Moses arose to go out to the tent, all of the people were concerned. Would God appear to him in the tent or not? Each man stood by the door of his own tent and watched. Before their eyes, they saw Moses and Joshua, who accompanied him, proceed to the door of the tabernacle and enter in. Then it happened. The cloud of God's presence descended to the door of the tent as it had in former days when Moses' tent was still in the camp. It meant that God had not forsaken them completely. He would still reveal himself to Moses and speak to him the words that they needed. In gratitude, the heads of the men of Israel bowed, and they worshiped.

In the tent, Moses slowly began to set forth his problem before the Lord. Neither he nor the people could do without the presence and revelation of the Lord. It would do them no good to be led to Canaan if the truth of God was not revealed unto them to feed and strengthen their souls. They needed God's presence. Carefully and deliberately Moses began to speak.

> 12. See, thou sayest unto me, Bring up this people: and thou hast not let me know whom thou wilt send with me. Yet thou hast said, I know thee by name, and thou hast also found grace in my sight.
> 13. Now therefore, I pray thee, if I have found grace in thy sight, shew me now thy way, that I may know thee, that I may find grace in thy sight: and consider that this nation is thy people. (Ex. 33:12–13)

The point that Moses wished to make was that he needed someone to strengthen and guide him if he was to lead the people. He could not do it alone. If God did not go with them, in their midst, revealing the way of truth, how could Israel ever be brought to the blessings of the promised land?

God, anticipating the conclusion of Moses' argument, immediately gave answer, "My presence shall go with thee, and I will give thee rest" (Ex. 33:14).

With unsurpassed joy Moses heard these words. A deep feeling of relief flowed into his soul. This was what he wanted to hear. In gratitude he answered, "If thy presence go not with me, carry us not up hence. For wherein shall it be known here that I and thy people have found grace in thy sight? is it not in that thou goest with us? so shall we be separated, I and thy people, from all the people that are upon the face of the earth" (Ex. 33:15–16).

Quietly and with love the Lord answered him, "I will do this thing also that thou hast spoken: for thou hast found grace in my sight, and I know thee by name" (Ex. 33:17).

With pleasure Moses heard these words, and yet, his problem still remained. What about the justice of God? His holiness? His glory? How could God dwell in the midst of a wicked people and not consume them in anger? Encouraged by the assurances of God's love, Moses found the boldness to make a most daring request. "I beseech thee, shew me thy glory" (Ex. 33:18).

As surprising as was the boldness of Moses' request, even more surprising was the answer. God replied,

19. I will make all my goodness pass before thee, and I will proclaim the name of the LORD before thee; and will be gracious to whom I will be gracious, and will shew mercy on whom I will shew mercy.
20. ...Thou canst not see my face: for there shall no man see me, and live.
21. ...Behold, there is a place by me, and thou shalt stand upon a rock:
22. And it shall come to pass, while my glory passeth by, that I will put thee in a clift of the rock, and will cover thee with my hand while I pass by:
23. And I will take away mine hand, and thou shalt see my back parts: but my face shall not be seen. (Ex. 33:19–23)

The camp of Israel was quiet that night and at peace. God would go on with them, even in their midst. However, we may imagine that, in the tent of Moses there was little in the way of sleep. On the morrow he was to go up into the mountain and stand before the glory of God. God would make known unto him how he could dwell in the midst of a sinful people and not consume them with his justice. God would reveal the working of his glory.

Early in the morning Moses arose and made his ascent into the mountain of God. There in the mountain Moses stood before God on a rock. There God descended in a cloud, and, while Moses was covered by his hand in a cleft of the rock, God passed by in all of his glory. Only after he had passed was the hand lifted, so that Moses might behold the back part of God's glory. No description is given us. Human words could never suffice to tell of the beauty seen that day. It remained a secret wonderment hid in Moses' soul. But neither does it matter; for the greater revelation of that day is recorded for us to read. As God passed by he spoke, and this is what he said:

6. The LORD, The LORD God, merciful and gracious, longsuffering, and abundant in goodness and truth,
7. Keeping mercy for thousands, forgiving iniquity and transgression and sin, and that will by no means clear the guilty; visiting the iniquity of the fathers upon the children, and upon the children's children, unto the third and to the fourth generation. (Ex. 34:6–7)

In this way alone God would continue to dwell in the midst of Israel, even by dealing with them according to his eternal decree of election and reprobation. Before, he had treated the nation as a whole as his covenant people. This he would do no more. Henceforth, he would make it evident that they were not all Israel that were of Israel (Rom. 9:6). He would have mercy upon whom he will have mercy. His forgiving grace and abundant goodness would be made known unto as many as he had chosen in love. They had been given eternally unto the Savior, who would bear the visitation of justice for their sins. But for the rest, their sins would be visited immediately by God's justice. Henceforth the journey of Israel would be marked by the judgments of God as he would cut off from her midst those who were hardened in the way of sin. He would visit the sins of the wicked even unto the third and fourth generations of their reprobate seed. Only through their judgment could Israel be saved.

With humility, Moses heard these words and "made haste, and bowed his head toward the earth, and worshipped" (Ex. 34:8).

Chapter 27

MOSES IN THE CLEFT OF THE ROCK

19. And [the Lord] said, I will make all my goodness pass before thee, and I will proclaim the name of the LORD before thee; and will be gracious to whom I will be gracious, and will shew mercy on whom I will shew mercy.

6. And the LORD passed by before him, and proclaimed, The LORD, The LORD God, merciful and gracious, longsuffering, and abundant in goodness and truth,

7. Keeping mercy for thousands, forgiving iniquity and transgression and sin, and that will by no means clear the guilty; visiting the iniquity of the fathers upon the children, and upon the children's children, unto the third and to the fourth generation.

10. And he said, Behold, I make a covenant: before all thy people I will do marvels, such as have not been done in all the earth, nor in any nation: and all the people among which thou art shall see the work of the LORD: for it is a terrible thing that I will do with thee. (Exodus 33:19; 34:6–7, 10)

Israel had come to a terrible impasse in her history. At Sinai the people had sinned a great sin, one that could not be forgotten and that even for the moment could not be passed over. They had ascribed the glory of the eternal God to a graven image of gold, and had worshiped that image with heathenish orgies of sin. They had provoked their God to anger. And, at the request of Moses, God had revealed his glory. The history of Israel would never again be the same. During the months gone by since Jehovah had visited them in the bondage of Egypt, they as a nation had tasted abundantly of his goodness and grace. It was not as though they deserved it, for the people had murmured and rebelled from the start. Already after Moses had first appeared before Pharaoh with God's command to let Israel go, they had brought their objection, "The LORD look upon you, and judge; because ye have made our savour to be abhorred in the eyes of Pharaoh, and in the eyes of his servants, to put a sword in their hand to slay us" (Ex. 5:21). Again, after they had been delivered from Egypt by the working of the power of God in the plagues and by the visitation of the angel of judgment and were brought to the impasse of the Red Sea, they complained because they had not been left alone to serve the Egyptians. Then at Marah, and in the wilderness of Sin, and at Rephidim, they had murmured and rebelled. Still, throughout, Jehovah had been merciful to them in spite of their murmuring. He brought them out of Egypt with a high hand; he gave them passage through the depths of the sea; he made the bitter water sweet, fed them with quails and manna, and brought forth for them water out of the rock. The faithfulness of Jehovah to his covenant and to the promises given to the fathers had been established beyond dispute. Moreover, these blessings had come upon the nation as a whole. Every member of the nation had been delivered from the bondage of Pharaoh, had passed through the bosom of the sea, had eaten the food and drank of the water that had been provided by God. The whole nation had from a typical point of view been treated as the chosen people of God.

Even while all of this was taking place, however, it was becoming evident that actually there was a deep rift that divided the camp into two different groups. On the one hand, there were the true children of Israel, who showed signs of true spiritual life. Indeed, these too were guilty of Israel's sins. Many of them in fact had joined in the murmuring and complaining that arose every time the way became hard. Others merely stood silently by while these sins were taking place and had become thereby silent partners in the rebellion. All made themselves guilty before the sight of God. But still, each time that God revealed himself in mercy and in power, these children of Israel turned in repentance from what they had done and cried to Jehovah for forgiveness. It was an indisputable sign that in them there dwelt the Spirit of God. But, on the other hand, there was another element in Israel of which this was not true. These were hardened, reprobate men. They were the ones who were always looking for an occasion to arouse the camp of Israel to murmur and complain. In turn, when the power of God's grace was clearly revealed, these men were displeased and fell into a sullen silence even while they were eating or drinking, partaking typically of Jehovah's deliverance. Finally, it was these who, in the very shadow of God's holy mountain, went all out. They took occasion at the extended absence of Moses to spread through the camp of Israel their miserable lies. They aroused the people to build the golden calf and to duplicate the wickedness of the heathen, causing one of the most wretched chapters in the history of the church to be written. While they were of Israel, they were not the true Israel. They could trace their generations back to the fathers, but they had none of the fathers' faith in the promises of God. They were children of the flesh but not of the promise.

And now, at Sinai, the cup of iniquity of many of them was just about filled. In fact, three thousand of them, by continuing their naked dancing in the face of Moses' reprimand, had filled their cup of iniquity and were cut down by the Levites' swords. Previously God had endured these men with much longsuffering, so that his love and faithfulness to the promise of the fathers might become clearly evident; but henceforth, after the sin at Sinai, he would be able to endure them no more. The path of Israel hereafter would be marked by judgment. This God made clear to Moses when he revealed to him his glory.

Before Jehovah revealed his glory to Moses, however, he guided him carefully in his work as mediator and intercessor for Israel until several facts stood out clearly before Moses' mind. The first fact was that if Moses would stand aside and forsake Israel as their intercessor, a type of Jesus Christ, the wrath of God's justice would destroy the nation in a moment (Ex. 32:7–10). The second fact was that Moses, being a mere man, could not make atonement for the sin of Israel but that the sin of Israel would surely be visited in the day of visitation (vv. 11–34). The third was that, if God would come again into the camp of Israel, he would come with a visitation of his justice, and people would be consumed by his wrath (33:1–3). The fourth was that, if God did not dwell in the midst of the camp of Israel, they might go on to the land of Canaan, and he would even lead them with his angel, but they would not experience the richness of the covenant blessing for which the presence of God in their midst was needed (vv. 12–17). Slowly God led Moses, through threatenings and promises, until these facts all stood out very clearly before Moses' mind. Finally, when all of this was clearly seen by Moses, there was still only one conclusion to which Moses could come: Israel needed the presence of God in the midst of them. This was true regardless of what the consequences might be. This fact he laid before the Lord, and the Lord consented to comply.

It was at this point that there burst forth from the lips of Moses the astounding prayer, "I beseech thee, shew me thy glory" (Ex. 33:18). This meant more than that Moses wished to see a glorious vision of heavenly light. Moses was troubled by all that he had learned. He wished to understand the greatness of God whereby all that he had learned could be maintained and the covenant of God with Israel still be kept. That was what he wanted to see.

God in answer said, "I will make all my goodness pass before thee, and I will proclaim the name of the LORD before thee; and will be gracious to whom I will be gracious, and will shew mercy on whom I will shew mercy" (Ex. 33:19). Indeed, there would be a limit beyond which Moses could not go, as God said: "Thou canst not see my face: for there shall no man see me, and live" (v. 20). Mere man can never come to understand the infinite God and his ways completely, but God would lead Moses into new truths that were wonderful in themselves.

The next day upon the mountain, God passed by in his glory

while Moses was kept hid in the cleft of the rock. Afterward Moses was allowed to gaze upon the back part, the reflection, of God's glory. There must have been some visible demonstration of the heavenly glory of God; but that was only secondary, emphasizing and illustrating the *word* that God spoke. For as the Lord passed by, he spoke:

6. The LORD, The LORD God, merciful and gracious, longsuffering, and abundant in goodness and truth,

7. Keeping mercy for thousands, forgiving iniquity and transgression and sin, and that will by no means clear the guilty; visiting the iniquity of the fathers upon the children, and upon the children's children, unto the third and to the fourth generation. (Ex. 34:6–7)

Before this truth, Moses bowed and worshiped.

This was the work of God's sovereign counsel in the work of predestination. There were in Israel those to whom God would be merciful and gracious for no other reason than that he in his sovereign good pleasure had determined to be merciful and gracious to them. They were a sinful people too; but God would reveal his grace and mercy to them by forgiving iniquity and transgression and sin. And, God said, he would do this without by any means clearing or passing over as though they did not exist, the sins of those who were guilty, anticipating thereby the day when he would reveal his mercy to his chosen by visiting the guilt of their sins upon his own Son. But, on the other hand, there were others in Israel whom God had not chosen in his sovereign good pleasure unto mercy. The guilt of their sins God would visit upon them, and their children, and their children's children unto the third and fourth generations after them. Through the early part of the journey, God had been longsuffering with these for his elect's sake, but he would be so no more. Henceforth the way of Israel would be marked with judgments of God upon the reprobate of Israel, who would fill their cup of iniquity. The sovereignty of God would cause a constant division in the camp, as he would separate the children of the flesh from the elect children of grace. This was the first implication of God's revelation of glory.

Moses must have seen the sorrow and hardship that the sovereign judgments of God would bring into Israel's camp. Nonetheless, in faithfulness, he had the grace to exclaim as he worshiped, "If now I have found grace in thy sight, O Lord, let my Lord, I pray thee, go among us; for it is a stiffnecked people; and pardon our iniquity and our sin, and take us for thine inheritance" (Ex. 34:9). Nothing was more important to him than that Jehovah should go in their midst, even if it must be unto the judgment and destruction of many. For that, he would repeatedly make his prayer.

There is a special beauty to God's answer: "Behold, I make a covenant: before all thy people I will do marvels, such as have not been done in all the earth, nor in any nation: and all the people among which thou art shall see the work of the LORD: for it is a terrible thing that I will do with thee" (Ex. 34:10). The visitations of God's justice would be terrible in the months and years to come, not only upon the nations of Canaan, but upon the reprobate of Israel itself. And yet this very work would be marvelous, such as the world had never seen. It anticipated the teaching of Isaiah, "Zion shall be redeemed with judgment, and her converts with righteousness. And the destruction of the transgressors and of the sinners shall be together, and they that forsake the LORD shall be consumed" (Isa. 1:27–28). By the judgments of God, Israel would henceforth be purged, and the true children of promise would be preserved. Thus alone could the covenant be eternally established.

Chapter 28

REFLECTION OF GOD'S GLORY IN THE FACE OF MOSES

29. And it came to pass, when Moses came down from mount Sinai with the two tables of testimony in Moses' hand, when he came down from the mount, that Moses wist not that the skin of his face shone while he talked with him.

30. And when Aaron and all the children of Israel saw Moses, behold, the skin of his face shone; and they were afraid to come nigh him. (Exodus 34:29–30)

For a second period of forty days and forty nights, Moses abode on Mount Sinai without food and drink communing with God. There upon the mountain, God revealed to Moses his glory in a vision that cannot be described and in words that are recorded for us to read yet today. God brought Moses to understand the greatness whereby he is gracious unto whom he will be gracious, and showeth mercy unto whom he will show mercy, and whom he will he hardeneth. God proclaimed his name unto Moses and said,

6. The LORD, The LORD God, merciful and gracious, longsuffering, and abundant in goodness and truth,

7. Keeping mercy for thousands, forgiving iniquity and transgression and sin, and that will by no means clear the guilty; visiting the iniquity of the fathers upon the children, and upon the children's children, unto the third and to the fourth generation. (Ex. 34:6–7)

Great were the implications of this revelation. God would perform marvels before his people, and terrible would be the work that he would do. Before this he had revealed himself as the God of faithfulness. He had kept Israel with his blessings, while with much longsuffering he bore with the wicked and their sin. This he would do no longer. Henceforth, as he went forth in the midst of Israel, he would reveal himself also as the God of holiness. In this holiness, indeed, he would continue to be merciful unto those of Israel whom he had chosen in his eternal, elective purpose. But he would also strike out with visitations of his holy judgment upon the wicked of the nation who had no part in him. The path of Israel henceforth would be marked by the blood of judgment. In holiness, he would establish the glory of his name. This was the glory that Moses contemplated upon the mountain for forty days and nights.

When Moses came up into the mountain, he had taken in his hands two tables of stone newly carved. They were the same shape and size as the others, which he had broken on the rocks below. God had commanded that he carve them and take them along. There, as Moses stood and watched, the ten words of God's law were engraved again by the finger of God upon the face of these tables of stone. The act of Moses in breaking the first tables had been rash, and now they had to be replaced. At the moment when he had broken them, it had seemed the only thing to do. To his mind they had lost their only use. He had been there with Israel when God had first spoken those words of the law from the peaks of the mount. Then he had received those commandments engraved by the hand of God upon those first two tables of stone. At the time, he had fully expected that by the law of God Israel would be led to righteousness and glory. By the grace of God, he thought, Israel would be enabled to keep the law and become a distinct nation, holy and different from all others. Could anyone, having been so richly blessed, fail to walk in obedience before God? And then he had descended the mountain with Joshua until they stood overlooking the camp where Israel, so soon after listening to the voice of God, was engaged in heathenish rites. Boldly, at the very foot of God's holy mountain, the people were breaking all of the commandments of the law. Moses had held in his hand the two tables of stone, a permanent record of the command-ments that God had spoken, but what good were they to a people who had broken them all before they were even brought? In holy indignation Moses had dashed them to pieces on the rocks below. Then he knew that Israel would never keep God's law. And to his mind it had seemed that the law had lost all its use.

But many things had happened since then, even though the time was not long. He had gone down into the camp and had found that even in their sin he continued to love them as the people of God. He could not reject them, even as he had professed to God while still upon the mountain. It was for their sake that he had broken apart the idol and cast its dust into the water so that they could taste the bitterness of their sin. It was for their sake that he had slain the three thousand men in holy indignation because they had continued in their sin before his righteous admonition. For their sake he had returned to God again seeking to discover the way of atonement for them. It was an inner compulsion of heart with Moses. He had to know how Israel could be saved from her sin and the promises of God be fulfilled. God heard his prayer and answered him. Slowly he led Moses into an understanding of his truth, and through it to a greater understanding of the place and purpose of his law. Already when he began to make his prayer, Moses realized of himself that the sin of Israel was too great merely to be overlooked, and God soon told Moses that the sin was too great for Moses to make atonement for it. Rather, if God were to go on in the midst of Israel, it could only be as a consuming fire in holiness and judgment. But Moses realized that Israel needed the presence of God, and he prayed for it. It was then, upon Moses' request, that God revealed his glory. He would go on in the midst of Israel, and in doing so he would reveal mercy to the elect children of Israel by forgiving their iniquity and sin. That he would do, not by merely overlooking their guilt. In the day of visitation, their sin too would be visited. But at the same time he would be a consuming fire of holiness and justice upon all who did not belong to them. He would visit their iniquity upon them and upon their children unto the third and fourth generations after them.

As for the second time Moses received the law written upon tables of stone, he realized much more what purpose it was given to fulfill. The law would never serve to make the children of Israel perfect. Their sin was much too deeply entrenched for the law to do that. Always they would be subject to temptation, and often they would go astray. As they had sinned once, they would do it in the future over and over again. But they needed the law just the same, for, as long as the law was there, the children of Israel would never be able to say that they did not know that their sinful deeds were wrong. Whenever they sinned, the law would be there to remind them of their guilt. This would be even more true when God would come to visit Israel in judgment. According to the law, his justice would be dispensed both in the chastisement of his chosen and in the punishment of the wicked. Each time the visitation of God appeared, the Israelite who knew the law would be convicted by his own conscience of his own guilt. That was the purpose of the law. It could not take away sin. It could not make the children of Israel righteous. It was a schoolmaster that would serve to teach them, over and over again, that they had no righteousness in themselves. In this way those who truly desired salvation would be brought more and more to look upon and to trust in the promise that had been revealed to the fathers. They would place their hope in the promised seed that through the marvelous working of Jehovah would be a blessing unto them. It was the blessing they could not find in themselves. Smitten by sorrow and repentance under the chastisement of the law, true Israel would turn to the glory revealed unto Moses, even the assurance that God would have mercy according to his good pleasure to forgive the iniquity of his people and prepare for them the way of salvation.

For forty days and forty nights Moses abode in communion with God on the mountain. During that time he did not eat, he did not drink, and he had no sleep; and yet his eyes were not dim, and his body was not exhausted with fatigue. He abode in the presence of God and partook of the meat of which Jesus was later to speak at the well of Sychar. The glory of God's presence sustained his body even as it gave strength to his soul. We know only very little of that which was revealed to Moses while there. He must have seen a heavenly vision of glory such as our eyes cannot imagine. He must have been told many wonderful truths about God and his counsel, which were never fully revealed again until Jesus Christ came to dwell in the flesh. Moses both literally and figuratively beheld the beauty of God. He experienced that which Paul described many years later when he wrote, "But we all, with open face beholding as in a glass the glory of the Lord, are changed into the same image from glory to glory, even as by the Spirit of the Lord" (2 Cor. 3:18).

As Moses stood there before the beauty of God, the skin of his face began to shine with a reflection of the glory of God that was being revealed to him. The truth of God entered in to fill his heart, and the beauty of God impressed itself upon his countenance. He was being given to experience a more intimate communion with God than any other saint or prophet of Old Testament times, and this could not leave him unchanged. Even when the forty days and nights were over, and he went down from the holy mountain, the glory of God's presence continued to radiate from his face. But it was God's glory and not his, and he was unaware of it.

Coming again to Aaron and the people, Moses thought to tell them immediately of all that he had learned, but the people backed away from him in fear. They saw that glory of God on Moses' face that he unconsciously bore. They saw that radiance of divine holiness and were filled with terror. Then Moses began to realize how greatly his appearance had been changed by standing in the presence of God. Only after he had taken up a veil and covered his face would the people allow him to come close enough to them to speak. This was a warning to Moses. He had learned many wonderful things about God and his glory; but, in the form that he knew them, they were more than the people were able to endure. The people of Israel were as children in matters relating to God. As children they had to be talked to and instructed. If he would tell them directly all that he knew, it would only fill their hearts with terror. He would have to speak to them in accord with their limitations as though through a veil. The tabernacle would have to be built in the form that had been revealed to him before. Civil and ceremonial laws would be given. These would serve as types and figures through which the truth would be brought gradually to find a place in believing hearts. But always the veil would be there. Only when Moses went into the presence of the Lord could it be taken away. There he would know perfect and free communion. He could speak openly from the feeling and understanding of his heart.

Many years and ages would pass before that veil would be taken away from the revelation of the glory of God. All through the old dispensation the people of God were limited to type and shadow, for, even though they advanced in the truth, it was all that they could endure. Only with the coming of Jesus and the gift of his Holy Spirit was the veil finally removed from God's glory, and we stand before it as Moses did, only far more so, to be transformed from glory to glory into the very image of God.

Chapter 29

THE TABERNACLE

17. And it came to pass in the first month in the second year, on the first day of the month, that the tabernacle was reared up.

34. Then a cloud covered the tent of the congregation, and the glory of the Lord filled the tabernacle. (Exodus 40:17, 34)

It was during the first forty-day stay on the mountain that God revealed to Moses the plan for his holy tabernacle. It was a wonderful plan for a beautiful tent constructed of the richest materials, through which Israel would be able to worship her God in truth. With the plan came the gracious promise that Jehovah would dwell among the children of Israel and would be their God. While Moses had rejoiced in the beauty of the plan unfolded by God, Israel had not been ready to receive it. Much had yet to transpire before the people would be able to appreciate the institution of the tabernacle and its worship. First there had to take place the sin of the golden calf and its grievous results. It was a sad and disappointing history through which they had to pass, but it was necessary for Israel to come to a full consciousness of her own innate wickedness and corruption. Once the people had come to a humble awareness of their own unworthiness, they would be able to appreciate the fact that God had made his dwelling in their midst—but not before.

Now this had all happened. Israel had sinned her great sin by imitating the orgies of the heathen in the very shadow of God's holy mountain. Only by the faithful intercession of Moses had she been saved from the judgment of God and eternal destruction. At the same time, Jehovah had made clear that, as he continued to go on in her midst, it would be in perfect holiness. He would have mercy upon whom he would have mercy, but he would also judge whom he would for the hardness of their hearts. This had been made perfectly clear to Moses during the second period of forty days, when the glory of God passed before him on the mountain. This time, when he returned, he did not find the people of Israel again engaged in sin. The consciousness of guilt weighed too heavily upon their hearts for them to be able to give themselves again to open abandonment and sin. When Moses appeared before them, the very reflection of the holiness of God from his face was more than their guilty hearts could endure. They pleaded with him to cover his face with a veil. The sinfulness of Israel was not yet gone, but they had come to a new spirit of humble repentance. Now they were ready to receive the holy tabernacle of the Lord, for the tabernacle was designed to be a blessing only unto those who came to it with humble and repentant hearts.

Calling the people together, Moses laid before them the need that they had for materials to build the tabernacle of God. Only the best and richest of materials could be used, for Jehovah could not be served through anything that was inferior and marred. Even more, it was required that all that was brought for this cause should be given with a willing and God-fearing heart. God could accept no gift that was given for any motive less than pure and undefiled love. Soon the many different materials needed for the tabernacle were being brought to Moses in abundant supply. All manner of jewelry made of gold and silver and precious stones was brought as willingly as it had before been brought to Aaron for the golden calf, but with a much deeper joy and confidence. The golden earrings given to Aaron had been offered recklessly in an abandonment to lust. Now all was being brought with hearts joyful and free, thankful for the privilege of giving their best to the Lord. In addition, there was brought fine linen of blue and purple and scarlet, goat's hair, skins of rams and badgers, shittim wood, brass, spices, and oil. All that was needed for the tabernacle was presented before Moses and much more besides.

Soon a great bustle of activity was to be seen throughout the camp of Israel. A feeling of vital concern for the sanctuary of God had entered and filled the hearts of the host of God's chosen people. It stirred them with a zeal of holy dedication. The dwelling place of Jehovah had to be built, and it was a work that had to be done exactly according to the pattern revealed upon the mountain. Everyone according to his or her personal ability wanted to serve this cause. Some worked in preparing the materials, metal and wood and fine-twined threads. Some worked in fashioning the material, molding, carving, weaving, and embroidering. Finally, there were two men, Bezaleel and Aholiab, who were especially qualified by God to put the last finishing touches upon each piece that was made, in order that it might conform in closest detail to the pattern that Moses had received from God. No piece could be too carefully wrought; no standard was too exacting; this was God's work, and it had to be good. Days and weeks and months passed by as Israel applied itself with diligence to the beauty of this task, and the people did not tire. So great was the zeal, that the time came when more than enough work had been done, and they had to be ordered to stop. At last each completed piece was deposited before Moses in the form that had been designated by God, and Moses declared it to be right. All had been done just as the Lord had commanded them, and Moses blessed the people for the faithfulness of their labor.

Nearly six full months had been spent in preparing the beautiful tapestry and furnishings for the tabernacle, but as yet none of the parts had been assembled. It remained for the day appointed by God that the tabernacle should be raised as a completed and holy sanctuary unto Jehovah. That date was of monumental importance, for God appointed it to be the day that marked the first anniversary of Israel's departure from Egypt. It was a day well chosen to remind Israel of the great blessings she had received.

Early in the morning of the appointed day, the children of Israel began to gather about the space that had been allotted for the tabernacle. As the people watched in solemn silence, the walls of the tabernacle were erected and the beautifully woven coverings of the tent were draped over them. Into the inmost sanctuary the ark of the covenant, with the carefully fashioned mercy seat, was placed, and the fine-twined linen veil was hung before it, so that henceforth no human eye but those of the high priest might gaze upon its glory. Next, the golden furnishings of the foremost sanctuary, the table of shewbread, the candlestick, and the altar of incense, were carefully put in place. Fresh bread was placed on the table; the lamps were lit; incense was offered upon the altar; and again a veil was stretched before them. Before the door of the tabernacle the altar of burnt offering was set up, and a burnt offering and a meat offering were offered upon it. Between the altar and the tabernacle, the laver of washing was placed, and around the tabernacle and its court a fine linen curtain was hung upon pillars of silver. Many, many different pieces were involved in all this. There was a place for everything, and each piece fit precisely into its place. There was wonderment just in watching the sanctuary rising smoothly and in order from the maze of materials that had been sitting all around. Finally, when the whole of the building had been erected, Aaron and his sons were called forth to be clothed in their rich, flowing robes, so that they might serve as a holy priesthood unto the Lord. The last finishing touch was applied when Moses took the oil of consecration and sprinkled it over all—over the tabernacle, over its furnishings, and over the family of Aaron who henceforth were to spend their lives in holy consecration to the Lord. This oil was a symbol of the Holy Spirit, by whose power alone this tabernacle could be dedicated in complete consecration to the pure and holy service of Jehovah God.

The blessing of God rested upon the work of Israel, they knew, for as soon as all had been consecrated, the cloud of his presence descended upon the tabernacle and his glory filled it throughout. Henceforth he would make his dwelling place in the inmost sanctuary upon the mercy seat. Jehovah had come to make his dwelling place in their midst. So great was his glory revealed in the tabernacle that day that even Moses could not enter in. Israel could only stand at a distance and worship.

Henceforth the tabernacle, and the temple that succeeded it, would be one of the richest blessings that the Old Testament church would ever have. In the tabernacle the gospel was set before them in terms that they, in their day of limited revelation, could understand.

In the tabernacle the truth of God's covenant of grace was symbolized, and from the tabernacle the actual experience of the covenant went forth. In the tabernacle God dwelt upon the mercy seat, between the two golden cherubim. His dwelling was in the very heart of Israel's camp. Whenever the children of Israel would look to the tabernacle, they received from its very presence the testimony that God was with them. Whenever the individual believer felt in his heart a need for spiritual strength and assurance, he could go to the tabernacle and commune with God through the ceremonial means that were instituted, and receive the testimony that he was accepted. It was as though God were continuously repeating his covenant promise to everyone who had eyes to see and hearts to understand, saying, "And I will establish my covenant between me and thee and thy seed after thee in their generations for an everlasting covenant, to be a God unto thee, and to thy seed after thee" (Gen. 17:7). God's faithfulness in friendship and love was set before their eyes to be seen through the power of faith; God was with them.

But the tabernacle was more than that. It set forth the gospel as a gospel of grace. It testified that the blessings of the covenant were a free gift of grace from God to his people, and not the other way around. As they came to the tabernacle, each step of the way testified of that. No sooner had they entered the court but they stood before the altar, testifying that, because they were sinners, they could stand before God only through a sacrifice of atonement in the shedding of blood. Even at that, they could go farther only through their representative, the priest, who was washed in the laver and could serve typically as their mediator before God. For them the priest could enter the sanctuary, where were the visible representations of the bread of life sufficient for the whole of God's church in the twelve loaves on the golden table, the light of covenant life shed abroad by the Holy Spirit in the seven golden lamps filled with the consecrated oil, and the intercessory means of acceptance for the prayers of God's people in the altar of incense, which gave forth a sweet-smelling savor before the face of God. Even more, within the inner sanctuary there was the ark of the covenant with its mercy seat, upon which rested the cloud of God's presence. The Angel of Jehovah dwelt there, filling the tabernacle with the glory of God. Once every year the high priest, as the mediator and representative of the people of God, was permitted to enter that holy sanctuary with the blood of the great day of atonement as a testimony that someday, when the blood of atonement was perfectly shed, the people of God would be brought into the very presence of God. The whole of the tabernacle gave a visible expression to the wonder of grace and blessing that one day would be fulfilled in the promised seed yet to come. In type and shadow it testified of Jesus Christ.

Considering all this, we can understand the psalmist who wrote, "One thing have I desired of the LORD, that will I seek after; that I may dwell in the house of the LORD all the days of my life, to behold the beauty of the LORD, and to enquire in his temple" (Ps. 27:4).

Chapter 30

ISRAEL'S WORSHIP

> Then Moses said unto Aaron, This is it that the LORD spake, saying, I will be sanctified in them that come nigh me, and before all the people I will be glorified. (Leviticus 10:3)

It was a glorious day in the camp of Israel when the tabernacle of Jehovah was assembled from its various parts, and the cloud of his presence descended to cover the tent, and the glory of the Lord filled the tabernacle. Not only was it the fruit of many months of dedicated labor, it was a rich unfolding of revelation concerning the gospel through which alone they could be saved. We must remember that Israel did not possess the fullness of doctrine and spiritual truth that we have today. A scant outline of God's grace and faithfulness in salvation was all that her people knew: a history of Seth's generations and of the fathers; the promises given to Adam, Noah, Abraham and Jacob; and the short revelations they had received themselves. But for the true believer in Israel, this was sufficient to fill him with hope and confidence. It was the strength of his life. The spiritual children of Israel spoke of these things often, and they longed to learn more. And there in the tabernacle that materialized before their eyes, this hope was being realized. The tabernacle set before them new details concerning God's plan of salvation, which they could see; and, believing them, they could be drawn into closer communion with God.

In large part, these people possessed a mentality and understanding that was different from ours. We live in a scientific, philosophical age and do our thinking by analyzing logical relationships with our minds. It is a sign, perhaps, of maturity, although often, like maturity,

unnecessarily cold. In contrast, the people of Israel were more simple and poetical. Their minds would visualize images and pictures, to
which they reacted with strong feelings. Thus, when they saw the tabernacle rise up before them, it stirred their hearts with feelings such as
we, very likely, can never completely understand.

What made the existence of the tabernacle so very impressive for
them was the lingering feeling of guilt that still hung as a shadow
upon their hearts. Under the shadow of Sinai, their outlook on God
and life had undergone a great, deepening change. In coming to
Sinai from Egypt they had felt self-assured and confident to a fault.
It had seemed to them that they were the people of God because of
some special virtue that was characteristic of them as a nation. And
then they had committed that sin. And God had revealed to them
that, were it not for his mercy revealed in Moses as their typical
mediator, they would be utterly destroyed. All they deserved was to
perish, and, in times to come, many of them would indeed perish
who did not belong to him in truth. It was that which made the tabernacle and the cloud that filled it with glory so amazing. It meant
that God had come to dwell in the midst of them while they were
yet sinners!

In this tabernacle a richness of detail concerning the covenant
of grace was set forth as never before. It all centered in the cloud of
Jehovah's presence, which dwelt in the inner sanctuary of that tent
upon the mercy seat, between the cherubim and above the tables
of the law. That cloud was glorious because in it was revealed the
Angel of Jehovah, the old dispensation form of Jesus Christ, revealing the grace of God in salvation to his people. Under the canopy
of the tabernacle, he held covenant fellowship and communion with
them as they were represented in the outer sanctuary of the tent. The
blessedness of their state was to be seen in the furnishings of that
room—the golden candlesticks, the table of shewbread, and the altar
of incense. The candlesticks filled the sanctuary typically with the
light of life fed by the oil of the Holy Spirit. The table held the bread
of life sufficient for all of Israel according to its tribes. From the altar

their prayers ascended as a sweet-smelling savor before the face of the Angel of God. All of Israel knew that these visible representations of their blessedness were there, not only because they had helped make them and seen them put in their place, but because their representatives, the priests, could enter to partake of their blessings. And the only thing that stood between the two sanctuaries of God and his people was the finely woven veil of blue, purple, and scarlet with its golden cherubim design. And even that separation was not total, for once every year their high priest could enter within the veil as a promise of even more perfect communion in ages to come.

Indeed, all of this blessedness would have seemed impossible for Israel in her present humbled state, were it not that her own approach to the sanctuary was also made plain. Before the entrance to the sanctuary stood an altar. Generally, the people knew what this meant, for the altar was an institution that had been used by their fathers ever since man's first fall into sin. For those who were burdened with the sorrow of guilt, it was a symbolic promise of God that he would provide for them a way unto the forgiveness of their sins. Not that their sin would be forgotten and thus God's justice denied. Rather, a substitute would be provided, represented by the animal victim that was slain, which would enter into the cause of death in their stead. Vicarious blood would wash away the guilt, and they would be counted free from every taint and stain of sin. To every saint who came to the altar believing, it was a source of inner righteousness and peace.

But now, as they stood that day before the newly erected sanctuary, Moses stepped forth to explain that God was giving to that altar a new dimension of meaning. Henceforth the sacrifices would be distinguished into different kinds, according to the needs and occasions for them. Carefully he explained. As before, there would be the burnt offering, only now its ritual would be more definitely defined. This was a sacrifice freely given by a believer burdened with the conviction of his sinfulness. It was not occasioned by any particular act of iniquity, but by the general sorrow for sin that is experienced by every child of God. The body of the victim was consumed upon the altar before the eyes of the offeror, who by it received the testimony that his curse was atoned for and his sin completely covered. To this was being added the new institutions of the peace offering and the meat offering. The peace offering was a sacrifice of thanksgiving, in which the greater part of the victim's flesh was given to the priest and the offeror for a joyful feast before the Lord. Combined with it was the meat offering of wine and cakes, oil, salt, and frankincense, and its greater portion was also given to the priest.

Finally, Moses gave them the institution of the sin and trespass offerings, which were to be offered by those who in ignorance or weakness had committed some particular sin. For each of these sacrifices, very particular rituals were provided, governing the choice of the victim, the laying of the offeror's hands upon the victim's head, the slaying of the animals, the manipulation of the blood, the burning and disposal of the victim's body, and the sacrificial meal that often followed. The animal victim was to be perfect, so as to symbolize a perfect redeemer. Through the laying of the offeror's hands on the victim's head, it was testified that his sin and guilt were transferred to the sacrifice. The slaying of the animal, together with the burning of its body, testified that the curse of sin was borne completely, while, in the sprinkling of the blood before the altar, the image of the victim and the priest merged almost into one as the typical mediator who stood before the sinner and his God. Finally, in the sacrificial meal the assurance was given that the very atonement that took away guilt was a blessed nourishment and strength for all who came in faith unto Jehovah in the tabernacle.

As one by one these institutions were given, it became increasingly evident that the priesthood was to fill a very important place in the worship of Jehovah in the tabernacle. Only in their charge could any of the sacrifices be offered, and by their hands the atoning blood was to be sprinkled and poured out according to the ritual of each offering, almost as if it were their own. The sacrifices and blood stood as types of the perfect Mediator and Redeemer to come.

As all of Israel watched, Aaron and his sons were summoned to Moses. They were appointed to be the priests of the Lord. First Aaron, and then his sons, were brought forth. They were commanded to wash themselves at the laver in the tabernacle's court. Before the people they were dressed in the beautiful priestly robes that had been prepared, and they were anointed with holy oil to signify that they were separated and qualified by the Spirit of God to live in complete consecration to the service of God. It was for them that the altar of the tabernacle was first brought into use with a sin offering, a burnt offering, and a peace offering offered for them by Moses, that their guilt might be completely covered. While the congregation watched, they ate the sacrificial meal and were commanded to spend the next week, seven complete days, within the doors of the tabernacle.

After the seventh day was completed, Moses called the elders of Israel, with Aaron and his sons, to the tabernacle. The time had come for the priests to take up the duties of their offices. Before, the sacrifices had been offered by Moses; henceforth, the priests would be in charge. Soon all of the congregation had come together to observe as once again a sin offering, a burnt offering, and a peace offering were prepared unto the Lord. Carefully Moses instructed them each step of the way. When all was ready, Aaron lifted his hands toward the people and blessed them, and he with Moses entered into the sanctuary of the Lord. When they came out again, they once more blessed the people. It was at that moment that the glory of the Lord appeared before them all, and the fire of God leaped forth to consume the burnt offering and the fat. It was an indisputable sign that God would work in the sacrifices, and Israel would indeed be blessed. The people fell to their faces and worshiped.

This was a joyful day for Israel—until also a somber note was added. Nadab and Abihu, Aaron's oldest sons, corrupted their newly acquired offices. As Israel feasted and rejoiced, they were carried away with the excitement of the occasion. Possibly under the influence of wine, they decided of themselves to offer incense to the Lord. Without requesting either permission or instructions, they proceeded to do just that. They took incense and censers, put fire to them, and entered the sanctuary of God. It was neither the proper time nor method. Incense was to be offered to God only in the morning and evening, and with a fire taken from the coals of the altar. It was strange fire that they brought, and the wrath of God was kindled. In a moment, the fire of God struck out and devoured them in their sin.

Soon a hushed silence had fallen over the camp. But it was the judgment of God, and it was just. Moses stepped forth and gave instructions. Aaron and the two remaining sons might not mourn the death of the brothers. It was the work of God, and in the functions of their sacred offices they might not appear sorrowful because of it. The cousins of the boys were called to carry the bodies away, but the ceremonies of the tabernacle had to continue.

There was a vivid lesson for Israel in this. The tabernacle and its ceremonies were rich in spiritual blessing. They set forth the gospel of salvation in figure and type. But they were not to be used presumptuously. God would guard his dwelling place, and he who used them in sin would be judged in his sin. As Moses said to Aaron, "This is it that the LORD spake, saying, I will be sanctified in them that come nigh me, and before all the people I will be glorified" (Lev. 10:3).

Chapter 31

TRUE ISRAEL, A HOLY NATION

1. And the Lord spake unto Moses, saying,
2. Speak unto all the congregation of the children of Israel, and say unto them, Ye shall be holy: for I the Lord your God am holy. (Leviticus 19:1–2)

One of the most beautiful and most expressive of the forms of worship instituted for Israel while encamped in the wilderness was that of the great day of atonement. It was a new institution related directly to the tabernacle in its typical function as the dwelling place of God. It presented one of the clearest revelations of the covenant of grace with the approach of God's people into the blessing of Jehovah's presence.

The great day of atonement came at the conclusion of the many laws that God had given concerning the tabernacle and its services. It served to give in fullest detail the meaning and significance of the altar and its sacrifices that were offered daily before the Lord. In terms as clear as could be given in the Old Testament shadows and types, it anticipated and foreshadowed the work of atonement that in the fullness of time would be realized by Christ.

Summoned by Moses, Aaron was called at the opening of the designated day to the tabernacle of God, there to wash himself at the laver in the court of the tabernacle and to dress himself in the holy garments of the high priest. With him were brought four sacrificial animals: a bullock, a ram, and two small he goats as similar in appearance and size as they could be, to be presented before the Lord. Between the two he goats a lot was cast to select the one as the scapegoat, or Azazel as it was known by the Hebrews, and the other as the Lord's.

First in the ceremonies of the day was the atonement that was made for the high priest himself and for his house. It was of utmost importance at all times that the priests of God should be free from all guilt when serving in their office as representatives of the people before God. Thus, in the first ceremonial function of the day, the bullock was slain as a sin offering for Aaron the high priest. Once this sacrifice was completed, he could go in his own behalf into the inmost sanctuary of the tabernacle, the Holy of Holies, to stand before the mercy seat in the presence of the Lord. Twice he went, once with a censer filled with burning incense, and once with the blood of the sacrificial bullock, to sprinkle it seven times before the mercy seat and also upon the mercy seat itself. The significance of this was evident. It meant that the atonement for the high priest was accepted of God and that he was worthy to serve as the servant of God in the main ceremony of the day.

The principal sacrifice of the great day of atonement centered in the two sacrificial he goats. These two young kids, as similar in size and appearance as possible, represented one sacrificial offering. They were two in number so that they could represent the two different aspects of blessing that arose from the atoning sacrifices made before God.

Once the ceremony for the high priest was completed, the first of these goats was slain as a sin offering for the people. As in all of the sacrifices, this typically and symbolically manifested the promise of God that he would exact punishment for the sins of believing Israel upon the substitute that was presented upon the altar—typically the goat in this case, in reality Jesus Christ at his coming in the fullness of time. With the blood of this sacrifice, the high priest could once again enter into the inmost sanctuary, the dwelling place of Jehovah, now as the representative of the people of Israel. This blood of Israel's sacrifice was also sprinkled upon the mercy seat and before it seven times. The symbolism of this was very beautiful. It meant that Israel, because of the atoning sacrifice, was accepted representatively in her priest, before the face of Jehovah her God.

When the high priest came forth from the tabernacle again, the second young goat was brought forth. This was the scapegoat or Azazel. Upon the head of the live goat, Aaron laid both of his hands and made confession of all of the sins and transgressions of Israel. Thereupon the goat was led out into the wilderness far from Israel's camp and left free to wander by itself. Symbolically, the sins of Israel were carried away into an uninhabited land, never to return again.

This ceremony gave to the sacrifices of the tabernacle a very rich revelation of meaning. While all of the sacrifices of the tabernacle represented symbolically the promise of God that the Redeemer to come would bear the guilt of Israel's sins before the wrath of God, this ceremony revealed to them in lucid, although figurative, terms the blessings that would arise from the sacrifice. On the one hand, the true children of Israel would be received with favor into the presence of God, and on the other hand, the guilt of their sins would be carried far away never to return to them again. Israel in that day could not know as clearly as we how this would be realized, but surely from this very beautiful ceremony the believers of Israel came to understand some of the blessedness that would be theirs in the coming of the true Redeemer. Through faith it was for them a source of comfort and peace.

Finally, the ceremonies of the day were brought to a conclusion when Aaron went again into the tabernacle to wash himself in the Holy Place, to put upon himself another change of garments, and to return to offer the ram as a burnt offering to the Lord. The burnt offering too was a sacrifice of atonement, but it included in it also the aspect of complete dedication to the Lord. Standing at the conclusion of the rituals of that great and significant day, the burnt offering gave expression to the truth that, through the means of the atoning sacrifice, Israel was presented as a nation dedicated and holy unto the Lord.

As the ceremony of the great day of atonement stood at the end of many lengthy commandments concerning sacrifices and the cleansing from sin, it formed the introduction to many laws that were to follow concerning Israel's responsibilities as the people who had been brought into communion with God. The gift of this typical gospel by which the believers in Israel received the promise of complete and perfect redemption was purely of grace, but for them it implied great responsibilities. Through atoning grace, they were the people of God, and to them was the command, "Ye shall be holy: for I the LORD your God am holy" (Lev. 19:2). There followed weeks and months through which the many implications of this were explained. Many religious, civil, and ceremonial laws were given that would guide Israel in her national life so that she might appear as a distinctive nation dedicated to the service of her God.

Among these were many laws that dealt with the relation of the people to their God. Some of them gave specific instructions for the keeping of special festivals and ceremonies through which the nation would conduct its religious worship. Others were enlargements of the first four commandments of the law. The importance of these commandments was brought very forcibly to the fore in the instance of a young man who sinned against the third commandment of the law. The young man was a son born from the marriage of an Israelitish woman to an Egyptian husband. While fighting with a man of Israel, this young man very determinately gave utterance to an angry and blasphemous harangue against the name of Jehovah. The people were shocked with what they heard, and the judges before whom he was brought were at a loss to know what the punishment should be. Finally, the case was brought to Moses, and he in turn laid it before the Lord. In answer the reply was given, "Bring forth him that hath cursed without the camp; and let all that heard him lay their hands upon his head, and let all of the congregation stone him. And thou shalt speak unto the children of Israel, saying, Whosoever curseth his God shall bear his sin" (Lev. 24:14–15). It was a warning to Israel that any purposeful transgression of God's sacred law was a most serious offense, and this principle should be maintained by exacting upon the perpetrator of such the most severe punishment for it. Only in this way would Israel remain a nation holy before the Lord.

There were also many laws given that had to do with the relation of the Israelite to his neighbor. These were, in effect, an enlargement upon the second table of the law. They touched upon many different aspects of human life. Extensive legislation was given concerning the holy institution of marriage. The relationship between man and woman was at all times to be kept clean from adultery and fornication. It was to be characterized by continence and faithfulness, in order that marriage might reflect the relationship of love between the Lord and his church. There were also laws relating to the neighbor in his life and his possessions. The neighbor was at all times to be respected in the position given him by God. No one by his own choosing had any right to harm or terminate the neighbor's life. No one might deal dishonestly so as to infringe upon the neighbor's rights of possession. Such actions were to be punished with severity. The neighbor's very reputation was to be respected in the use of words. Notably these rights extended even to the poor, to slaves, and to strangers. The poor were to be cared for in love. The slaves were to be treated kindly and respected in their rights. All were to be respected as creatures of God. Generally, all of these laws followed the principle so often quoted in the New Testament scriptures: "Thou shalt love thy neighbour as thyself: I am the Lord" (Lev. 19:18).

Finally, God prescribed laws governing the relation of the Israelite to the land. This was in itself a promise, for as yet the nation of Israel had never owned a land that she could call her own. But to them was the promise. As the seed of Abraham, they would inherit the land of Canaan. The laws given to govern the manner in which the land was to be kept held the clear implication that Israel would not be left an outcast and a wanderer. Israel should be prepared to enter into her promise and to treat it as a land held in stewardship for the service of Jehovah God.

"Ye shall be holy: for I the Lord your God am holy" (Lev. 19:2). This was Israel's command. She was a nation that formed the peculiar possession of God. She formed a nation born again unto covenant life in highest liberty before God. It was not a liberty of the flesh to live according to the whims of the sinful flesh. Rather, the flesh in its sin was to be bound, so that wickedness might not bring forth the fruits of confusion and death. The liberty of Israel was a liberty of the heart that lived in peace and love before the blessings of her God.

But Israel as a nation was God's chosen people only in type. There were many in her midst who would not submit to the binding of the flesh. To them the law was but a scourge that drove them deeper into sin. And even for the faithful, the law was only a schoolmaster that taught them of the terribleness of their sins and brought them to cry the louder to God for the full realization of the promise through which the law would be written with love in the heart.

Chapter 32

DEPARTURE FROM SINAI

11. And it came to pass on the twentieth day of the second month, in the second year, that the cloud was taken up from off the tabernacle of the testimony.

12. And the children of Israel took their journeys out of the wilderness of Sinai; and the cloud rested in the wilderness of Paran. (Numbers 10:11–12)

Finally the time had come for Israel to leave the mount of Sinai and to proceed on the way to the promised land. Over one full year had passed since they had left the land of Egypt, and the greater part of that year had been spent encamped at the foot of Sinai. During that time many things had happened to deepen the spiritual understanding of those who held to Jehovah their God with true faith, while, at the same time, many others who had not that faith had been repeatedly offended and made more bold and ready to rebel. In the months to come, it was destined by God to become even more clearly evident that the word of God works both ways to expose the inner secrets of men's hearts, whether they be good or whether they be evil.

Before Israel could proceed on her journey, however, it was necessary that some extensive preparations should be made.

First of these preparations was the numbering of the people. This was more than a mere counting of individuals. It was a census of the adult male members of the nation according to their tribal positions. The total number of such persons was more than 600,000, exclusive of the tribe of Levi, and was arranged in groups of ten, one hundred, and one thousand, as Jethro had suggested. In Israel the tribal family structure of the nation was of utmost importance. In the order of tribes and families, the children of Israel had been called upon to pay the atonement money of the tabernacle. Now, in the same order, the census of the people was taken. It was to be used in arranging the camp of Israel about the tabernacle, to determine their order in travel, and to determine the number and order of the fighting men as they prepared for the conquest of Canaan. But more important than all this was the fact that this family census reminded the Israelites that their place in God's chosen nation was because they were descendants of Abraham, Isaac, and Jacob. Therefore the Lord would dwell in the midst of them, and each family could have its place among the tribes encamped about the tabernacle. And therefore they could go forth to fight in battle without fear, because God would be with them and would give them the promised land. They were the children of God's covenant.

Kept separate from the rest of the tribes in this census was the tribe of Levi. This tribe was set aside and dedicated to the service of God in the tabernacle in the place of the firstborn sons of the nation who were preserved from death by God at the first passover in Egypt. Not only was Levi counted separately in the census, but it was given to dwell closest to the tabernacle, surrounding it on every side. The whole life of this tribe was to be different, for unto Levi was given the exclusive care of the tabernacle and its services. As a tribe it was separated to be holy unto the Lord.

Still a few more things remained to be done. First, the princes of the various tribes brought offerings to the Lord for the service of the tabernacle. Together they offered six wagons, in which the various parts of the tabernacle could be carried on their journey. Individually each prince offered in behalf of his tribe one silver charger, one silver bowl, a golden spoon, and a burnt offering, a sin offering, and a peace offering. Through these offerings they testified of their concern for the services of the tabernacle. Also two silver trumpets were made to be used as signals for the various activities of the nation. The sound of the trumpet throughout scripture is symbolic of the word of God, and so was it also then. Finally, during this time, the first memorial celebration of the passover took place. Already in Egypt God had commanded that the passover should be kept as an annual feast unto the Lord in remembrance of the deliverance that he had wrought. It was fitting that, just as the original passover preceded the departure from Egypt, so the first celebration of it took place just prior to the departure from Sinai. At last the camp of Israel was cleansed and preparations for the journey were made.

It was an excited and eager group of people that once again packed its belongings in preparation for travel. The extended hardships of the wilderness made them ever more appreciative of the promise of God to bring them into the promised land. There they would have prosperity and blessings as never before. Repeatedly eager eyes were cast toward the cloud of Jehovah that hung above the tabernacle. It was that cloud that would show them when the time for journey had really come. In that cloud was the Angel of Jehovah, revealing to them the will of the Lord. As long as it stood above the tabernacle, they were to stay in the camp, but when it lifted and moved before them, the signal for travel would be given. That cloud would guide them upon the proper route through the desert's trackless waste, even as at night it would provide them with light throughout the camp. It was the indisputable proof of the presence of Jehovah in their midst. Because of it their inheritance was sure, and they had nothing to fear. God would surely fulfill all he had promised.

All during the stay at Sinai, Hobab, Jethro's son and Moses' brother-in-law, had made his home in Israel's camp. He had come with his father and had remained after Jethro left. During the stay at Sinai, he had rendered many invaluable services. Familiar with the wilderness in which they were camped, he had been able to show the Israelites the few places in the locality where water and pasture for the cattle could be found. His services had become even more dedicated because there had developed within his heart a true appreciation for the nation of Israel as Jehovah's chosen people. Now, however, as the camp was being taken up, he thought that the time had come for him to return to his home. But with this, Moses disagreed. Not only did he feel that Hobab's services would be needed as they continued their wilderness journey, but he also felt that Hobab had become spiritually one with God's covenant people, and his life in the future should be united with them. Thus Moses said to him, "We are journeying unto the place of which the Lord said, I will give it you: come thou with us, and we will do thee good: for the LORD hath spoken good concerning Israel" (Num. 10:29).

Hobab was hesitant, for he did not feel that he actually belonged to Israel and that their future could be his. He answered Moses, "I will not go; but I will depart to mine own land, and to my kindred" (Num. 10:30).

But Moses was confident. He felt convinced that the spiritual relationship of the heart was stronger than even a direct relationship of blood. Thus he replied again, "Leave us not, I pray thee; forasmuch as thou knowest how we are to encamp in the wilderness, and thou mayest be to us instead of eyes. And it shall be, if thou go with us, yea, it shall be, that what goodness the LORD shall do unto us, the same will we do unto thee" (Num. 10:31–32). Already in the typical times of the old dispensation, it was essentially true that anyone who was dedicated in the service of Jehovah was a true member of God's covenant people, regardless of his blood. Hobab believed this word of Moses, continued on with Israel, and was received as a living member of the covenant.

Early one morning, after all preparations had been completed, the children of Israel arose to see that the cloud of God's presence had lifted and was going before them into the wilderness. Slowly the various tribes arranged themselves in a lengthy column for the march. In the foremost portion, the various parts of the disassembled tabernacle were borne by the children of Levi. There was a new orderliness in their journeying that had not been there before the encampment at Sinai, even as there was a new appreciation in the hearts of the spiritual members of Israel for the grace of God that upheld and guided them as they went. Israel was being prepared more and more as a nation peculiar unto the Lord.

At Sinai the whole national life of Israel had taken on a new ceremonial dimension. All centered in the ark of the covenant, above which the Lord dwelt in the inner sanctuary of the tabernacle. It was this ark that led the children of Israel in their journey, borne upon the shoulders of the Levites. Each morning as the ark was taken up by its bearers, Moses would stand before it and say, "Rise up, LORD, and let thine enemies be scattered; and let them that hate thee flee before thee" (Num. 10:35). In turn, each evening when it was set down, he would say, "Return, O LORD, unto the many thousands of Israel" (v. 36). Israel was never allowed to forget that through the ark Jehovah went forth in their midst.

However, it was not long after Israel had taken up its journey again that the eagerness of the people began to waver and die. Once again they began to taste the rigor of their travels, and they found it hard. And now the terrain was becoming even more rugged than that over which they had passed before. True, there was still ample evidence of God's presence and of his grace that cared for them. The cloud still protected them from the scorching heat of the desert sun. Their clothing and sandals were miraculously preserved from wear and damage. Each day there was ample manna to eat and water to drink. But to all of these things they had become so accustomed that they hardly noticed them anymore. The fact was that their travel was difficult, the way was rough, dreary, and hot. This was that "great and terrible wilderness, wherein were fiery serpents, and scorpions, and drought" (Deut. 8:15). This was fuel to kindle the ire of the chronic complainers in the camp. But a few days had passed before the joyful procession of God's chosen people that had left their camp at Sinai was transformed into a long column of dissident, despondent people. Then, as always, there was a hardened core of rebellious people in Israel who laid hold upon the least opportunity to agitate against the way of the Lord. As so often before, Israel once again revealed itself susceptible to this poison of sin and murmured against her God.

Moses had been informed, however, upon Mt. Sinai that God would no longer bear with such manifestations of sin in silence.

His presence would be a dividing force within the camp, having mercy upon whom he would have mercy but visiting the iniquities of countless others. Now it was becoming evident what this meant, for suddenly the fire of God descended from heaven and began to burn among the people in the outskirts of the camp. It was a divine fire, flashing like lightning and searching out those who were the hardened leaders in this new manifestation of sin. It burned and consumed until the people, humbled in fear, began to cry unto Moses for deliverance. Not until Moses bowed and prayed and interceded for them did that fire of judgment cease to burn and consume among them.

All this was but the beginning of a new phase of Israel's life that would continue on into the future. The presence of God among them was a blessing unto the fulfillment of his covenant unto every true child of Abraham who was elect according to God's promise, but, at the same time, countless numbers in that nation who were Abraham's children only outwardly according to the flesh would be consumed by God's judgment, They were not all Israel that were of Israel; many would perish in God's anger, that the elect might be saved through judgment.

Chapter 33

MOSES' DESPAIR

11. And Moses said unto the Lord...

14. I am not able to bear all this people alone, because it is too
heavy for me. (Numbers 11:11, 14)

With Israel in the wilderness, there was a mixed multitude of
people that had come along from the land of Egypt. They
were not of the seed of Abraham. There is not great certainty as
to what their nationalities actually were. Some may well have been
Egyptians, perhaps mostly of the lower classes. But most of them
were of diverse national backgrounds, slaves that had been bought or
captured by the Egyptians in years gone by. And even as their nationalities were diverse, so were their reasons for going along with Israel.
A few, no doubt, went along because they had heard and believed in
the spiritual heritage of Israel as God's chosen people. Believing in
God, they were attracted to God's people even though outwardly, it
seemed, they could never belong to them. But these were the exception. Most of them saw the exodus of Israel as an opportunity for
themselves also to escape the bondage of the Egyptian taskmasters. In
addition, they saw the hope of also entering into the promised land
of which the Israelites spoke. For merely earthly, material consider-
ations, they followed after Israel, but because of their lack of feeling
for Israel's true status as Jehovah's covenant people, they could never
in any real sense feel themselves one with the nation. They merely
straggled along, more and more withdrawing together into a group
separate from the rest. Especially after a definite order of marching
and camping was instituted at Sinai, they were left to straggle far

beyond and to pitch their tents far out on the outskirts of the camp. Sadly, they discovered that even under the blessings of God, the way of God's people through this world is always hard. Having no inner spiritual strength, they were more miserable than all of the rest.

This mixed multitude of people became a great cause of trouble for Israel as time went on. Their portion of the camp became a breeding place for rebellion. Actually, the lot of these people was greatly improved through their attachment to Israel. No longer were they held in slavery and bondage; they ate also of the manna, and all of their needs were supplied; their human rights and freedom were respected. But it is deeply seated in the nature of man not to be satisfied with life as it is, no matter how good it may be. Only by the influence of the Spirit of God can one resist this, and those people did not have that. No matter in which way the Lord led Israel, there was something about it that was hard, and that for them was ample reason to complain. When camped at Sinai, they had no doubt objected to remaining so long in one place. When Israel moved on again, they complained for the hardness of the way, until the fire of God burned in the outskirts of the camp where their tents were pitched. Often these murmurings spread into Israel proper and instigated major crises in the camp.

Thus, as soon as the fire of judgment was quenched in the wilderness of Paran, these people were ready with still another complaint. For over a year they had eaten little besides the manna furnished each morning by God. It was truly an extraordinary food, wholesome, tasty, and nourishing. Its flavor was mild, so that even when eaten continuously it did not nauseate the stomach, and it could be prepared in various ways. But these people remembered the more exotic foods of Egypt, the fish, cucumbers, melons, leeks, onions, and garlic, and their hearts longed for them with their lusty tangs. Soon the spirit of discontent had spread from the mixed multitude throughout the camp. The people began to imagine all kinds of evil effects that were coming upon them because of the manna. It was not sufficient for their needs, they claimed, and was robbing them of their strength. With tears streaming from their eyes, they turned to Moses and cried, "Who shall give us flesh to eat? We remember the fish, which we did eat in Egypt freely; the cucumbers, and the melons, and the leeks, and the onions, and the garlick: but now our soul is dried away: there is nothing at all, beside this manna, before our eyes" (Num. 11:4–6).

Moses was a man of great spiritual stature and extraordinary patience. Time and again he had borne with Israel in its weakness and pleaded their cause before Jehovah. Even at Sinai, when Israel had sinned its great sin, he had become angered but had remained faithful in his dedication and had interceded on Israel's behalf. From that time on, he had known that Israel would never be free from wickedness, and he could only look forward to repeated evidences of it. But still, though expecting it, he could never be fully prepared. He was only a man, and the time was sure to come when even his patience would reach its end. Now it happened. This was too much. It was not another instance of gross immorality that did it. It was but another case of the perpetual complaining that came so relentlessly upon him. At last his courage broke, and he fell into the black depths of despair. Turning to God, he cried out in plaintive anguish,

11. Wherefore hast thou afflicted thy servant? and wherefore have I not found favour in thy sight, that thou layest the burden of all this people upon me?

12. Have I conceived all this people? have I begotten them, that thou shouldest say unto me, Carry them in thy bosom, as a nursing father beareth the suckling child, unto the land which thou swarest unto their fathers?

13. Whence should I have flesh to give unto all this people? for they weep unto me, saying, Give us flesh, that we may eat.

14. I am not able to bear all this people alone, because it is too heavy for me.

15. And if thou deal thus with me, kill me, I pray thee, out of hand, if I have found favour in thy sight; and let me not see my wretchedness. (Num. 11:11–15)

There was sin in this cry of Moses. He had fallen into the same pit of unfaithfulness that he found so repulsive in the people. And he knew better. How often had he not told the people that the way of the Lord was good and his grace sufficient for all their needs? It was just that he felt so all alone in teaching the people and withstanding their sin. His courage had finally broken, for he was only a man. It was not a time for accusation and admonition. Even as he spoke, Moses knew in his heart that what he did was wrong. He did not have to be reminded. God's answer to him was gentle and kind, filled with divine love.

16. Gather unto me seventy men of the elders of Israel, whom thou knowest to be elders of the people, and officers over them; and bring them unto the tabernacle of the congregation, that they may stand there with thee.

17. And I will come down and talk with thee there: and I will take of the spirit which is upon thee, and will put it upon them; and they shall bear the burden of the people with thee, that thou bear it not thyself alone. (Num. 11:16–17)

It was a remarkable thing that was to happen in Israel. It had always been a rare thing for a man to be blessed with the spirit of prophecy in Israel so as to be able to instruct the people concerning the things of God with authority. In recent years, Moses had been the only one to have been thus enabled. He alone was able to teach the people. But now God promised to give this same spirit to seventy more. With new hope and courage in his heart, Moses went forth to gather the seventy together. He knew his men well, and with little trouble was able to select those who could best help him in his work. As he selected them, he told them to come to the tabernacle, and soon the men were gathered there. There the cloud of God's presence descended, and even as God had said, the spirit of prophecy that had before rested on Moses alone came upon all the rest. It was evident, for, as one by one they spoke, the beauty of God graced their words. It was true of all seventy, save two.

For some unexplained reason, two of the appointed men had not appeared at the tabernacle. Perhaps they were timid or duty detained them in the camp. They were Eldad and Medad. Suddenly there appeared before the tabernacle a young man. He had been with Eldad and Medad, and they too had begun to prophesy even where they were. Joshua, on hearing this, was deeply concerned lest these men should be usurping a privilege that had always belonged to Moses alone. In agitation he cried, "My lord Moses, forbid them" (Num. 11:28).

The answer of Moses ranks as one of the greatest manifestations of spiritual life found in scripture: "Enviest thou for my sake? would God that all the LORD's people were prophets, and that the LORD would put his spirit upon them!" (Num. 11:29). It is like the wonderful confession of Paul to the Philippians: "Notwithstanding, every way, whether in pretence, or in truth, Christ is preached; and I therein do rejoice, yea, and will rejoice" (Phil. 1:18). Even more, it is like the answer of Jesus to John, who forbade a man who did not follow with them from casting out devils in Jesus' name. Jesus' answer was, "Forbid him not: for he that is not against us is for us" (Luke 9:50). It is a mark of true, godly love when a person with a great spiritual blessing similar to one's own is looked upon not as a competitor but as an occasion for great joy because he serves to the advancement of God's kingdom. Would that all of God's people could feel that love.

But that was not all that God said to Moses. He spoke also concerning the sin of the people:

18. And say thou unto the people, Sanctify yourselves against to morrow, and ye shall eat flesh: for ye have wept in the ears of the LORD, saying, Who shall give us flesh to eat? for it was well with us in Egypt: therefore the LORD will give you flesh, and ye shall eat.

19. Ye shall not eat one day, nor two days, nor five days, neither ten days, nor twenty days;

20. But even a whole month, until it come out at your nostrils, and it be loathsome unto you: because that ye have

despised the LORD which is among you, and have wept
before him, saying, Why came we forth out of Egypt?
(Num. 11:18–20)

To Moses such provision seemed impossible, so he replied, "The
people, among whom I am, are six hundred thousand footmen; and
thou hast said, I will give them flesh, that they may eat a whole
month. Shall the flocks and the herds be slain for them, to suffice
them? or shall all the fish of the sea be gathered together for them, to
suffice them?" (Num. 11:21–22).

But why should Moses doubt? As God answered him, "Is the
LORD's hand waxed short? thou shalt see now whether my word shall
come to pass unto thee or not" (Num. 11:23).

Soon there sprang up a strong wind, and a dark cloud appeared
on the horizon. It was a cloud of quails that then settled on the
ground for miles around the camp. For a day and a half, the people
went out to gather great piles of birds to be dried in the sun for the
meat that they desired. And then the manna stopped for thirty days.
The people had nothing but meat to eat, just as they had wanted.
But this food was not suited for a steady diet. Before long it began to
nauseate their stomachs. And they suffered, besides, more than just
the natural results of their own folly. God in his anger struck out at
the camp with a great plague. Soon many became violently sick and
countless died, especially of those who had been the leaders in the
murmuring rebellion. With one swift stroke the Lord had revealed to
them the wickedness and folly of their sin. He made them to suffer
by giving to them that which they in their own carnal wisdom had
desired; and he revealed to them once more that through judgment
he would divide them, by having mercy upon whom he would have
mercy and by visiting the iniquity of countless others upon them.

"And he called the name of that place Kibroth-hattaavah [the
graves of lust]: because there they buried the people that lusted"
(Num. 11:34).

Chapter 34

JEALOUSY OF MIRIAM AND AARON

And Miriam and Aaron spake against Moses because of the Ethiopian woman whom he had married: for he had married an Ethiopian woman. (Numbers 12:1)

It is a very brief insight that the scriptures give into Moses' personal life when they inform us that he "had married an Ethiopian woman" (Num. 12:1); but the implications of it are of considerable interest.

We know that, sometime after fleeing from Pharaoh, Moses was first married in Midian to Zipporah, Jethro's daughter. Although we perhaps have no reason to doubt that she, like her father, worshiped the true God, it appears that in all respects the marriage was not completely successful. It evidently was impossible for her to understand why the nation of Israel should be considered the peculiar people of God in distinction from all others. Because of this, she was not able to uphold and strengthen her husband in his work, but in fact often opposed him. When he was called by God to return to Egypt and his people, she went along only reluctantly. When God met them on the way with the demand that their children should be circumcised, she agreed to do it only after God threatened her husband with death—and even then she could not refrain from giving utterance to bitter complaints. With this it became evident to Moses that, if Zipporah went along with him to Egypt, she would be more of a hindrance to him in his work than an aid. As a matter of discretion, Moses returned her with the children to the care of her father to wait for him until the deliverance from Egypt had been completed.

It was after the deliverance from Egypt, as Israel was approaching

Mt. Sinai, that Jethro came to bring Zipporah and the children back to Moses. Beyond that, we read nothing more of her. She made no significant contribution to her husband's work as leader to the children of Israel. Zipporah never came to understand the deep spiritual nature of her husband's work and was never one with whom he could consult or share his problems. For this he looked to his brother and sister, Aaron and Miriam, who were well able to strengthen and encourage him because both were blessed with a special measure of the Spirit of God, Miriam as a prophetess and Aaron as God's high priest elect. This continued until Zipporah died, perhaps during the encampment at Sinai. It was soon after Israel had resumed its journey that Moses married again, this time to an Ethiopian woman.

We have noted in the past that there was a mixed multitude of people that followed Israel out of Egypt. These were people of many different nationalities who, like the Israelites, had been oppressed by the tyrannical Egyptians. Many if not most of them were opportunists, who thought that in following the Israelites they could greatly improve their own status in life. Being purely carnal in their goals, they were an endless cause of trouble to God's people. Nonetheless, there were also others, people who had come to see and believe in the greatness and wonder of Israel's God. To them nothing was more important than to live in as close a contact as possible to the people that belonged to that God. They were themselves children of God at heart, and their presence was a blessing and source of strength to the children of Israel. Surely it was to this group that the Ethiopian woman belonged.

In this marriage Moses found for himself a helpmeet and companion such as he had never had in Zipporah. The Ethiopian woman possessed an understanding of and appreciation for the distinctive position and calling of Israel that was far greater than that of many actual Israelites. With her Moses could speak freely of the many problems and burdens that rested upon his heart, and she would understand. Her presence was for Moses a constant source of encouragement and strength. It meant, however, that Moses no longer felt the need for the companionship of Aaron and Miriam as he had before. Soon he was making many decisions by himself concerning which formerly he would have consulted them. This was hardly to their liking. They had come to assume it to be their prerogative to advise Moses in the affairs of the nations. Now they felt that their rightful position had been usurped by another. Especially Miriam began soon to assume a very invidious attitude toward Moses' wife. With the backing of Aaron, she voiced her complaint.

It seemed almost, however, that Miriam had a point that was valid, at least enough so for her to convince herself that the cause that she upheld was really righteous. This Ethiopian woman was not, after all, a descendant of Abraham. In fact, she was not even of Shem, but of the family of Gush, the son of Ham. It had been Abraham's children alone that had been separated as the people of God and had been commanded to keep themselves separate and distinct. Already Abraham had commanded that his son should never marry a woman of the Canaanitish race. Could it possibly be right, then, for Moses to marry a woman of a foreign race? Was he not guilty of ignoring the commandment of God and of corrupting Abraham's seed?

But in this there was one thing that Miriam forgot. The separation of God's chosen people was essentially a spiritual distinction and not racial. It was true that, in a typical sense, God had separated Abraham's descendants as a peculiar nation; but this typical distinction was subject to and for the service of a much more important spiritual distinction, for the service of those who were truly the children of God in their hearts. Thus those who continued in wickedness among them were commanded to be cut off from the nation even if they were descendants of Abraham after the flesh, while allowance was made that those of the Gentiles who believed in God could easily be taken in. This was well understood throughout the greater part of the old dispensation. Already Abraham had been commanded to circumcise his servants, regardless of their racial background. When the passover was instituted, allowance was made for the stranger also to partake of it if he believed and was circumcised. In later years,

Rahab and Ruth were taken readily into the nation, because it had become perfectly evident that they believed in God. And undoubtedly there were many others. It was not until many years later, when the hypocritical pride of the Pharisees gained power, that it became a very hard and difficult thing for a believing Gentile to be united with their nation. But Miriam anticipated their prejudices, not for spiritual reasons as she liked to think, but to excuse a personal jealousy that had arisen in her own soul.

Moreover, Miriam was not one to stop with just a bitter attack upon Moses' marriage. She knew that Moses, having taken the Ethiopian woman to wife, was not apt to put her away. And because of that woman, she and Aaron had lost a position of great influence in Israel. Miriam wanted that restored. Soon her bitterness led her on to a more serious attack. It was her claim that, after all, Moses did not even have the right to assume the leadership of Israel alone. She was a prophetess in Israel, and Aaron was the high priest. Did not that give them a right to have a part in the important decisions concerning the nation? When Moses failed to consult them, was he not doing wrong? Rallying Aaron to the cause, she stood up with him to express her thoughts. "Hath the LORD indeed spoken only by Moses? hath he not spoken also by us?" (Num. 12:2).

We read at this point in scripture, "Now the man Moses was very meek, above all the men which were upon the face of the earth" (Num. 12:3). The purpose is to give us a feeling for the reaction of Moses to this attack. Through his intimate communion with God, Moses had become very bold in opposing that which was evil and in upholding that which was good; but at the same time he had become ever more conscious of his own personal limitations and sin. He was very conscious of his own inability to lead the children of Israel by himself, and it was far from him to deprecate in any way the gifts of others. Now that a personal attack had been made against his ability and right to lead the nation by himself, and coming from those whom he loved so dearly and whose gifts he appreciated so much, it was more than he could do to answer. Had it been an attack directly against God, coming even from Miriam and Aaron, he would have denounced it. But being directed so personally against him, he was silent.

But the Lord in heaven also heard Miriam and Aaron's accusation, and he did not hesitate to give answer. He came directly to Moses and Aaron and Miriam and said, "Come out ye three unto the tabernacle of the congregation" (Num. 12:4).

No doubt the situation had quickly become more serious than Aaron or Miriam had anticipated. Soon they found themselves standing at the door of God's tabernacle with the cloud of God's holy presence hovering before their faces. It was a fearful sight to behold, and then the voice of God was heard.

6. Hear now my words: If there be a prophet among you, I the LORD will make myself known unto him in a vision, and will speak unto him in a dream.
7. My servant Moses is not so, who is faithful in all mine house.
8. With him will I speak mouth to mouth, even apparently, and not in dark speeches; and the similitude of the LORD shall he behold: wherefore then were ye not afraid to speak against my servant Moses? (Num. 12:6–8)

No, God did not deny that he had given his Spirit also to Miriam and Aaron and had revealed through them his word and will. But at no time did that give them the right to presume to be equal to Moses. Moses had been appointed to be God's typical deliverer and mediator in Israel and had been honored by God with most intimate communion. In speaking against Moses, their attack was upon God.

It was then that a most fearful thing happened. The cloud of God's presence withdrew away from the tabernacle and without the camp. The anger of the Lord was kindled. Aaron and Miriam had corrupted not just themselves, but also the nation to which they belonged. God would not dwell with Israel as long as such corruption remained in the camp. When Aaron turned to look at Miriam, he saw the reason even more clearly: Miriam had become leprous, white as snow. The law had clearly stipulated that leprosy was a sign of moral corruption. Those afflicted with it must be driven out of the camp.

Suddenly Aaron realized the magnitude of the sin in which they had engaged. Miriam had led the way, but he had consented to follow. Now he saw the results clearly demonstrated before his eyes, and Miriam felt it on her own body. Turning to Moses, Aaron pleaded in her behalf, "Alas, my lord, I beseech thee, lay not the sin upon us, wherein we have done foolishly, and wherein we have sinned. Let her not be as one dead, of whom the flesh is half consumed when he cometh out of his mother's womb" (Num. 12:11–12).

Now the true excellence of Moses' office came into clear relief. He was Israel's typical mediator, and it was he that prayed for the sister who had rebelled against him, "Heal her now, O God, I beseech thee" (Num. 12:13).

To this prayer God listened, and Miriam was healed, but not without qualifications. The Lord said to Moses, "If her father had but spit in her face, should she not be ashamed seven days? let her be shut out from the camp seven days, and after that let her be received in again" (Num. 12:14).

For seven days Miriam sat alone without the camp contemplating the shame that she had brought upon herself. And for seven days Israel remained, without continuing its journey, to contemplate the seriousness of rebellion against the servant who was appointed by God.

Chapter 35

EVIL REPORT OF TEN SPIES

20. And I said unto you, Ye are come unto the mountain of the Amorites, which the LORD our God doth give unto us.
21. Behold, the LORD thy God hath set the land before thee: go up and possess it, as the LORD God of thy fathers hath said unto thee; fear not, neither be discouraged.
22. And ye came near unto me every one of you, and said, We will send men before us, and they shall search us out the land, and bring us word again by what way we must go up, and into what cities we shall come. (Deuteronomy 1:20–22)

At last, well over one year after leaving the land of Egypt, the children of Israel approached the borders of Canaan. Coming from the south, they found no barriers between them and the promised land. Moses stood before them and said, "Ye are come unto the mountain of the Amorites, which the LORD our God doth give unto us. Behold, the LORD thy God hath set the land before thee: go up and possess it, as the LORD God of thy fathers hath said unto thee; fear not, neither be discouraged" (Deut. 1:20–21).

The people, however, were not so sure. They held within themselves an underlying skepticism concerning the ways of the Lord. They were not at all sure that the promised land was as rich and good as God had said it was. Neither were they so sure that they would be able to capture the land, even with the help of God. The trouble was that they held deep within them a gnawing desire that God should be found to be wrong. This had been developing throughout the wilderness journey. Time and again they had passed through critical junctures where Jehovah had been vindicated at their expense. Now

they were suffering from a badly wounded pride. It had come to the
point where no price seemed too great if only they could vindicate
themselves at the expense of God. They longed to be able to say
that God was wrong and they were right. It was their bitterly sinful
human nature that wanted the will of God to prove itself of none
effect. Surely, this was not all clearly defined in their own minds. If
accused of it, they would have denied it. In fact, there were some in
Israel that felt this only vaguely and in conflict with the pure desires
of their sanctified hearts. Still, there were only too many in Israel
who held this as the basic motivation of their lives. They were reprobate people who hated God more than anything else. Still, even they
were careful not to expose themselves openly. They came to Moses
with what might well have appeared to be an innocent suggestion.
"We will send men before us, and they shall search us out the land,
and bring us word again by what way we must go up, and into what
cities we shall come" (Deut. 1:22).

For Moses, the true reason for this request was inconceivable.
Filled as he was with the love of God, he could not imagine such
wickedness in his brethren who had seen so much of the greatness of
God. The worst that he could suspect was that they were timid and
afraid because of the uncertainty of the way that lay before them.
For the relieving of such fear, the suggestion of the people appeared
good. He had no doubt that such a scouting expedition would find
the land to be fully as rich and good as God had promised. Neither
could he conceive it possible that the people should doubt the ability
of their God to overcome all resistance, no matter how great, when
they had witnessed and experienced so many of his marvelous works.
And it would be to their advantage to know the lay of the land into
which they were going and the nature of its fortifications. He was
more than willing to comply with this apparently innocent request.

Nevertheless, Moses was careful. He went to the Lord and presented the suggestion of the people to him. God, indeed, knew the
motivations that were behind it, but he was also willing that the

true sinfulness of the people should be exposed. He answered Moses, "Send thou men, that they may search the land of Canaan, which I give unto the children of Israel: of every tribe of their fathers shall ye send a man, every one a ruler among them" (Num. 13:2).

Soon Moses was making the appointments. Of every tribe he took a responsible leader whose opinion would be respected by the people. His instructions for them were very specific.

17. Get you up this way southward, and go up into the mountain:
18. And see the land, what it is, and the people that dwelleth therein, whether they be strong or weak, few or many;
19. And what the land is that they dwell in, whether it be good or bad; and what cities they be that they dwell in, whether in tents, or in strong holds;
20. And what the land is, whether it be fat or lean, whether there be wood therein, or not. And be ye of good courage, and bring of the fruit of the land. (Num. 13:17–20)

The duty of the twelve was to bring an objective report of what they found in the land, nothing more and nothing less.

With their duties clearly spelled out, the twelve appointed spies left the camp of Israel. They followed their instructions carefully, traveling the length and breadth of the land, observing the people and their homes, the cities and their fortifications, the land and its fertility. What they saw far exceeded their greatest anticipation both as to the fertility of the land and as to the strength of the people. As required, they noted the strongholds of the country and gathered the choice of its fruits, even when one cluster of grapes required two men to carry it on a pole between them. Finally, after forty days, they returned to give their report to Moses, to Aaron, and to the people. With the fruits of the land spread out before them—grapes, pomegranates, and figs—they gave their report:

27. We came unto the land whither thou sentest us, and surely it floweth with milk and honey; and this is the fruit of it.

28. Nevertheless the people be strong that dwell in the land, and the cities are walled, and very great: and moreover we saw the children of Anak there.

29. The Amalekites dwell in the land of the south: and the Hittites, and the Jebusites, and the Amorites, dwell in the mountains: and the Canaanites dwell by the sea, and by the coast of Jordan. (Num. 13:27–29)

To all appearances the report given by the spies was an objective report such as Moses had commanded them to give. Nevertheless, there was a very subtle argument implied in the manner in which the report was given, and it was well adapted to impress the prejudices of the speakers upon the people who listened. They began by reporting on the fertility of the land. Without attempting to hide the truth, they reported as though to confirm the veracity of the promises of God. It was indeed a land flowing with milk and honey. But soon they passed on from this to add a "nevertheless...moreover...and..." argument. Point was heaped upon point stressing the fearful strength of the country. The people were strong; the cities were fortified and great; many fearful nations were there to defend it all. The report had its desired effect. Vivid imaginations conjured before the minds of the people visions more terrible than even the report of the spies warranted. The courage of the people melted, and a restless, troubled spirit spread through the camp. The conviction was set that Canaan was after all only an impossible dream.

It was Caleb, himself one of the spies, who first caught the implication of the report that their spokesman was giving. He saw that the report was being adapted, not to confirm the truthfulness of their God, but to carry the thoughts of the people away from him so as to make them tremble before the greatness of the enemies. It was an evil report that was being given, designed to stir up the people in rebellion. Courageously he spoke up to contradict the implication of the report as it had been given. "Let us go up at once, and possess it; for we are well able to overcome it" (Num. 13:30).

For a moment it almost seemed as though the move of Caleb

would be successful. It was the first definite statement of advice that came from any of the spies, and the people listened. For a short time a quieter attitude appeared to have settled upon the people. But it was then that the true motivation of the majority of the spies revealed itself. They were satisfied to state their point by mere subtle implications as long as no one opposed them; but as soon as Caleb spoke up, they cast all subtlety aside and spoke out directly. "We be not able to go up against the people," they vehemently responded, "for they are stronger than we" (Num. 13:31). So determined were they to gain their point that truth was no longer of any great concern. With determined exaggeration they began to add new and almost-unreasonable slants to their report. "The land through which we have gone to search it, is a land that eateth up the inhabitants thereof; and all the people that we saw in it are men of a great stature. And there we saw the giants, the sons of Anak, which come of the giants: and we were in our own sight as grasshoppers, and so we were in their sight" (vv. 32–33). Under their imaginings the land began to appear in the minds of the people with a ferocity unheard of and unimagined.

With this, all semblance of calm and reasonable thinking was disrupted. As usual, the people were much more impressed by the wild, fanatic predictions of wicked men than by the positive exhortations of faith. Soon wild sobbing and weeping was to be heard throughout the camp. A confused uproar broke forth on every side. Strong condemnatory invectives were to be heard on every side, denouncing Moses and Aaron and even Jehovah their God. Exclamations of evil were to be heard on every side. Here one cried, with strained reasoning, "Would God that we had died in the land of Egypt!" Another added, "Or would God we had died in the wilderness!" (Num. 14:2). Another asked, "And wherefore hath the LORD brought us unto this land, to fall by the sword, that our wives and our children should be a prey? were it not better for us to return into Egypt?" (v. 3). A fourth gave answer, "Because the LORD hated us, he hath brought us forth out of the land of Egypt, to deliver us into the hand of the Amorites, to destroy us" (Deut. 1:27). On every side was to be heard the despairing cry, "Whither shall we go up? our brethren have discouraged our heart, saying, The people is greater and taller than we; the cities are great and walled up to heaven; and moreover we have seen the sons of the Anakims there" (v. 28).

Vainly Joshua and Caleb circulated among the people, trying to calm their fears. Their argument was sound,

7. The land, which we passed through to search it, is an exceeding good land.
8. If the LORD delight in us, then he will bring us into this land, and give it us; a land which floweth with milk and honey.
9. Only rebel not ye against the LORD, neither fear ye the people of the land; for they are bread for us; their defence is departed from them, and the LORD is with us: fear them not. (Num. 14:7–9)

But this was not what the people wanted to hear. They found a strange delight in the bitter cry of rebellion. In their hearts they felt sure that this time the Lord had been proved wrong, and they liked it. The answer of the people was that Joshua and Caleb should be stoned.

Within the hearts of the people there had emerged a new plan. They said to each other, "Let us make a captain, and let us return into Egypt" (Num. 14:4). They wanted to be free from the way of the Lord. The promise of that was sweeter to them than the fertility of the land before which they stood.

And from heaven the Lord God heard the wickedness of the people and was wroth.

Chapter 36

ISRAEL'S REBELLION AND
THE KINDLING OF GOD'S WRATH

20. And the LORD said, I have pardoned according to thy word:
21. But as truly as I live, all the earth shall be filled with the glory of the LORD.
22. Because all those men which have seen my glory, and my miracles, which I did in Egypt and in the wilderness, and have tempted me now these ten times, and have not hearkened to my voice;
23. Surely they shall not see the land which I sware unto their fathers, neither shall any of them that provoked me see it. (Numbers 14:20–23)

It was a troubled spirit that moved through the camp of Israel. God had brought them to what appeared to be an utterly impossible situation. Spies had been sent to find out what the land of Canaan was like, and, upon returning, the great majority of them had agreed that the land was impossible to conquer. Only two out of the twelve had felt that they could take the land, and that was merely on the basis of a faith that Jehovah could do what was apparently impossible to them. Once the people saw what stood before them, a cry of anguish went up from their lips. Agitation moved in waves throughout the nation. A movement quickly gathered strength to do away with Moses and Aaron and to return en masse to the land of Egypt. Openly the people wept, but inwardly they were really pleased. This was exactly what they wanted. So often they had been proved wrong by Jehovah, and now the tables were turned. Now it seemed quite evident that Jehovah was in the wrong. His promises to them could not be kept. That was a soothing balm to their wounded pride. It gave added strength to the volume of their complaints. The more Moses and Aaron and Joshua and Caleb circulated through the camp telling them not to rebel, the louder their cries of anguish became. They had a good case, they thought, and they were not going to let it rest. Boldly they picked up stones and told them to be silent or suffer death.

And then God came. His glory shone in all of its holy brilliance before the tabernacle, and a hushed silence settled over the camp. This the people had not expected. Somehow they had felt that in the difficulty of the situation he would not dare to appear. Or, if he did, that it would be to beg and to plead that they would help him along in this time of trouble. But now they gazed upon the full glory of God as so often before. They never could get used to that glory. Before it they trembled, in spite of all they had said.

Once again the drama of God's righteousness was repeating itself. His wrath was kindled and would not be silent. When Moses appeared before him, God spoke, "How long will this people provoke me? and how long will it be ere they believe me, for all the signs which I have shewed among them? I will smite them with the pestilence, and disinherit them, and will make of thee a greater nation and mightier than they" (Num. 14:11–12).

Just as before at Mt. Horeb, Moses found himself standing in the position of a mediator between Israel and God's holy wrath, a type of the true Mediator to come. The people had sinned a great sin; and if he would stand aside, the justice of God would consume them in a moment. The seriousness of the situation brought from within him the deepest love that he felt. Nothing could detract him from it, not even the possibility of highest exaltation for him and his own children. Only one thing finally mattered to Moses, and that, he quickly expressed.

13. Then the Egyptians shall hear it, (for thou broughtest up this people in thy might from among them;)
14. And they will tell it to the inhabitants of this land: for they have heard that thou LORD art among this people, that

thou LORD art seen face to face, and that thy cloud stan-
deth over them, and that thou goest before them, by day in
a pillar of a cloud, and in a pillar of fire by night.

15. Now if thou wilt kill all this people as one man, then the
nations which have heard the fame of thee will speak, saying,

16. Because the LORD was not able to bring this people into
the land which he sware unto them, therefore he hath slain
them in the wilderness.

17. And now, I beseech thee, let the power of my LORD be
great, according as thou hast spoken, saying,

18. The LORD is longsuffering, and of great mercy, forgiving
iniquity and transgression, and by no means clearing the
guilty, visiting the iniquity of the fathers upon the children
unto the third and fourth generation.

19. Pardon, I beseech thee, the iniquity of this people according
unto the greatness of thy mercy, and as thou hast forgiven
this people, from Egypt even until now. (Num. 14:13–19)

This was the deepest love of Moses' heart. It was true that he loved
Israel, the people that he led. It was true that he loved the promise of
God to bring them into Canaan land. But more than anything else,
he loved his God and was jealous for the glory of God's name. He
desired with all his heart that the goodness of God should be revealed
and maintained unto the ends of the earth. For this he first pleaded,
and from this derived all the rest. There was nothing on Israel's part
that could be pleaded as an excuse for what they did. There was no
virtue on Israel's part that warranted that their sin should be overlooked. There was only one thing that demanded Israel's preservation.
God had promised forgiveness and redemption, and for his name's
sake Moses pleaded, "Pardon, I beseech thee, the iniquity of this people according unto the greatness of thy mercy" (Num.14:19).

The intercession of Moses was good and in accord with God's
own purpose. The answer God gave to Moses immediately: "I have
pardoned according to thy word" (14:20). But there was also more
that had to be considered for the glory of his name. As he had also

said on Horeb's mountain, he could not allow sin to go unpunished. His justice also had to be maintained. Thus he went on to add,

21. But as truly as I live, all the earth shall be filled with the glory of the LORD.
22. Because all those men which have seen my glory, and my miracles, which I did in Egypt and in the wilderness, and have tempted me now these ten times, and have not hearkened to my voice;
23. Surely they shall not see the land which I sware unto their fathers, neither shall any of them that provoked me see it:
24. But my servant Caleb, because he had another spirit with him, and hath followed me fully, him will I bring into the land whereinto he went; and his seed shall possess it.
25. …Tomorrow turn you, and get you into the wilderness by the way of the Red sea.

27. How long shall I bear with this evil congregation, which murmur against me? I have heard the murmurings of the children of Israel, which they murmur against me.
28. Say unto them, As truly as I live, saith the LORD, as ye have spoken in mine ears, so will I do to you:
29. Your carcasses shall fall in this wilderness; and all that were numbered of you, according to your whole number, from twenty years old and upward, which have murmured against me,
30. Doubtless ye shall not come into the land, concerning which I sware to make you dwell therein, save Caleb the son of Jephunneh, and Joshua the son of Nun.
31. But your little ones, which ye said should be a prey, them will I bring in, and they shall know the land which ye have despised.
32. But as for you, your carcases, they shall fall in this wilderness.
33. And your children shall wander in the wilderness forty years, and bear you whoredoms, until your carcases be wasted in the wilderness.
34. After the number of days in which ye searched the land, even forty days, each day for a year, shall ye bear your iniquities, even forty years, and ye shall know my breach of promise.

35. I the LORD have said, I will surely do it unto all this evil congregation, that are gathered together against me: in this wilderness they shall be consumed, and there they shall die. (Num. 14:21–25, 27–35)

The history of Israel had come to a very critical juncture. Ten times the people had rebelled against their God, and ten in the Old Testament typical language was the number of completeness. Theirs was a complete rebellion. And over against them God would maintain his glory. In faithfulness to his promises, he would pardon and save the nation. But he would also be faithful to his justice. No one would be allowed to think that God overlooked Israel's sin and allowed it to go unpunished. Those who had sinned this great sin would not be allowed to enter the rest of the promised land. For many this would be a judgment. They were inwardly enemies of God and, wandering in the wilderness, would die in their sins. For some who had joined this rebellion against their better judgment, it would be a chastisement to remind them of their unworthiness and turn them in repentance to God. Forty years Israel must wander in the wilderness and only the few faithful, such as Joshua and Caleb, would be preserved to enter the promised land.

The true depth of Israel's iniquity came to light when Moses informed the people of this which the Lord had said. A deep mourning fell over the camp, but it was not a mourning of repentance. As long as the opportunity was there for them to enter the land, they found a certain pleasure in refusing to go. Now that the way was closed, they wanted the land as never before. Their mourning was that of a people who felt themselves greatly misused. This was their trouble all along. They just did not want the way of Lord. What the Lord commanded they did not want, because the Lord had commanded it, and for no other reason. All of their heated reasoning was but a making of excuses to justify the basic wickedness of their hearts.

Suddenly the feelings of the camp took an entirely different tack. Those who before had been so determined to appoint a new leader and return to Egypt now exclaimed that they had to enter the land of Canaan and that they had to do it right away. With God they would not go near the land, but without him they felt no restraint. Even more, they would do so under the pretense of religious dedication. Like a wave they began to move, all the time muttering the cry, "Lo, we be here, and will go up unto the place which the LORD hath promised: for we have sinned" (Num. 14:40).

Aghast at their inconsistent folly, Moses tried vainly to stop them.

41. Wherefore now do ye transgress the commandment of the LORD? but it shall not prosper.
42. Go not up, for the LORD is not among you; that ye be not smitten before your enemies.
43. For the Amalekites and the Canaanites are there before you, and ye shall fall by the sword: because ye are turned away from the LORD, therefore the LORD will not be with you. (Num. 14:41–43)

It was a pitiful sight. Without order, without preparation, and without plan, the children of Israel moved en masse toward the strongly fortified borders of Canaan. But what was far more serious, they went without their God. It was but a small group of faithful that remained behind with the ark of God, looking on in anguished horror at the mass of Israel's fighting men rushing toward Canaan as cattle to the slaughter. And then from the hills came the Amalekites and the Canaanites. Strong, hardened warriors, they swept through the host of Israel as a tide of death. In what seemed but a matter of moments, the great nation of Israel was scattered. As the spies had reported, from a human point of view the strength of Canaan formed an impenetrable barrier. Without faith in their God, Israel before them was as nothing. The people fled for their lives unto Hormah.

Forty years the children of Israel were given to wander in the wilderness and contemplate their presumptions and folly. They had yet to learn that without their God they were as good as dead.

Chapter 37

REBELLION OF KORAH, DATHAN, AND ABIRAM

1. Now Korah… and Dathan and Abiram…
2. …rose up before Moses, with certain of the children of Israel…
3. And they gathered themselves together against Moses and against Aaron, and said unto them, Ye take too much upon you, seeing all the congregation are holy, every one of them, and the LORD is among them: wherefore then lift ye up yourselves above the congregation of the LORD? (Numbers 16:1–3)

During the wilderness journey, there were many in Israel who were children of God in name but not at heart. This became ever increasingly evident. Through the months and years the great and marvelous works of God were multiplied one upon the other. In fact, the very continued existence of such a great nation in that arid, barren land was an astounding miracle in itself. But this did not mean that the respect and gratitude of the people increased accordingly. Rather it was their indifference, discontent, and rebellion that increased. In Israel there was a hardened core of reprobate men, and this was the natural reaction of their hearts to the greater revelations of the Lord.

It was not long after Israel was turned back from the borders of Canaan that another rebellion arose in the camp. Four of Israel's malcontents had found sympathy in each other for their mutual complaint. They were Korah, Dathan, Abiram, and On. Together they were agreed that they had good reason to complain, for they felt that they had not received the positions and recognition in Israel that they deserved. The most outspoken and the leader of them was Korah, a Levite of the family of Kohath. As such he took part in some of the most important functions of the tabernacle. It was an important position in itself. But, as is so often the case, a little taste of honor begat the desire for more. He looked upon Moses and Aaron and could see no reason why their still higher positions should not be his. And the feeling of Dathan, Abiram, and On was much the same. They were of the tribe of Reuben. They could not forget that Reuben had been the oldest son of Jacob, and they thought it quite unjust that the highest positions in the nation had been given to Levi.

Sharing their dissatisfaction together, the four men soon became very bitter. Neither did they find it difficult to kindle the same feeling in others. No less than 250 of the princes of the nation were soon gathered to their cause. It was the working of sinful pride. Men never find it difficult to feel bitterly discontented with the place that the Lord had given them. A little taste of glory so easily whets the appetite for more and produces a bitter discontent when it is not immediately obtained. On this the devil thrives. Of these men it appears that only On came to an understanding of the wickedness of their movement and forsook it in repentance.

These men, each prompted by his own personal ambitions, were united in one primary goal. They had to remove Moses and Aaron from their positions of political and religious authority. Moreover, their attempt to do this had to be more than just a personal attack. Israel was a religious nation, and any action of such great importance would have to have a religious justification. And for men as determined as they were, this was not hard to find. They lay hold upon the promise of God given at Mt. Sinai, "And ye shall be unto me a kingdom of priests, and an holy nation" (Ex. 19:6). Their reasoning was simple. Because all of God's people were priests, it was presumptuous for Moses and Aaron to set themselves above the rest. It was an implied denial of the word of God. What these men failed to consider was not only that Moses served as mediator between Israel and God upon the people's own request, but even more that both Moses and Aaron were appointed to their positions by the same God who had spoken this promise. But the men were not interested in understanding the will of God; they wanted only to justify their own sinful desires. Thus they came to Moses and Aaron and laid down their accusation: "Ye take too much upon you, seeing all the congregation are holy, every one of them, and the Lord is among them: wherefore then lift ye up yourselves above the congregation of the Lord?" (Num. 16:3).

Moses had learned through long experience how to cope with rebellious people. He knew better than to answer them in a heat of anger or to engage them in an extended debate. First he bowed before the Lord in prayer, and then he rose to answer Korah and his company.

5. Even to morrow the Lord will shew who are his, and who is holy; and will cause him to come near unto him: even him whom he hath chosen will he cause to come near unto him.
6. This do; Take you censers, Korah, and all his company;
7. And put fire therein, and put incense in them before the Lord to morrow: and it shall be that the man whom the Lord doth choose, he shall be holy: ye take too much upon you, ye sons of Levi. (Num. 16:5–7)

With this, Moses put them to the test. If it were true that all the people were holy without exception and regardless of their spiritual attitude of the heart, and if it were so that such an innate holiness of the people held precedence over all of the rest of the word of God, then all had a perfect right to take the holy censers of the priest and stand before the face of God. But if this were not true, their action would be a terrible presumption that would surely bring down upon them the wrath of God. Through this test it would be made known who were truly holy before the Lord. But Moses warned them, "Ye take too much upon you."

Neither did Moses allow his warning to rest with that. He separated out the leaders of the movement according to their individual responsibility and warned them personally. First he spoke to Korah, who as a Levite already served in the tabernacle of God and therefore had the best reason to understand the seriousness of their claim. He warned him,

9. Seemeth it but a small thing unto you, that the God of Israel hath separated you from the congregation of Israel, to bring you near to himself to do the service of the tabernacle of the LORD, and to stand before the congregation to minister unto them?

10. And he hath brought thee near to him, and all thy brethren the sons of Levi with thee: and seek ye the priesthood also?

11. For which cause both thou and all thy company are gathered together against the LORD: and what is Aaron, that ye murmur against him? (Num. 16:9–11)

But Korah was determined and would not listen.

Next Moses sent for Dathan and Abiram, who were Reubenites, and whose sin therefore was of a different motive. But the men felt their inability to defend themselves before Moses and sent the answer back,

4. We will not come up:

5. Is it a small thing that thou hast brought us up out of a land that floweth with milk and honey, to kill us in the wilderness, except thou make thyself altogether a prince over us?

6. Moreover thou hast not brought us into a land that floweth with milk and honey, or given us inheritance of fields and vineyards: wilt thou put out the eyes of these men? we will not come up. (Num. 16:12–14)

Not knowing how to defend their new claim, they fell back upon all of the old, personal accusations against Moses: in taking them from Egypt he had taken them from a good land; for the sake of his own glory he was willing to sacrifice the lives of the people; he had not and never would bring them into the promised land; and with his words he only blinded the eyes of the people, and therefore they would not come to talk to him personally. Dathan and Abiram had set for themselves a goal of sin, and they would give no one the opportunity to try to deter them from it. Out of love for their personal ambitions, they forsook all love for God, for his word, for his people, and for truth.

Troubled by the hardness of the men, Moses once again called them all together to reemphasize the seriousness of the test to which they would be put on the morrow. To them he said again, "Be thou and all thy company before the LORD, thou, and they, and Aaron, to morrow: and take every man his censer, and put incense in them, and bring ye before the LORD every man his censer, two hundred and fifty censers; thou also, and Aaron, each of you his censer" (Num. 16:16–17). In a nation that had tasted so often of the terrible judgment of God, it would have been expected that they would think twice before performing an act of such presumption. But the men were determined to follow through every implication of their sinful claim.

Morning came and found Korah, Dathan, and Abiram with their 250 followers gathered before the tabernacle. In their hands were the holy censers that were ordained only for use by the priests. Nearby stood the people of the nation, waiting with mixed feelings to behold the outcome of this latest attempt to take over the leadership of the nation.

First God spoke to Moses and Aaron. "Separate yourselves from among this congregation, that I may consume them in a moment" (Num. 16:21). In this he assured them once again that they, as typical mediators, were all that stood between the nation and destruction. They were not only the leaders of the nation, but as types of Christ they were also the nation's saviors. In faithfulness to their calling, they fell on their faces before God and prayed in Israel's behalf: "O God, the God of the spirits of all flesh, shall one man sin, and wilt thou be wroth with all the congregation?" (v. 22). Their prayer was not for the hardened wicked but for the true congregation of the Lord. God heard their prayer, and there could be no doubt about the validity of their offices.

The time had come for the test. The men had presumed to appear in the presence of God with the holy censers of the priesthood in their hands, and now the Lord would speak as to whether they were received or not. Moses turned to the congregation and spoke, "Depart, I pray you, from the tents of these wicked men, and touch nothing of theirs, lest ye be consumed in all their sins" (Num. 16:26). Defensively and defiantly, Korah, Dathan, and Abiram had withdrawn to their own tents. Warned by the words of Moses, the people removed themselves, until the three tents stood out as islands in the sea of people. By the tents stood the three men with their families, except for the children of Korah who, being older, had rejected the cause of their father. Once again Moses spoke to the congregation,

28. Hereby ye shall know that the LORD hath sent me to do all these works; for I have not done them of mine own mind.

29. If these men die the common death of all men, or if they be visited after the visitation of all men; then the LORD hath not sent me.

30. But if the LORD make a new thing, and the earth open her mouth, and swallow them up, with all that appertain unto them, and they go down quick into the pit; then ye shall understand that these men have provoked the LORD. (vv. 28–30)

For a moment there was a terrible silence, and then there came the sound of the earth tearing asunder. Before the eyes of the people, three great pits opened up to swallow Korah, Dathan, and Abiram, and all that they possessed. The judgment of the Lord had spoken.

In utter fright, the mass of people turned and ran. Their sympathies with the men had been all too great. With burning consciences, they feared "lest the earth swallow us up also" (Num. 16:34). But even as they ran, the judgment of God spoke yet once more. The fire of the Lord swept down and consumed the 250 men who had joined cause in the rebellion.

Still one more thing remained to be done. The 250 golden censers that the men had used were gathered at the command of God. They were hallowed instruments, and from their gold were made plates of gold to cover the altars of the tabernacle. It was a memorial to the people of the judgment of God upon those who presume to be holy of themselves apart from the word and commandments of God. Even in those early days the error of Pelagius would not be endured.

Chapter 38

THE BUDDING OF AARON'S ROD

7. And Moses laid up the rods before the Lord in the tabernacle of witness.
8. And it came to pass, that on the morrow Moses went into the tabernacle of witness; and, behold, the rod of Aaron for the house of Levi was budded, and brought forth buds, and bloomed blossoms, and yielded almonds.
9. And Moses brought out all the rods from before the Lord unto all the children of Israel: and they looked, and took every man his rod. (Numbers 17:7–9)

Before the very eyes of Israel the earth had opened up its mouth and in one moment swallowed up Korah, Dathan, and Abiram with their families because of their rebellion against Moses and Aaron. Struck with fear, the people had turned and fled lest they too should be swallowed alive. Nor was that the extent of God's judgment. As the people fled, the fire of God had fallen from heaven and consumed the 250 men who had joined cause in Korah's rebellion. Finally, at the command of God the 250 golden censers that the men had carried were gathered together and beaten into covers for the altar to serve as a memorial to the people of this great and terrible judgment that had taken place. It was to serve as a testimony to anyone besides the priests who might presume to offer incense before the Lord.

However, Korah, Dathan, and Abiram had held a very fond place in the hearts of the people. There had been a very special appeal in the cause they had sought to defend. They had claimed that Moses and Aaron did not have any more rights to leadership than did any of the people because all of the congregation was holy before the Lord. This the people had liked. It had a certain religious sound and yet was much easier for them to receive than Moses' repeated admonitions accusing them of sin. For the moment the people were silenced by the judgments that fell on the rebels before their very eyes, but they were still not ready to let the ideas of Korah and his company go. By morning their courage had returned, and they were ready to believe that it was some magical power of Moses and not really the wrath of God that had done away with those men. The more they talked it over among themselves, the more the thought appealed to them, until at last they gained sufficient boldness to stand before Moses and Aaron and accuse them to their faces, "Ye have killed the people of the Lord" (Num. 16:41).

Progressively the wickedness of Israel was becoming more and more apparent. It had been evident, of course, from the very beginning of the exodus that they were a sinful people, for they had always murmured and complained at the way of the Lord. Still, for a long time it had seemed to be nothing more than a weakness on the part of the people that would eventually be overcome. They had appeared to be affected by the works of God and subject to Moses' instruction. However, as time went on, matters were becoming worse instead of better. The works of God were becoming ever greater, the instruction of Moses was becoming more pointed, but the people were less and less responsive. The more apparent it became that the true blessing of God was spiritual for the heart, the less the people wanted of it. They became ever bolder in the way of rebellion, and this in spite of the fact that God's judgments were coming ever closer with greater destruction. It was an evil generation that Moses led. A very large percentage of them were of reprobate heart. The clearer the word of God became to them, the less they wanted of it. There was but one end to which they could come: to fall under the judgment of Jehovah's just wrath. They had no true part in Jacob, and the judgment of God struck out again and again to cut them off. And so now once more the anger of the Lord was kindled, and he spoke to Moses saying, "Get you up from among this congregation, that I may consume them as in a moment" (Num. 16:45).

But the fact remained that Israel was the people of God. As a nation they were the typical participants in God's covenant. God had promised to keep that covenant unto all generations. This Moses knew. If Israel were destroyed, the covenant of God would have proved to be of none effect, and the name of Jehovah, who had established that covenant, would be forever discredited. In spite of the unworthiness of the people, the honor of Jehovah had to be maintained. Even more, Moses realized that, although so many in Israel were rebellious of heart, there were a few, a small remnant according to election that still feared God from the heart. These he could not forsake. Neither could he forget the children of the next generation that had not yet joined themselves to the sins of their fathers. For all these reasons, Moses could not stand aside unto the destruction of the nation. With Aaron he fell on his face before God in intercession.

But the anger of God was kindled, and already judgment stalked the camp. Already at Marah, God had said, "If thou wilt diligently hearken to the voice of the LORD thy God, and wilt do that which is right in his sight, and wilt give ear to his commandments, and keep all his statutes, I will put none of these diseases upon thee, which I have brought upon the Egyptians: for I am the LORD that healeth thee" (Ex. 15:26). In this the people had notably failed, and now the plague from God was felt upon their bodies. It was a terrible disease spreading throughout the camp and carrying death on every side. There was no doubt. The people knew. The judgment of God was upon them.

But even in the judgment of God there is mercy. He uses his revelations of wrath to bring forth the gospel unto them that are able to receive it. So was it here in the wilderness. Many hardened men were falling under the plague by the hand of God's wrath. The whole nation seemed to stand on the brink of destruction. But the scene was set for a wonderful, typical revelation of the gospel. The rights of the high priest's office had been questioned. Now, as death swept over the camp, God would make it perfectly clear that Aaron's position in the office was not only right, but was also absolutely necessary. He was the priest appointed by God, and only he could save the people from the death that they deserved. Moses sent Aaron immediately to take his holy censer and to fill it with burning incense. By this incense the prayers of the high priest on behalf of the people were typified. With it Aaron went forth into the camp, passing between those who had been smitten by the plague and those who had not, between the living and the dead. As he did so, the plague was stopped. It brought to the people an indisputable proof of the fact that only the typical office of the high priest stood between them and destruction. Israel's salvation existed only in the perfect atonement to be made by the true High Priest that was to come.

Once again a rebellion of the people was silenced. Fourteen thousand seven hundred people besides Korah, Dathan, and Abiram and their 250 followers had died by the fierce wrath of God's judgment. By indisputable signs it had been established that Moses and Aaron functioned in their offices by authoritative appointment from God. Israel was indeed a holy nation, but only because of the typical offices of Moses and Aaron and the promised Redeemer whom they typified. But God was not ready to leave it at that. There was yet one more sign that he would give to the people.

Summoning Moses to him, God gave to him careful instructions.

2. Speak unto the children of Israel, and take of every one of them a rod according to the house of their fathers, of all their princes according to the house of their fathers twelve rods: write thou every man's name upon his rod.

3. And thou shalt write Aaron's name upon the rod of Levi: for one rod shall be for the head of the house of their fathers.

4. And thou shalt lay them up in the tabernacle of the congregation before the testimony, where I will meet with you.

5. And it shall come to pass, that the man's rod, whom I shall choose, shall blossom: and I will make to cease from me the murmurings of the children of Israel, whereby they murmur against you. (Num. 17:2–5)

It was a solemn meeting that brought the children of Israel together once again. They had stood on the brink of death, and only by the official priestly functions of Aaron had they been saved. They were no longer in any position to challenge his rights and would perhaps have preferred to let the matter rest. But God had called them to receive one more sign. With troubled conscience they listened as the sign was set forth.

It was a simple sign that was given. From the head of each tribe of Israel there was taken a rod. Each rod was to stand as a symbol of the tribe from which it was taken, and upon each rod was written the name of the father of the tribe. The only exception to this was the rod of Levi. Because Aaron was head of that tribe by special appointment of God, because he functioned as the high priest of the nation before God, and because his right to that office had been a matter of dispute, Aaron's name was written upon that rod instead of Levi's. Finally, these rods were laid together over night in the tabernacle before the sanctuary of God.

The next morning the leaders of Israel were again summoned to stand before the tabernacle. As they watched, Moses entered the tabernacle and brought forth the rods that had lain all night in the sanctuary. All of the rods were the same as they had been the day before except for the rod of Aaron. From Aaron's rod there had sprouted forth branches of fresh growth, bearing buds, blossoms, and even almonds. From a dead branch there had come forth new life.

To the children of Israel the implications of this sign were disconcerting. They had held strongly to the teaching of Korah that the whole congregation was holy before God. This holiness they had considered to be an innate characteristic of their nation, which gave to them all a right to stand in the presence of God. Even after Korah had died in judgment they had not abandoned that notion. Now, through the signs of the rods, God had revealed to them what they were in his presence—nothing but dead wood, as was represented in their rods. There was only one evidence of life in all of Israel: that was in Aaron and the priesthood. To him God had given life, and apart from him all of Israel was dead. Troubled by the sign, the people cried out unto Moses in fear, "Behold, we die, we perish, we all perish. Whosoever cometh any thing near unto the tabernacle of the LORD shall die: shall we be consumed with dying?" (Num. 17:12–13). The people had caught the full implication. As they were, they were not holy, and they had no right to draw nigh unto the presence of God. Under his justice they could only taste death.

The real trouble in Israel, however, was that they found no comfort in this sign. They could not identify themselves with the life of the priest. They were so determined to stand on their own pride that, when God gave a testimony of life through their priesthood, they felt it to be unto their condemnation rather than unto their salvation. Only the few who were true believers in Israel felt themselves to be one with the priest that God had given them. In his life they had life, and through him they were united to the perfect Priest who was yet to come.

Chapter 39

THE FALL OF MOSES

7. And the Lord spake unto Moses, saying,
8. Take the rod, and gather thou the assembly together, thou, and Aaron thy brother, and speak ye unto the rock before their eyes; and it shall give forth his water, and thou shalt bring forth to them water out of the rock: so thou shalt give the congregation and their beasts drink.
9. And Moses took the rod from before the Lord, as he commanded him.
10. And Moses and Aaron gathered the congregation together before the rock, and he said unto them, Hear now, ye rebels; must we fetch you water out of this rock?
11. And Moses lifted up his hand, and with his rod he smote the rock twice: and the water came out abundantly, and the congregation drank, and their beasts also. (Numbers 20:7–11)

Slowly the years passed while Israel waited to enter the promised land. This was the burden of punishment that they had to bear for rejecting the way of the Lord. One by one the members of that generation fell in the barren waste of the wilderness to be replaced by the new generation that had not taken part in their fathers' sin. Finally only a handful of the older generation was left. Forty years had passed, and the time drew near for them to take up the last lap of the journey. Through the years the people had scattered out through the surrounding territory of the desert. Now once again they were called together into the wilderness of Zin at Kadesh. This was a new generation of Israelites. Some of them had been small children during the early part of the wilderness journey; most of them had been born here on the borders of Canaan while Israel waited to enter in; none of them had lived and shared in the wickedness of Egypt like their fathers who had fallen in their sin. These had been raised under God's law with the promise ever present before their minds. There was a new zeal and dedication such as had never pervaded the nation before. They looked forward with enthusiasm to the promises that set them apart from all other nations of the world.

It was here, however, in Kadesh that a great sorrow was brought into Moses' life. Miriam, Moses' sister died. It was a great loss for Moses and also for the nation. Miriam had been active in the affairs of the nation from her youth. It was she who had watched the infant Moses in his ark on the shore of the Nile and had negotiated with Pharaoh's daughter for the child's care. Through the wilderness journey she had served as a prophetess before the Lord. She had contributed to the women of Israel a certain leadership that no man could ever supply. She had guided the women in song and dance and worship of the Lord. Her death left a certain vacuum in the camp, and all Israel stopped to observe it. But it was Moses and Aaron who felt the absence of their sister more than anyone else.

Hardly had the burial of Miriam taken place when an even greater burden entered Moses' life. In a way it was nothing new. The people were suffering for lack of water. All through the forty years of waiting to go into Canaan they had managed to find enough water for themselves and their flocks. Now, just as they were ready to move on to the land of plenty, a drought settled down around them. It brought to the people an almost frantic sense of frustration. Morning after morning the people arose to find the manna upon the ground to give them their needed food; but when the sun arose it was always in a cloudless sky that showed no sign of giving the water that they also needed to live. Death seemed to be closing in upon them with its cruel grip of thirst. Would the promise of God in the end prove to be too late and in vain?

Frightened and dismayed, the people turned again to Moses to vent upon him their frustration. They cried,

3. Would God that we had died when our brethren died before the LORD!

4. And why have ye brought up the congregation of the LORD into this wilderness, that we and our cattle should die there?

5. And wherefore have ye made us to come up out of Egypt, to bring us in unto this evil place? it is no place of seed, or of figs, or of vines, or of pomegranates; neither is there any water to drink. (Num. 20:3–5)

With a cruel shock these words fell upon the ears of Moses and sunk into his consciousness. It was the very familiarity that hurt. It stung like the lash of a whip. Almost forty years before, he had heard this same language from the lips of their fathers. He had tried everything in his power to show them the evil of talking like that. He had pleaded; he had scolded; he had punished; he had prayed for them. It all had been in vain. They had continued in their rebellion until God had refused to them the right to enter the promised land. Now they had waited all of this time for the old, rebellious generation to perish and for a younger, guiltless generation to take its place, and the same old thing was starting all over again. New fears began to lay hold upon Moses' heart. Could it be that this new generation was no better than the old? Had he waited patiently through all these years only to see a new generation repeat the sins of their fathers and, like them, be barred from the promised possession? He was already approaching one hundred and twenty years of age, and he could not live long enough to see yet another generation replaced by the hand of God. Might it be that, after all, he would never come to see the promised land? His soul was left cold by the very thought.

Still, Moses was a man of much spiritual experience. He knew better than to respond to the demands of the people impetuously. With Aaron his brother he left the assembly of the people and retired to the tabernacle of the congregation to consult with the Lord in prayer. In humility they prostrated themselves in God's presence expressing their dependence upon him. In grace God answered and revealed his glory unto them.

The instructions that the Lord gave to them were simple: "Take the rod, and gather thou the assembly together, thou, and Aaron thy brother, and speak ye unto the rock before their eyes; and it shall give forth his water, and thou shalt bring forth to them water out of the rock: so thou shalt give the congregation and their beasts drink" (Num. 20:8).

To Moses and Aaron these instructions of God were disappointing. They did not seem to fit the seriousness of the situation as they saw it. The two brothers were convinced that the nation of Israel was standing at a very critical juncture. If this new generation would repeat the sin of their fathers and continue on this way of rebellion that they had begun, it would surely lead to catastrophe. They too would eventually be turned back from the borders of Canaan. It did not seem to them that, when God said merely to go and to speak to the rock, that would supply sufficient warning for the people. They would have liked something stronger. Even the sign of Rephidim, where the rock was struck as a sign of judgment seemed more emphatic in its warning than this. How could just speaking to the rock ever affect the rebellious hearts of these people? Moses and Aaron were dissatisfied.

Nevertheless, it was an almost natural response on the part of Moses and Aaron to obey the commands that came to them from the Lord. They returned to the people and instructed them to assemble themselves before a high rock cliff that stood nearby in the wilderness. Even as they assembled the people, however, the two men continued to be troubled about the command of God. Finally they decided, after deliberating together, that Moses would have to add the warning for which the Lord had not provided. The people could not be left off so easy. Moses would have to let them know that they were walking in a way of rebellion and sin.

Finally the people were gathered together before the rock. Agitated but determined, Moses stepped forth before them. Rarely before had he stood before the people under circumstances such as this. Through conscious deliberation he had decided to go beyond the command of God to say and do what he thought was best. It made a difference. He possessed calmness and certainty before. Usually he spoke deliberately with conviction. Now agitation was to be seen on his face, and when he spoke, the words were curt and harsh. "Hear now, ye rebels; must we fetch you water out of this rock?" (Num. 20:10). And then it was done. Once having said that in that spirit, Moses could not turn back. It just was not possible for him to speak quietly to the rock as God had commanded. Rather, in his anger he lifted the rod that was in his hand and brought it down with all of his might upon the rock as though he were striking the rebels themselves. Once and once again he did it, until water gushed forth and the people had plenty to drink.

Quickly the people stooped to wet their dry lips and throats; but somehow it did not satisfy as might have been thought. There was a tension in the air that was hard to explain. Especially was this felt by Moses. He had passed through many troubled times with Israel, but never before had he felt like this. Indeed, God had not denied him the miracle. Before the people he had not been put to shame. But maybe, he thought, it would have been better if God had left him vainly beating the rock without effect. Now he felt as though God had been shamed because he had perverted the divine command. He stood there now as the greatest rebel of them all.

Could either Moses or Aaron have been surprised when God came to them again and spoke? "Because ye believed me not, to sanctify me in the eyes of the children of Israel, therefore ye shall not bring this congregation into the land which I have given them" (Num. 20:12).

These were harsh words, but they were just, and they were true. Moses and Aaron had sinned a great sin. Entrusted with the word of God, they had changed and perverted it according to their own discretion. In doing this, they had actually substituted their word, the word of man, for the gospel of God. The rock was, in type and in figure, a picture of the promised redemption, a picture of the Christ to come. There had been a day when God desired to reveal to Israel that the Christ would bear the stripes of their sin. Thus Moses had been commanded to strike the rock at Rephidim. But now it was the will of God to reveal that just a word spoken sincerely in prayer would bring forth God's blessing upon his people. When Moses refused to speak to the rock but instead struck it, he was thereby denying that the prayer of a righteous man could be effective enough. He was denying the validity of the gospel. This had to be punished. All must know that no one, not even Moses, could be allowed to change the word of God. Because he had tried to do that, Moses was denied the right to enter the land of promise. God would be justified also in him.

"This is the water of Meribah; because the children of Israel strove with the LORD, and he was sanctified in them" (Num. 20:13).

Chapter 40

THE DEATH OF AARON

23. And the Lord spake unto Moses and Aaron in Mount Hor, by the coast of the land of Edom, saying,
24. Aaron shall be gathered unto his people: for he shall not enter into the land which I have given unto the children of Israel, because ye rebelled against my word at the water of Meribah. (Numbers 20:23–24)

It was a stringent measure of judgment that fell to Moses and Aaron at the waters of Meribah. They had disobeyed the commandment of the Lord. To them it had seemed a matter of discretion. When the people had murmured rebelliously for lack of water, God had commanded them to go out into the wilderness and to speak to the rock there. They had felt that this was much too lenient. To them it seemed important that there should be at least a sign of judgment condemning the people for their sin and warning them of the wrath of God. It was this that moved Moses to strike the rock in anger rather than speaking to it as God had commanded. It was a great sin. Regardless of how good their intentions might seem to have been, they had perverted the way of God. For men in their position of leadership and influence, it was inexcusable. With quick justice God pronounced the verdict, "Because ye believed me not, to sanctify me in the eyes of the children of Israel, therefore ye shall not bring this congregation into the land which I have given them" (Num. 20:12).

For Moses and Aaron, there was no more painful verdict that could be given. For all of their lives they had looked in hope to the land of promise. Even more, the last forty years of their lives had been spent in working for the fulfillment of that hope. No one had been more tireless in encouraging the people to hold to the faithfulness of God in confidence that he would give them the land of Canaan. When, while standing at the very entrance to the land of Canaan all the people had rebelled and refused to enter in, Moses and Aaron had been among the few that had remained faithful. And now, just as the entrance was to be realized, they were being deprived of the privilege so dear to their hearts.

We are not given the details, but we do know that a number of times Moses petitioned the Lord if this verdict might not be changed. It was to no avail. The judgment of God had been given and could not be reversed. The sin that Moses and Aaron had committed was a great sin, greater than might at first be thought. The seriousness of their offense derived from the positions that they filled. Both Moses and Aaron, each in his own official capacity, stood as a representative of God before the people and as a type of Jesus Christ. Their words and deeds were sealed by the authority of God before the people. When therefore they agreed together to present to the people something different than God had commanded under the official seal of their offices, they became guilty of putting themselves in the place of God and substituting their word for his. It was a sin that could not be overlooked or ignored. It was a sin that could not go unpunished. As they had so often announced the judgment of God upon Israel for the sin of the people, so, with the same measure, their sin also had to be judged. To have exempted them from punishment would have made God a respecter of persons. This he could not be.

Now that the time had come for Israel to actually enter the promised land, Moses and Aaron's exclusion from it only intensified. It was for this that they had lived in hope since as little children they had sat in the home of faithful Amram and Jocabed. For it they had expended the strength of their lives, resisting both the wicked hatred of Pharaoh and the murmuring unfaithfulness of the people. For forty years they had patiently waited while the older, rebellious generation died in the wilderness, and all the time they had been left to believe that, with Joshua and Caleb, they would be allowed to enter in. And now, just when the time was ripe, this entrance was denied. Nor were they allowed to forget the promise toward which the people were heading. They were still the leaders of the nation. Upon them fell the responsibility of preparing to enter Canaan and of leading the Israelites on the way, even while they knew that they themselves would not be allowed to enter in. Daily their failure in service was brought again before their minds. They were unworthy of entering Canaan. To the people it was a warning of the seriousness of sin.

Continuing faithfully in his labors, Moses addressed a message unto the king of Edom requesting permission to pass through his land. Because this was the seed of Esau, Jacob's brother and Isaac's son, Israel was forbidden to fight with them at this time. It was a friendly request that Moses sent.

14. Thus saith thy brother Israel, Thou knowest all the travail that hath befallen us:
15. How our fathers went down into Egypt, and we have dwelt in Egypt a long time; and the Egyptians vexed us, and our fathers:
16. And when we cried unto the LORD, he heard our voice, and sent an angel, and hath brought us forth out of Egypt: and, behold, we are in Kadesh, a city in the uttermost of thy border:
17. Let us pass, I pray thee, through thy country: we will not pass through the fields, or through the vineyards, neither will we drink of the water of the wells: we will go by the king's high way, we will not turn to the right hand nor to the left, until we have passed thy borders. (Num. 20:14–17)

With the Edomites, however, there was no sympathy for Moses' request. It was true that they were brothers with Israel through Isaac, but for Israel they held no love. They were true children of their father Esau. The underlying desire of Esau's life had always been to prove that he could get along without the aid of the God upon whom his fathers, Isaac and Abraham, had always relied. He had been a proud man who had always hated God and hated his brother Jacob for Jacob's covenant relation with God. This hatred he passed on to his children. Thus the message of Moses that was actually intended to create sympathy in the Edomites based on the mutual relationship of their fathers to the God of Abraham only aroused the old animosities anew. The answer they gave was brief, "Thou shalt not pass by me, lest I come out against thee with the sword" (Num. 20:18).

To Moses and the children of Israel this answer came as a shock. They could not understand the deep-seated hatred that smoldered in the hearts of the Edomites. All they could imagine was that the Edomites were afraid that the children of Israel would damage their land. Once more they sent their messengers with their promises. "We will go by the high way: and if I and my cattle drink of thy water, then I will pay for it: I will only, without doing anything else, go through on my feet" (Num. 20:19).

The laconic reply came back, "Thou shalt not go through" (Num. 20:20). Even more, to support their reply, the Edomites sent forth their armies to see that Israel did not trespass upon their land. It was a strong band of experienced fighters filled with the fierce pride and hatred of their father. They were determined in their opposition to Israel and Israel's God.

It is almost with surprise that we find Israel commanded to turn back from the borders of Edom. After all, we know from scripture that Edom was a reprobate nation. Already before Esau was born, this was foretold to Rebecca when God said to her, "Two nations are in thy womb, and two manner of people shall be separated from thy bowels; and the one people shall be stronger than the other people; and the elder shall serve the younger" (Gen. 25:23). In Malachi this is explained to mean,

3. And I hated Esau, and laid his mountains and his heritage waste for the dragons of the wilderness.
4. Whereas Edom saith, We are impoverished, but we will return and build the desolate places; thus saith the LORD of

hosts, They shall build, but I will throw down; and they shall call them, The border of wickedness, and, The people against whom the LORD hath indignation forever. (Mal. 1:3–4)

We wonder, therefore, why God did not send forth the armies of Israel to destroy this wicked nation. But the time was not ripe. Nothing would be done that might seem to give Edom an excuse to live in hatred toward Israel. It had to become evident that Edom's hatred came, without provocation, from the wickedness of the heart. Then in the proper time God would descend upon them in judgment. But until that time Israel was commanded to turn away from Edom's borders.

And also there was another reason. This new route brought Israel to the foot of Mount Hor. It was necessary for them to pass that way. It was God's will that upon that mountain Aaron, the high priest, should be taken away.

There at Mount Hor, God came and spoke to Moses and Aaron together. Mercifully God did not speak to Moses alone, as he usually did, for that would have necessitated Moses' passing the message along to his brother. It would have been a duty too painful for him. The word of God was short and to the point.

24. Aaron shall be gathered unto his people: for he shall not enter into the land which I have given unto the children of Israel, because ye rebelled against my word at the water of Meribah.
25. Take Aaron and Eleazar his son, and bring them up unto Mount Hor.
26. And strip Aaron of his garments and put them upon Eleazar his son: and Aaron shall be gathered unto his people, and shall die there. (Num. 20:24–26)

Obediently the three men commanded by God took their departure from the camp and together ascended the mount. It was a sad journey that they took. Even the people in the camp, although they had not been told what was to happen, could not help but feel that there was something very ominous in what was taking place. The fact that Aaron wore the rich robes of his high priestly office implied that what was to happen was important, and the steps of the three men making their way up the mountain could hardly help but betray that there was no joy or promise in what was to take place. But the concern of the people in their ignorance could not begin to compare with the sorrow of the three men who knew what was to happen. There was the younger man, Eleazar. With love and admiration he had often watched his father performing the duties of his office. He had observed the duties and responsibilities time and time again. Now all was to fall upon his shoulders, and his father would not be there to help him. The anticipation could only make him tremble. But even heavier was the burden that rested upon Moses. Through all of his labor, Aaron had been a companion near to help him. As brothers they had labored together in love. Aaron's hope, as his, had been to enter the land of Canaan, and now Moses had to watch while Aaron's life was taken away with the goal unaccomplished. But the greatest sorrow was that of Aaron. His death pointed out for all to see his sin, his weakness, his limitation. In the function of his office he had fallen short, and his untimely death without the borders of Canaan testified to all that he had been a failure. Another must take his place in entering the land of promise.

In solemn silence the three men went about their duty upon the mountain. With only the heavens watching on, the robes of office were transferred from father to child. All wished that the time was not quite yet. All knew that it could not be other. God had spoken, and in faithful obedience they accepted it as good. We do not know what final parting words were spoken. We do not know what final prayers were uttered. But there upon the mountain one of the great saints of Israel was taken into rest.

There was sorrow in Israel's camp when Moses and Eleazar returned without Aaron. For thirty days they mourned his death. The fact of his death was for the nation an occasion of grief. The time and the manner was a warning of the seriousness of sin.

Chapter 41

THE BRAZEN SERPENT AS
A REVELATION OF THE GOSPEL

14. As Moses lifted up the serpent in the wilderness, even so must the Son of man be lifted up:
15. That whosoever believeth in him should not perish but have eternal life. (John 3:14–15)

At times the hope of the children of Israel to enter the promised land must have appeared almost futile to them. It had been full forty years since they had come into the wilderness from Egypt, and according to God's own words it was time for them to enter Canaan. But the land of Edom stood between them and the entrance into Canaan. The king of Edom forbade them passage through his land, and the Lord forbade them to fight. It meant that they had to circumvent the whole of the land of Edom, an extensive additional journey. When they wanted so badly to be traveling north, they found themselves heading south, back through the barren wilderness. Each step of the way brought them farther from the longed for goal. It was discouraging, to say the least.

Nor was this the full extent of their discouragement. No sooner had Israel come together and begun to travel again than Arad, king of the Canaanites, came against them unexpectedly with his armies and took some of them captive. They had done nothing to provoke him other than beginning to travel again. But that was all it took. Israel still had to learn how bitterly they were hated by the people of every land. The nations had all heard about Israel and the works that Israel's God could perform. None of them had gods as powerful as he. When these nations heard that Israel was coming to settle and live in the land of Canaan, they were afraid. During the forty years while Israel was waiting on Canaan's borders, they became uneasy and on edge. Their hatred for Israel grew and became so intense that, once Israel began to move again, they attacked Israel wildly and without a cause. This intense hatred Israel would experience more and more as they went on.

Still it was not under this attack of Arad that Israel faltered. Their strength was sufficient to go as they should to the Lord. Before the Lord they made a vow, "If thou wilt indeed deliver this people into my hand, then I will utterly destroy their cities" (Num. 21:2). It was an expressed willingness to serve as the instrument of judgment in the hand of God whereby the cities of this sinful nation would be destroyed. God heard this vow and gave to them a great victory. By them the cities of Arad were utterly destroyed.

It was not, however, until they began to journey again that the courage of the people finally broke. Back they were led among the rough and barren crags that surrounded Mount Seir of Edom. The sun was hot; the ground was dry; the way was steep and rough; and all of the time they were going farther and farther away from the land of promise. It could be seen on the faces of the people; they were sullen and sad. At last it began to be heard; the voice of murmuring was being raised. At first it was just an undertone of hushed whispers, but louder and louder it became. Finally it was brought to Moses, a cry of anguish and pain, "Wherefore have ye brought us up out of Egypt to die in the wilderness? for there is no bread, neither is there any water; and our soul loatheth this light bread" (Num. 21:5).

This was the cry of a different generation from that with which Moses had traveled before. And there was a difference. The former generation had been raised in Egypt, and from the Egyptians they had learned much as to the ways of sin. In that generation there had been many who had come along merely out of the hope of material advancement. Many of them had been spiritually hard, and for that very reason they had perished without the land of promise. This new generation had been raised under the law of God within the realm of the covenant. They knew the terrible wrath of God against sin from the desolate wilderness in which their parents were made to perish. We know for a fact that in the history of the church there were few generations more spiritual than this one. And yet, as they began their journey, it was in the same weakness and rebellion as their parents had so often shown. They complained about the way in which they were led as though their God were cruel to them and his way unjust.

This could not be allowed to go unanswered. The reply of the Lord came quickly. The wilderness in which Israel had now lived for so many years was the natural habitat of the serpent. Always there were snakes around, and many of them were poisonous. But always there was also the miracle of Israel's survival in that desert. God by his power preserved them from all of the dangers of that wild land. Even the serpents were restrained, so that Israel passed by their holes and remained untouched by their fangs throughout those wilderness years. That was, until they had committed this sin of rebellion. Suddenly God lifted his restraint. Even more, he sent a special breed of poisonous snakes directly into the camp. They were fiery serpents, in appearance perhaps but especially in their bite; quickly a burning inflammation set in, soon to be followed by a painful death.

There was a very definite symbolism in this judgment sent by God. From the fall of Eve in the Garden of Eden, the serpent has stood as a symbol of sin. The inflaming, killing result of its poisonous bite closely parallels the working of sin. Once sin has found its way into man's moral system, it spreads, inflaming man's sinful passions. It brings with it death, true spiritual death, separation from God and his favor. There is only one thing that can stay the working of this moral decay: the miracle of God's salvation given by grace. Only God can save man from this fiery death.

Once this punishment had been given, the true distinctiveness of this generation from that of their fathers became apparent. The sin committed was outwardly no different; but the former generation under punishment of their sin had hardened themselves again and again, while this generation bowed in repentance for what they had done. Those long years of waiting in the wilderness had had their effect. This generation was not too proud to acknowledge its own weakness as their fathers had been. The prayer with which they came to the now aged Moses was beautiful in its plaintive cry. "We have sinned, for we have spoken against the LORD, and against thee; pray unto the LORD, that he take away the serpents from us" (Num. 21:7).

This was a prayer that could not go unanswered. Moses brought it in their behalf to God, and he withdrew the serpents from their midst. But the answer of God went far beyond that which the people had asked. There were still in the camp many of those who had been bitten and in whom even now the poison of death was at work. God made provision also for them. To Moses he said, "Make thee a fiery serpent, and set it upon a pole: and it shall come to pass, that every one that is bitten, when he looketh upon it, shall live" (Num. 21:8).

Moses must have worked quickly. He took a rod of brass and, heating it, bent it into the shape of a snake. This brazen serpent he lifted up on a pole above the camp. The call went out through the camp summoning all that had been bitten by the serpents to come and look upon the serpent that Moses had made. Here was a marvelous thing to behold: people in all stages of this deadly pain coming to the place where Moses had set up this pole. Many of them no doubt had to be carried by friends and relatives, they were so weak from the working of the poison. But regardless of how close to death they were, in the instant that they looked upon the serpent hanging from the pole they were healed. No one could doubt the miracle that was being wrought.

And still it was more than just the healing of some seriously sick people that happened that day. There was a revelation that was taking place. God was speaking to Israel, explaining to them the wonder of his infinite love. These were a people used to the language of symbolism, much more so than we are today. In this that was happening there was a truth that the true, spiritual children of Israel could well meditate upon as they proceeded on their way.

The first symbolic element in the events of that day was, of course, in the relation between the serpent and sin. Those people did not have nearly as much sacred history to remember as we do, and thus, in what they did know, the account of the fall occupied a very important part. They remembered well the word of God to the serpent:

14. Because thou hast done this, thou art cursed above all cattle, and above every beast of the field; upon thy belly shalt thou go, and dust shalt thou eat all the days of thy life:
15. And I will put enmity between thee and the woman, and between thy seed and her seed; it shall bruise thy head, and thou shalt bruise his heel. (Gen. 3:14–15)

Whenever they saw a serpent, they were reminded of Satan himself and the constant enmity between him and God. When all through the wilderness God restrained the serpents on the way from harming them, it was a sign of God's favor and grace. And when they saw this restraint removed and fiery serpents begin to invade their camp, it was as though Satan and his angels had descended upon their camp. The curse of sin held them under its power. But they knew better than to think that it was just a physical thing, injected as venom into the blood. It was spiritual in their hearts. Thus they turned in repentance to God.

But most beautiful of all were the resultant instructions given to Moses by God, the instructions to make a brazen serpent and to raise it up above the camp upon a pole. This too was a symbolism that they knew. That which was lifted up upon a tree was accounted accursed; it was lifted up as an unholy thing from off the earth. This was in the nature of a promise from God. He was not merely healing them from the poison of the serpents. That could have as well been done in some other and more simple way. God was bringing to them, in terms they could well understand, that he was lifting from their midst the curse.

There was, however, still one more fact that entered in: the healing result of this blessing came only to those who looked upon the serpent. Whether any failed to do this in Israel's camp, we do not know. Probably not. But regardless, the typical fact was there, that only those who looked upon that accursed tree and saw the curse of sin suspended there were healed.

In type and shadow, according to the understanding of the people, God was revealing the gospel. It is the same gospel that we know now in fulfillment. God has hung our curse upon the tree. As many as look upon it and see it with the eyes of faith, they are healed from the wound of the devil.

Chapter 42

BALAAM COVETS BALAK'S PROMISED REWARD

2. And Balak the son of Zippor saw all that Israel had done to the Amorites.
3. And Moab was sore afraid of the people, because they were many: and Moab was distressed because of the children of Israel.
5. He sent messengers therefore unto Balaam the son of Beor to Pethor, which is by the river of the land of the children of his people, to call him, saying, Behold, there is a people come out from Egypt: behold, they cover the face of the earth, and they abide over against me:
6. Come now therefore, I pray thee, curse me this people; for they are too mighty for me: peradventure I shall prevail, that we may smite them, and that I may drive them out of the land: for I wot that he whom thou blessest is blessed, and he whom thou cursest is cursed. (Numbers 22:2–3, 5–6)

The journey of Israel was extended considerably by the fact that they were refused permission to travel through either the land of Edom or the land of Moab, and God had forbidden them to fight for this right. They were forced to circumvent these lands almost completely, involving many more miles of travel. But this was the way that the guiding cloud led them, and that way they went. The way was hard. Finally, however, they had bypassed those lands almost completely, and they were approaching the borders of the land of Ammon. To Sihon, the king of Ammon, they addressed a request such as they had done before to Edom and Moab. In the name of

Israel the messengers said, "Let me pass through thy land: we will not turn into the fields, or into the vineyards; we will not drink of the waters of the well: but we will go along by the king's high way, until we be past thy borders" (Num. 21:22).

The steady approach of the children of Israel, however, was making the inhabitants of Canaan nervously afraid. The size of the nation in itself was foreboding, and the destructive power in which Israel had left the land of Egypt was far from forgotten. Everyone was quite aware of Israel's intentions to settle in the land of Canaan. The closer the Israelites came, the more uneasy they became. When, therefore, Sihon received the messengers of Israel and heard of their request to enter into his land, he was frightened and unable to believe that they intended only to pass through and leave him and his people unmolested. To him it was quite evidently a deception, and he sent the messengers back with a harsh refusal. Even more, he gathered his people together and told them to prepare for battle. He would not give the Israelites time to work out whatever plans they might have and so gain an advantage. He would take the offensive and attack the Israelites where they were. It was a move of wild desperation.

Thus it was that the children of Israel found themselves engaged in battle much sooner than they had expected. But God was with them, and they were in no need for elaborate preparations. Not only did they repel the first attack of Sihon, but they went on to follow with one victorious battle after another until the whole of the land of the Amorites was subjected. Even more, when Og, the king of the neighboring land of Bashan, saw the moving power of the Israelites, he too gathered together his armies and sent them against the children of Israel. Soon they too were conquered, and still another land was subjected under the people of God.

All this was taking place on the northern edge of the land of Moab, and there was considerable misgiving that arose in the hearts of the Moabites because of all they saw. Finally the battles were over, their neighbors had been utterly destroyed, and the children of Israel moved to an encampment on the very plains of Moab across the

Jordan River from Jericho. Balak, the king of Moab, was clearly frightened. He could only imagine that Israel would next turn against him and his people. Neither was there any doubt in his mind that he would never be able to withstand their power. He realized that it was not just the armies of Israel with which they would have to contend, but also Israel's God. If he were to meet their force it would have to be on the same level.

Far away at Pethor in Mesopotamia there was living one of the strangest figures of that day. Actually, he was a very remarkable man, a man familiar with the revelation of God as it was known. In itself, that was not as strange as it might seem. It is apparent from the histories of Job, Melchizedek, and Jethro that there were various communities scattered throughout the world in that day where the true worship of Jehovah was still maintained. Balaam had very likely lived in such a community. There he had learned and become unusually well acquainted with the word of God. In fact, this was so much true that God had used him from time to time in the capacity of a prophet. In this way he had served to express the blessings and cursings of God upon various individuals and perhaps even upon nations. Invariably his blessings and cursings came to pass, and soon his reputation spread far and wide through the nations. Thus it was that Balak, in the distant land of Moab, had come to hear about him. Even more, when it became apparent to him that the true nature of Israel's power was spiritual, he determined to send for Balaam and answer the God of Israel with a curse of a similar nature. What Balak did not realize was that the source of Balaam's strength was the very same God by whom Israel was blessed.

Soon the messengers of Balak were on their way. When they came finally to Balaam, they presented to him the request of their king.

5. Behold, there is a people come out from Egypt: behold, they cover the face of the earth, and they abide over against me:
6. Come now therefore, I pray thee, curse me this people; for they are too mighty for me: peradventure I shall prevail, that we may smite them, and that I may drive them out of

the land: for I wot that he whom thou blessest is blessed,
and he whom thou cursest is cursed. (Num. 22:5–6)

With them the messangers carried evidence of large rewards that would be given to Balaam if he would comply with this request. It was clear that Balak was ready to pay dearly for his services.

It is not unlikely that Balaam was acquainted with the history of the children of Israel to which the messengers referred. The exodus of Israel from Egypt was spectacular enough for all the world to take note. If he was, then he knew also that Israel's strength was from the same God from whom he received his power. But Balaam was a careful man, and the proffered reward looked good to him. He answered the men, "Lodge here this night, and I will bring you word again, as the LORD shall speak unto me" (Num. 22:8).

During the night, God came and spoke to Balaam. The conversation that followed showed clearly God's concern for the mission of these messengers. That was his inquiry: "What men are these with thee?" (Num. 22:9).

To this Balaam answered very correctly, "Balak the son of Zippor, king of Moab, hath sent unto me, saying, Behold, there is a people come out of Egypt, which covereth the face of the earth: come now, curse me them; peradventure I shall be able to overcome them, and drive them out" (Num. 22:10–11).

The answer of God left no doubt as to what the facts were. He answered Balaam, "Thou shalt not go with them; thou shalt not curse the people: for they are blessed" (Num. 22:12).

The next morning Balaam briefly told the messengers that he could not go with them. He did not explain that the children of Israel could not be cursed because they were blessed of God. He merely said, "Get you into your land: for the LORD refuseth to give me leave to go with you" (Num. 22:13). He felt bad, and he did not wish to go any further into the matter. That was the strange part about Balaam. Although he knew the Lord so well and had an extensive understanding of revelation, his appreciation for it was only intellectual and passing. His real love was not for the word of

God but for the recognition he gained when serving as a prophet of that word. He knew better than to go in direct opposition to God's command, but that did not mean he liked it. His heart was sad as he watched the messengers with their rich gifts disappearing into the distance.

Balaam's feelings, however, were not hid from the messengers of Balak. When they made their report, they were able to assure the king that Balaam was not as indifferent as his mere words might tend to indicate. To Balak it seemed evident that Balaam was just holding out for a higher wage, and Balak was willing to go a long way to meet this. He quickly sent another embassage of more important men with more appealing promises. Their message was this, "Let nothing, I pray thee, hinder thee from coming unto me: for I will promote thee unto very great honour, and I will do whatsoever thou sayest unto me: come therefore, I pray thee, curse me this people" (Num. 22:16–17). Balak knew how to appeal to a man's natural desires.

When messengers once more appeared at Balaam's door, it was evident that he was perturbed by their presence. On the one hand, he knew that he could not grant their wish. Thus he said to them immediately, "If Balak would give me his house full of silver and gold, I cannot go beyond the word of the LORD my God, to do less or more" (Num. 22:18). Still, it was not that their new offer did not have appeal to him. He wanted the reward badly. So he finally went so far as to suggest, "Now therefore, I pray you, tarry ye also here this night, that I may know what the LORD will say unto me more" (v. 19).

To Balaam, the new answer of the Lord came as a surprise. "If the men come to call thee, rise up and go with them; but yet the word which I shall say unto thee, that shalt thou do" (Num. 22:20). From it he should have realized that he would never be able to satisfy Balak and collect the reward, but he thought enough of his own ingenuity to expect that, if only he could get to Moab, he would be able to find some way to turn the trip to his profit. He was a happy man when he set out on his journey the next morning.

God, however, did not leave him without a warning about any mistaken intentions he might have. Balaam was deep in thought as to how he could evade the blessing of God upon Israel and so turn this journey to his profit, when suddenly the ass upon which he rode turned from the way and into a field. Impatiently Balaam smote the ass to bring it again to the road. They had not gone much farther, however, when the ass again swerved, crushing Balaam's foot against the wall of a vineyard. Incensed, Balaam struck the animal again to return it to the way. And then when finally, in a narrow place between two walls, the ass stopped and fell to its knees, throwing Balaam to the ground, it was too much. Enraged, he took his staff and began to beat the beast. So beside himself was he that it did not even strike him as unusual when the dumb beast spoke, "What have I done unto thee, that thou hast smitten me these three times?" (Num. 22:28). In anger Balaam merely replied, "Because thou hast mocked me: I would there were a sword in mine hand, for now would I kill thee" (v. 29).

It was then that God opened the eyes of Balaam to see what the ass had seen all the time. There before him was the angel of the Lord, with a drawn sword in his hand. Trembling Balaam spoke, "I have sinned; for I knew not that thou stoodest in the way against me: now therefore, if it displease thee, I will get me back again" (Num. 22:34). In his heart he knew that he was proceeding on a very precarious way, for his desire was to go against the will of the Lord. However, he also knew better than to oppose the Lord openly, and he offered to turn back, even though his desire was to go on.

But no, it was also God's will that he should proceed. So the angel instructed him, "Go with the men: but only the word that I shall speak unto thee, that thou shalt speak" (Num 22:35). Let Balaam remember the angel of judgment that overshadowed his path. If he opposed the will of God it would be to his own destruction. He was a man under judgment, not under grace.

Chapter 43

BALAAM'S PROPHETIC PROPHECY

> 7. And he took up his parable, and said, Balak the king of
>   Moab hath brought me from Aram, out of the mountains of
>   the east, saying, Come, curse me Jacob, and come defy Israel.
> 8. How shall I curse, whom God hath not cursed? or how shall
>   I defy, whom the LORD hath not defied? (Numbers 23:7–8)

Balaam arrived in the land of Moab firmly determined in one way
or another to bring a curse upon Israel. He knew it would not be
easy. God had said to him before he left Aram, "Thou shalt not curse
the people: for they are blessed" (Num. 22:12). And he knew that,
as a prophet, he was powerless to say one word different from what
God had placed in his mouth. He remembered only too well the
angel of judgment with a sword in his hand who had appeared first
to his ass and then to him as though to warn him that, if he changed
the word of God in one bit, it would be to his own destruction.
Still he was determined. Balak had offered him a great reward, and
he wanted it very badly. He was quite sure that he could get it, not
by perverting the word of God, but by convincing God that Moab
ought to be blessed and Israel cursed.

Balak, of course, had no idea of the difficulties that confronted
Balaam. He was sure that Balaam was able to bless or curse whomever
he chose. When at first Balaam had refused to come, Balak thought
it was only because he was holding out for higher pay. In fact, it irri-
tated Balak just to think that anyone might consider him unwilling
to pay what his services were worth. But now Balaam was come, and
Balak hurried to the border city to meet him. Still, he could not help
but chide Balaam for his hesitation. "Did I not earnestly send unto

thee to call thee? wherefore camest thou not unto me? am I not able indeed to promote thee to honour?" (Num. 22:37).

Balaam immediately detected the confidence that Balak had in him, and it bothered him. He was afraid that Balak would expect too much, too soon, and too easily. Carefully he tried to warn him: "Lo, I am come unto thee: have I now any power at all to say any thing? the word that God putteth in my mouth, that shall I speak" (Num. 22:38).

But Balak was not daunted. Eagerly he took Balaam to Kirjath-Huzoth near the camp of Israel. Once they were there, and unbeknownst to Balaam, he offered a sacrifice of joy to his god. This did not fit with the plans of Balaam, but he did not know of it until the sacrificial meat was brought to him to eat.

Early the next morning they went together to a mountaintop overlooking the camp of Israel. There Balaam began putting his plan into action. He commanded seven altars to be built and seven oxen and seven rams prepared for sacrifice. He knew that Jehovah was pleased with sacrifices and that seven was a favorite, covenant number. When all was ready, he and Balak brought the sacrifice of an ox and a ram to each altar. His hope was to induce Jehovah to be favorably disposed to Moab by this sacrifice by its king.

While the sacrifices were yet burning, Balaam said to Balak, "Stand by thy burnt offering, and I will go: peradventure the LORD will come to meet me: and whatsoever he sheweth me I will tell thee" (Num. 23:3). Balaam felt rather safe that in the presence of these sacrifices God would say something favorable or, at worse, nothing at all. Slowly he went higher up the peak to wait for God to speak. Soon God did come, and immediately Balaam set forth his cause, "I have prepared seven altars, and I have offered upon every altar a bullock and a ram" (v. 4).

Meanwhile, Balak and the princes of Moab who had come with him were waiting for Balaam's return in eager anticipation. They had seen how carefully he worked and had no doubt that it would be rewarded. Attentively they listened when at last Balaam did return and spoke:

7. Balak the king of Moab hath brought me from Aram, out of the mountains of the east, saying, Come, curse me Jacob, and come, defy Israel.

8. How shall I curse, whom God hath not cursed? or how shall I defy, whom the LORD hath not defied?

9. For from the top of the rocks I see him, and from the hills I behold him: lo, the people shall dwell alone, and shall not be reckoned among the nations.

10. Who can count the dust of Jacob, and the number of the fourth part of Israel? Let me die the death of the righteous, and let my last end be like his! (Num. 23:7–10)

Astonishment was written all over the faces of Balak and his princes. They might well have burst forth in anger, were it not for fear that they had for Balaam and his strange power. Still, the dismay could not be hidden. Balak cried out, "What hast thou done unto me? I took thee to curse mine enemies, and, behold, thou hast blessed them altogether" (Num. 23:11).

To this, Balaam had only one answer. He was himself deeply disappointed. Lamely he said, "Must I not take heed to speak that which the LORD hath put in my mouth?" (Num. 23:12).

The cold grip of fear was laying hold again upon Balak's heart. Now more than ever he felt the need for a curse to be pronounced upon the nation of Israel. Possibly, he thought, Balaam was too much impressed by the size of the nation and the orderliness of Israel's camp. Turning again to Balaam he said, "Come, I pray thee, with me unto another place, from whence thou mayest see them: thou shalt see but the utmost part of them, and shall not see them all: and curse me them from thence" (Num. 23:13).

Together they went to the field of Zophim at the top of the mount of Pisgah. From there they could see only part of Israel's camp, and, at that, the outer part, where the unorganized mixed multitude dwelt that had so often been a snare to Israel's moral life. There once again they built seven altars and offered a bullock and a ram upon each. Then Balaam said to Balak, "Stand here by thy burnt offering, while I meet the LORD yonder" (Num. 23:15).

When Balaam returned, Balak was waiting even more anxiously than before, but without the former confidence. Before him Balaam stood in prophetic ecstasy and spoke:

18. Rise up, Balak, and hear; hearken unto me, thou son of Zippor:
19. God is not a man, that he should lie; neither the son of man, that he should repent: hath he said, and shall he not do it? or hath he spoken, and shall he not make it good?
20. Behold, I have received commandment to bless: and he hath blessed; and I cannot reverse it.
21. He hath not beheld iniquity in Jacob, neither hath he seen perverseness in Israel: the LORD his God is with him, and the shout of a king is among them.
22. God brought them out of Egypt; he hath as it were the strength of an unicorn.
23. Surely there is no enchantment against Jacob, neither is there any divination against Israel: according to this time it shall be said of Jacob and of Israel, What hath God wrought!
24. Behold, the people shall rise up as a great lion, and lift himself as a young lion: he shall not lie down until he eat of the prey, and drink the blood of the slain. (Num. 23:18–24)

A stunned silence hung heavy over the group of Moabitish nobles gathered there to listen, broken only by the anguished cry of Balak the king. "Neither curse them at all, nor bless them at all" (Num. 23:25).

For this, Balaam had only one answer, "Told not I thee, saying, All that the LORD speaketh, that I must do?" (Num. 23:26).

Both Balaam and Balak were on the verge of complete despair. Their present state was much worse than the first, and well they might have wished that they had never started on this course. But now they could hardly refrain from going on. In desperation Balak suggested once more to Balaam, "Come, I pray thee, I will bring thee unto another place; peradventure it will please God that thou mayest curse me them from thence" (Num. 23:27).

This time they went to the top of mount Peor, and again they built seven altars and offered a bullock and a ram upon each. But Balaam's confidence was waning, and he was almost beginning to hope that God would not come to speak to him. As though to discourage the Lord from speaking, this time he set his face toward the wilderness instead of toward the mountain peaks. But once more God came, and Balaam returned to Balak in a state of prophetic ecstasy.

3. Balaam the son of Beor hath said, and the man whose eyes are open hath said:

4. He hath said, which heard the words of God, which saw the vision of the Almighty, falling into a trance, but having his eyes open:

5. How goodly are thy tents, O Jacob, and thy tabernacles, O Israel!

6. As the valleys are they spread forth, as gardens by the river's side, as the trees of lign aloes which the LORD hath planted, and as cedar trees beside the waters.

7. He shall pour the water out of his buckets, and his seed shall be in many waters, and his king shall be higher than Agag, and his kingdom shall be exalted.

8. God brought him forth out of Egypt; he hath as it were the strength of an unicorn: he shall eat up the nations his enemies, and shall break their bones, and pierce them through with his arrows.

9. He couched, he lay down as a lion, and as a great lion: who shall stir him up? Blessed is he that blesseth thee, and cursed is he that curseth thee. (Num. 24:3–9)

It was all more than Balak could take. To him it seemed to be nothing short of treachery, and his anger could restrain itself no longer. Hitting his hands together in rage, he cried out at the top of his voice, "I called thee to curse mine enemies, and, behold, thou hast altogether blessed them these three times. Therefore now flee thou to thy place: I thought to promote thee unto great honour; but, lo, the LORD hath kept thee back from honour" (Num. 24:10–11). Sarcasm dripped from his voice, for he was quite convinced that the fault was more Balaam's than the Lord's.

Balaam knew better. He was as disappointed as Balak was, for there was nothing he desired more than to curse Israel and so gain the honor that Balak offered. But God prevented him from doing what he wanted. All that he could do was to repeat again what he said so often before, "Spake I not also to thy messengers which thou sentest unto me, saying, if Balak would give me his house full of silver and gold, I cannot go beyond the commandment of the LORD, to do either good or bad of mine own mind; but what the LORD saith, that will I speak?" (Num. 24:12–13).

Chapter 44

BALAAM'S FINAL ATTEMPT TO BRING GOD'S WRATH UPON ISRAEL

1. Israel abode in Shittim, and the people began to commit whoredom with the daughters of Moab.
2. And they called the people unto the sacrifices of their gods: and the people did eat, and bowed down to their gods. (Numbers 25:1–2)

1. And the LORD spake unto Moses, saying,
2. Avenge the children of Israel of the Midianites…

8. And they slew the kings of Midian…:, Balaam also the son of Beor they slew with the sword. (Numbers 31:1–2, 8)

Balak had hired Balaam the prophet to come from Aram in the East to curse the children of Israel encamped on the borders of his land. The attempt had been made and had failed utterly. Three times Balaam had fallen into prophetic ecstasy, and each time he had pronounced richest blessings upon Israel in the name of God. At first Balak was only dismayed, but finally he became infuriated. Beating his hands together in fury he cried out, "I called thee to curse mine enemies, and, behold, thou hast altogether blessed them these three times. Therefore now flee thou to thy place: I thought to promote thee unto great honour; but, lo, the LORD hath kept thee back from honour" (Num. 24:10–11).

Balaam too was disappointed. He wanted the promised reward of Balak very badly. Lamely, he could only reply, "Spake I not also to thy messengers which thou sentest unto me, saying, If Balak would give me his house full of silver and gold, I cannot go beyond the commandment of the LORD, to do either good or bad of mine own mind; but what the LORD saith, that will I speak?" (Num. 24:12–13). But that was not all. Before they realized it, Balaam was once again caught up in prophetic ecstasy, and he continued to speak, "And now, behold, I go unto my people: come therefore, and I will advertise thee what this people shall do to thy people in the latter days" (v. 14). There followed what was by far the most remarkable prophecy of all. In it he foretold the coming of the Messiah as "a Star out of Jacob" and "a Scepter...out of Israel" (v. 17). But, even more, he foretold that the coming of this Messiah would be to the judgment not only of Moab, Edom, Amalek, and other nations, but also of the future kingdom of Ashur (Assyria) and, in fact, the kingdom of the Antichrist. Israel, through its king, would dominate the history of the world until its end. When this prophecy was finished, there was nothing more to be said. Balaam arose and went his way.

Balaam's mind, however, would not allow him any peace over the whole matter. He was not used to failure, and this failure had been so utterly complete. Even as he left Balak his mind was trying to figure out why he did not succeed. As he rode, his mind went back through all his old experiences in this line, when suddenly there came to him a significant realization. All those nations that were cursed of God had been so cursed because they had given themselves to iniquity, idolatry, and fornication. Yet, in trying to curse Israel, he had ignored the integrity of Israel's religious life completely. All at once his mind was alive with things that he should have done. But maybe it was not too late, and he could recoup his losses still. Quickly he turned his beast about to return. But he did not go to Balak in Moab. The Moabites would not have the full confidence in him anymore that would be needed. Rather, he turned to the wild, roving tribes of the Midianites. Although they had little to lose to Israel, they hated the Israelites with a zeal. In addition, they were morally indifferent enough to cooperate in this new plan and would be able to convince the Moabites to lend their cooperation too.

Soon he came to the princes of Midian and laid before them his plan. They in turn went with him to the princes of Moab to gain also their cooperation. The plan was very simple. Before, they had tried to purchase the favor of Jehovah for themselves by the means of sacrifices and burnt offerings. That had failed. It had not dimmed Jehovah's favor in Israel. Now they would work to turn Israel away from Jehovah. If his people would be unfaithful to him and his commandments, then surely God would curse them.

To the children of Israel it was a strangely new and different experience that suddenly began to take place. Ever since their beginning as a nation they had been hated by everyone they met. The Egyptians had hated them, and when they left Egypt, the new nations they met hated them just the same. They had become used to it and had expected it wherever they went. It was, therefore, quite an unexpected surprise when one day a group of young women of the Moabites and Midianites appeared at their camp with gestures of friendship and kindness. They came and mingled freely with the girls of Israel. It seemed almost too good to be true. The young women of Israel had never experienced such open friendliness from daughters of strangers. Day after day they came, until the friendships became very firm. Soon it was not only the young women but also the young men of Israel who were entering into these friendships with the daughters of Moab and Midian. It was then that the situation took a much more serious turn.

Before long the young women of Moab and Midian were inviting the young men of Israel to their homes. There they were treated with the utmost hospitality, even to the point of being invited to take part in their religious ceremonies and festivities. This was for the men of Israel a new and entirely different experience. The religious worship of these nations had little resemblance to the solemn ceremonies of Israel that were used in the worship of Jehovah. They were more pageants of sheer pleasure, dedicated to the heathen god Baalpeor. In them, carnal lust knew no bounds, even to the point where the women openly prostituted themselves in the name of Baalpeor. All this could only have shocked the moral senses of the Israelites. But they had gone too far in their friendships to draw back. Soon many of them were engaging in these heathenish ceremonies with carnal abandonment.

It seemed that Balaam had at last calculated correctly. Through friendship, Israel had been beguiled into such sin as was abhorrent to its God. The people had made themselves unsavory in his sight, until his fierce anger was kindled against them. Suddenly there was sweeping through the camp a great plague, threatening to destroy the nation. It was the righteous anger of God expressing itself against Israel's sin.

For Moses and the people, the whole situation had developed quite without their realization. They had hardly seen the danger in the proffered friendship of the girls of Midian and Moab. Before they were aware of it, many of their men had fallen deeply into sin, and the wrath of God was kindled against them. Only after the killing plague was upon them did they stop to take notice of what was being done, and then they hardly knew what to do about it. It was God who finally came to Moses and told him how Israel might yet be saved from destruction. "Take all the heads of the people, and hang them up before the LORD against the sun, that the fierce anger of the LORD may be turned away from Israel" (Num. 25:4).

With a heavy heart, Moses called together the heads of the people and passed on the command that God had given him, "Slay ye every one his men that were joined unto Baalpeor" (Num. 25:5). The command came as a shock. It seemed almost too much. Those who had sinned were many, and they came from almost every family in the nation. Could they turn their own swords against their own flesh? And not only that, but once slain, the bodies had to be hung up before the sun as a sign that they were considered accursed. In shocked silence the people stood around in groups without courage to proceed.

It was then that the extent to which sin had permeated Israel suddenly came to light. At the very time when the plague of judgment was devastating the nation because of its sin, Zimri, a young prince of the tribe of Simeon, entered the camp, and with him he had a young Midianitish woman named Cozbi. His intentions were very evidently immoral. He made no secret of it. It was as though he openly was challenging the validity of God's law and its moral standards. While all the people looked on, he led the heathen woman into the chambers of his own tent.

It was Phinehas, the grandson of Aaron, who was shocked into action. With such audacious sins being practiced openly in the camp, it was no time to hesitate for lack of courage. In righteous indignation he took a javelin and followed the couple into the tent. Without mercy he struck them both through with the javelin so that they died.

This was the sort of righteous courage from which Israel could take an example. In recognition of it, God caused that the plague of destruction should be immediately stopped within the nation. Even more, he established with Phinehas an everlasting covenant of peace. His seed would inherit the covenant of an everlasting priesthood.

But the matter of this sin was still not settled. Also the Midianites who had instigated the whole affair under the leadership of Balaam had to be punished. The following instructions were issued to Moses by God: "Vex the Midianites, and smite them: for they vex you with their wiles, wherewith they have beguiled you in the matter of Peor, and in the matter of Cozbi, the daughter of a prince of Midian, their sister, which was slain in the day of the plague for Peor's sake" (Num. 25:17–18).

The preparations for obeying this command were necessarily slow and difficult. Israel had never before stood before the need of engaging offensively in battle. First, a numbering of the people had to be taken, and it had to be determined which of the men were able to go out into battle. When this was finally accomplished, God commanded Moses to take one thousand men from each tribe to fight against the army of Midian. It must have seemed like a hopelessly small force, but this would only serve to establish the better that the strength of Israel was in its God.

Into the battle came the armies of Midian with five kings at their head. Also with them they took Balaam the son of Beor. We may well imagine that it was not by choice on his part. But the Midianitish kings were still of the notion that Balaam had within him the power to bless their every effort. By forcing him to take part in the battle, they thought to insure his blessing upon them and their fighting.

What Balaam had forgotten was the vision of the angel that accompanied him from Aram. It had warned him that, in all that he did, God's angel would be there to judge him with righteous judgment. As long as he had not misrepresented God's word to Balak, he had remained untouched. But what he had not taken into consideration was that when he had plotted to beguile Israel into sin, God's judgment would fall not only upon those who sinned, but also upon the one who led them that way. He had succeeded in bringing God's wrath upon Israel, or at least upon the sinners in Israel, but at the same time he made himself guilty and ripe for judgment. Without his own choice he was carried into battle, and with the five kings of Midian he perished. It was the angel of judgment working righteousness over the wicked.

Chapter 45

MOSES NOT ALLOWED TO ENTER

23. And I besought the LORD at that time, saying,
24. O LORD God, thou hast begun to shew thy servant thy greatness, and thy mighty hand: for what God is there in heaven or in earth, that can do according to thy works, and according to thy might?
25. I pray thee, let me go over, and see the good land that is beyond Jordan, that goodly mountain, and Lebanon.
26. But the LORD was wroth with me for your sakes, and would not hear me: and the LORD said unto me, Let it suffice thee; speak no more unto me of this matter. (Deuteronomy 3:23–26)

Israel was encamped on the plains of Moab closely bordering the river Jordan. They had only to look across the expanse of the river and they could see the promised land that they had come so far and waited so long to inherit. Even more, they had been given a foretaste of the power with which they would enter that land. Not only had they won great victories over the armies of Og king of Bashan and Sihon king of the Amorites, but they had gone forth to punish and destroy the Midianites for the sin that they had instigated in Israel at the suggestion of Balaam. There could no longer be any doubt for them, or for anyone else, that the power of God was with them.

Every day the excitement and anticipation was growing stronger in the camp of Israel as events pointed more and more to their entrance into the promised land. Everything seemed to say that the time was near.

One of the first such events took the form of a crisis. One day the heads of the tribes of Reuben and Gad came to Moses and Eleazar the priest and announced their desire not to pass over the River Jordan at all. They had been looking at the land of Bashan and of the Amorites that they had conquered and had decided that it was as good a land for their cattle as they could ever desire. To Moses the words were like treason. Violently he reacted, "Shall your brethren go to war, and shall ye sit here? And wherefore discourage ye the heart of the children of Israel from going over into the land which the LORD hath given them? Thus did your fathers, when I sent them from Kadesh-barnea to see the land" (Num. 32:6–8). He could not understand that any should be hesitant to enter the land of promise. To him, lack of courage was the only real reason that they could have had for their request. Stung by the severity of Moses' attack, the leaders of Reuben and Gad quickly modified their request.

16. We will build sheepfolds here for our cattle, and cities for our little ones:

17. But we ourselves will go ready armed before the children of Israel, until we have brought them unto their place: and our little ones shall dwell in the fenced cities because of the inhabitants of the land.

18. We will not return unto our houses, until the children of Israel have inherited every man his inheritance (vv. 16–18).

With this condition understood, Moses gave his reluctant approval. It was another event that served to stress for Israel the importance of the promised land that they were about to inherit. With the conclusion of this event, there came to Moses an overwhelming realization of the difficulties that were still lying ahead of Israel. Problems would continue to arise, requiring bold and courageous leadership. All the time, moreover, he could not forget that he would not be allowed to provide that leadership. God had told him that he could not enter the promised land. Nor would God allow him to forget this. He came to him again and said,

12. Get thee up into the mount Abarim, and see the land which I have given unto the children of Israel.

13. And when thou hast seen it, thou also shalt be gathered unto thy people, as Aaron thy brother was gathered.

14. For ye rebelled against my commandment in the desert of Zin, in the strife of the congregation, to sanctify me at the water before their eyes: that is the water of Meribah in Kadesh in the wilderness of Zin (Num. 27:12–14).

In concern for Israel, Moses answered back, "Let the LORD, the God of the spirits of all flesh, set a man over the congregation, which may go out before them, and which may go in before them, and which may lead them out, and which may bring them in; that the congregation of the LORD be not as sheep which have no shepherd" (Num. 27:16–17).

To this the Lord gave immediate answer.

18. Take thee Joshua the son of Nun, a man in whom is the spirit, and lay thine hand upon him;

19. And set him before Eleazar the priest, and before all the congregation; and give him a charge in their sight.

20. And thou shalt put some of thine honour upon him, that all the congregation of the children of Israel may be obedient.

21. And he shall stand before Eleazar the priest, who shall ask counsel for him after the judgment of Urim before the LORD: at his word shall they go out, and at his word they shall come in, both he, and all the children of Israel with him, even all the congregation (Num. 27:18–21).

In obedience to God, Moses did as he was commanded. He took Joshua and set him before Eleazar and before the congregation of Israel. There he laid his hands upon Joshua to symbolize that his position and authority was being laid upon Joshua. Joshua was to take Moses' place before the children of Israel.

This was a difficult ceremony for Moses to perform, perhaps

one of the most difficult in all of his life. Moses' life from its very beginning had been centered in the hope of return to the promised land. From his very earliest years he had been schooled in the promise by his faithful parents. Through the years in Pharaoh's court he had nurtured that hope until he had become convinced that God was preparing him to perform an important part in the redemption from Egypt. For a time, the hope had dimmed as he fled an exile to Midian, but even then there was always the possibility that he could join his nation should they pass through the wilderness on the way to Canaan. When, finally, God had extended to him that almost unbelievable calling, and he actually went forth to give leadership to Israel, his hope grew clearer and more vivid than ever before. During the years that he guided Israel through the wilderness, his calling had brought him before countless trials that defied human faithfulness and courage. Still he had endured. It was the power of faith that had upheld him with strength from on high. Holding firmly to God's promise, he had gone on in the assurance that Israel's return to Canaan would surely come to pass because the word of the Lord had promised it.

And now, suddenly, in the closing stages of the journey Moses found this promised land slipping away from him. God, in faithfulness to his promise, was still giving it to Israel, but Moses personally was being denied it in his earthly life. He had sinned by striking the rock at Meribah instead of speaking to it as God had commanded, and because of that he was being denied the right of entering Canaan. He might go up to the very edge; he might gaze upon it from across Jordan's waters; but he might not enter in. This was God's judgment upon his sin.

One can hardly imagine a greater disappointment than Moses must have felt. From the moment that God pronounced this judgment, he knew that it was right, but that did not take away the longing that he had always nurtured in his heart as a good thing. The hope of his life lay fractured and hurting in his heart, never to be realized. Surely he was not above the rebellious feeling that God was unjust in punishing him so severely for so little. How often must he not have cried out in anguished repentance for his foolish lapse of obedience. And then, as the time for Israel to cross over Jordan came near and he saw the anticipation of the people growing more eager, how lonely he must have felt because he was to be left behind. And when troubles arose, as those with Reuben and Gad, which only his decisive and determined leadership could straighten out, did he not wonder how Israel could do without that? And can we blame him for thinking those thoughts? But God's word was unwavering. The leadership of Israel had to be turned over to another, even at this critical juncture of affairs.

For Moses it was almost too much. It seemed almost impossible for him to reconcile himself to this judgment of God. Again and again he found himself crying out through tears to God.

24. O LORD God, thou hast begun to shew thy servant thy greatness, and thy mighty hand: for what God is there in heaven or in earth, that can do according to thy works, and according to thy might?

25. I pray thee, let me go over, and see the good land that is beyond Jordan, that goodly mountain, and Lebanon. (Deut. 3:24–25)

Moses knew well how effectual the fervent prayer of a righteous man could be. Often he had prayed in almost impossible situations, and God had listened to answer him in grace. Through his prayers, Israel had repeatedly been saved. But for this prayer, as earnest as it was, there was no such answer. Rebukingly God replied, "Let it suffice thee; speak no more unto me of this matter" (Deut. 3:26).

To Moses, these words seemed harsh, but they were God's words, and they were final. And when he at last reconciled himself to this end, he saw also the reason for it. At the close of his earthly sojourn he could say to Israel, "But the LORD was wroth with me for your sakes, and would not hear me" (Deut. 3:26). It was not because God hated Moses and sought vengeance upon him that he would not allow Moses to enter Canaan. Moses was a child of his love, and before divine justice his guilt was completely covered by the redemption of the promised blood. But still, for the sake of Israel, Moses could not be allowed to enter in but must perish east of Jordan.

It was just exactly because Moses was so close to God at all times that when he sinned, his judgment had to be so severe and so definite. Israel must be given no occasion to accuse God of being a respecter of persons. Time and again Moses had been used as an agent of God to announce judgments upon those who had erred and broken his commandments. To serve in this capacity was a privilege but also a great responsibility. He could never be allowed to leave the impression that, because of his intimate relationship with God, he was above living as purely as he demanded from others. When, therefore, Moses fell openly into public sin and rebellion, God could not allow it to appear for a moment that he was less strict with his demands upon Moses than upon others. For the sake of Israel, that she might be spared from any misconceptions, God imposed upon Moses a public punishment for his error, and from it God would not relent, even when Moses' repentance was sincere and his prayers long and repeated.

Even more, however, was this punishment necessary because of the danger that confronted the future generations of Israel. As time passed by, the danger would become very great that Israel would begin to look back upon Moses as a man worthy of special recognition and of worship. There would be a tendency to put Moses in the place that belongs to God. It was necessary, therefore, that Israel should be left with one indisputable testimony of the fact that Moses was only a man and imperfect. Should anyone ever feel inclined to deify Moses, he would always stand before the fact that, as important as Moses was as a servant of God, he could not enter the land of promise because he had sinned. For the sake of Israel and its future generations, this testimony had to be allowed to stand, so that to God alone the glory of all ages might be given.

Chapter 46

THE DEATH OF MOSES

5. So Moses the servant of the LORD died there in the land of Moab, according to the word of the LORD.

10. And there arose not a prophet since in Israel like unto Moses, whom the LORD knew face to face. (Deuteronomy 34:5, 10)

The journey of Moses' earthly life was all but ended. It had been a long life and eventful, with many strange and different paths to be traveled. But now he had journeyed as far as he could go. Israel, the nation that he loved so dearly and had led so far so tenderly, must go on without him. He had prayed that it might be different. Repeatedly he had cried to God to forgive his sin and allow him to go on over Jordan to finish the work now so nearly completed. But it had been denied him. All that remained now was for him to speak his parting words to Israel, to ascend the mountain appointed by God, and there within sight of Canaan to die.

It must have been with a heavy heart that Moses called the people of Israel to him, and with heavy hearts that the people came. Moses knew, and the people knew, that they could go no farther together. The parting could not be easy. Though the people had often murmured against Moses, there had developed a deep and abiding love between them. Now their parting was bound to hurt, but it could not be avoided. Moses had much on his heart that had to be said. A few words would not suffice. His parting words constituted three different discourses, spread over days and weeks of time. They fill most of the book that we call Deuteronomy.

The first discourse of Moses contained a review and a reminder of all that the Lord had done for their nation in the past. There were no longer many living of those who had taken part in the original exodus from Egypt, only those who had been under twenty years of age at the time. It was necessary, therefore, that Moses should remind them of the marvelous works that Jehovah performed on their behalf as he brought their fathers to the very gates of Canaan. He reminded them again of the repeated sins of their fathers that had kept their nation now for forty years from entering the land of promise. And in conclusion he urged them to learn from the lesson of their fathers and to go forth in obedience to Jehovah their covenant God.

The second discourse of Moses in a large part constituted a repetition of the laws that had been given to Israel at Sinai and thereabouts. And still it was much more than a repetition; it was more of an interpretation and application of the law. From this portion the book of Deuteronomy receives its name meaning "the second law." In it Moses stressed the principle of the law, as he said, "Hear, O Israel: The LORD our God is one LORD: and thou shalt love the LORD thy God with all thine heart, and with all thy soul, and with all thy might, and these words, which I command thee this day, shall be in thine heart" (Deut. 6:4–6).

The third and final discourse turned to a consideration of the future. It gave commands to Israel concerning the recognition of the law with its blessings and cursings when they should come to mounts Gerizim and Ebal in the land of Canaan. But what was more; it gave them remarkably detailed prophecies of what would happen to their nation in future ages when they would fall into the ways of sin.

Through the days and weeks in which these discourses were being delivered, Moses gradually began to warm again to the wonderful truth that he, for the last time, was being given the opportunity to proclaim. He lived again in memory the trials and hardships of the exodus, with the wonderful works of deliverance wrought by Jehovah on their behalf. His heart thrilled anew, as point by point, he again instructed the covenant people in the deep spiritual wisdom of

God's law. He felt, more than ever before, the serious responsibility that fell to Israel to keep that law and the immensity of blessings and cursings that would come as a result upon the nation. The more Moses spoke, the more he gradually forgot about himself and his impending death. His mind became filled with concern for Israel, his beloved nation, and all of his last effort was put into impressing upon the people the importance of abiding in complete obedience to Jehovah. As time went on, and his death approached closer, his enthusiasm seemed to grow ever stronger, instead of waning, as might have been expected. When finally he came to the end of his discourse, there was no longer any tone of bitter resignation; he concluded as though with a shout of triumph, with a song of exaltation. It was a wonderful hymn of praise that broke forth from Moses' lips:

1. Give ear, O ye heavens, and I will speak; and hear, O earth, the words of my mouth.

2. My doctrine shall drop as the rain, my speech shall distil as the dew, as the small rain upon the tender herb, and as the showers upon the grass:

3. Because I will publish the name of the LORD, ascribe ye greatness unto our God.

4. He is the Rock, his work is perfect: for all his ways are judgment; a God of truth, and without iniquity, just and right is he. (Deut. 32:1–4)

Not only did Moses sing this song, he insisted that the people learn it and sing it after him. It was a glorious psalm-praise and the last words of instruction that Moses left with the people whom he loved so dearly. It expressed as nothing else the note of triumph that characterized his life now unto the very end.

One thing only remained now for Moses to do. Turning to each of the tribes of Israel individually, he pronounced the blessing of God upon them. It was much like the pronouncements of a father over his children, and was reminiscent of the blessings that Jacob, many years before, had pronounced upon the fathers of those same tribes. For forty years, Moses had been in very fact as a father to the whole of the nation of Israel. The parting words that he now spoke were filled with all the tender concern that he felt for this people that he had guided so carefully through all of the dangers of the wilderness. But even more, he spoke to them as a prophet of God, so that Israel might be assured that all that he spoke concerning her was truth. His words were not such as could be ignored. These were the last words of God to be spoken through Moses his servant. Especially the closing words were filled with glorious promise:

27. The eternal God is thy refuge, and underneath are the everlasting arms: and he shall thrust out the enemy from before thee; and shall say, Destroy them.
28. Israel then shall dwell in safety alone; the fountain of Jacob shall be upon a land of corn and wine; also his heavens shall drop down dew.
29. Happy art thou, O Israel: who is like unto thee, O people saved by the LORD, the shield of thy help, and who is the sword of thy excellency! and thine enemies shall be found liars unto thee; and thou shalt tread upon their high places (Deut. 33:27–29).

While these words were still echoing in the ears of all Israel, Moses turned to leave the plains of Moab where they were camped and began to climb the slopes of Nebo. And, somehow, in that departure there was not the undertone of extreme sadness that might have been expected. It was an old man whom they were watching, but his shoulders were still strong and upright. The head was white with age, but it was held as firm and confident as ever. So often Israel had watched the figure of Moses making its way up among the mountain peaks, and now, as always, it seemed that he was going with the purpose of communing with his Maker. He had left them with a message of joyful promise, and the same confidence seemed to carry him on as he ascended before their eyes closer and closer to heaven. It might have been a lonesome figure disappearing alone in the distance, except that all Israel knew so well that he went in communion with Jehovah.

Also for Moses there had come a new assurance and confidence that he had not expected. To leave the nation of Israel so close to the goal of all his labors had appeared to him an almost impossible thing. But as he had sought to encourage the children of Israel at his departure, he had found himself to be strengthened and encouraged as much as anyone else. He had left the camp of Israel, but he was not alone. The Lord was with him, and he had found peace with the fact that he could not enter the earthly Canaan. His thoughts were turned more and more to the better Canaan, where he would soon find his dwelling place, and its promise was more than enough to comfort his soul. Arriving at the top of Nebo, Moses looked out across Jordan to the land beyond with peaceful satisfaction. The air was clear, and even from this great distance the land was beautiful to behold. Its verdant green was rich and fruitful-looking, as a land that was blessed by the hand of the Lord. It was enough for Moses just to know that soon his people would enter in and possess that land. God stood by his side and said, "This is the land which I sware unto Abraham, unto Isaac, and unto Jacob, saying, I will give it unto thy seed: I have caused thee to see it with thine eyes, but thou shalt not go over thither" (Deut. 34:4).

There, with that beautiful vision before his eyes, Moses died. It was a quiet and peaceful death. We are told, as though with special significance, that it was by the "word of the LORD" (Deut. 34:5), and the old Jewish Rabbis liked to render this "by the kiss of the LORD." In a very special sense, God gathered Moses into death. There were no natural causes; God just determined that it was time for Moses to be taken from this earth. And God also provided for his body, burying it in a sepulcher not known unto man.

It was finally the children of Israel, and not Moses, who found this death to be most painful. Gradually they began to realize what it would mean not to have Moses with them anymore. Although Joshua would carry on Moses' work, he would never really take

Moses' place. Moses was a unique figure in the history of the church. Never again would there be a mere human prophet who would know the Lord so intimately, face to face. His life, in so many respects, had been a visible demonstration of the grace of God and of the gospel. He was a mediator through whom Israel had stood before the greatness of the living God. Henceforth they could only look forward to the day of which Moses spoke when he said to them, "The LORD thy God will raise up unto thee a Prophet from the midst of thee, of thy brethren, like unto me; unto him ye shall hearken" (Deut. 18:15). He would be the fulfillment of that of which Moses was only the type.